The Story of
Queen Helene of Adiabene
NEZIRAH

The
Story of
Queen Helene
of Adiabene

Nezirah

Tzirel Greenberg

Copyright © 2016 by Tzirel Greenberg

ISBN 978-1-60091-438-6

All rights reserved. No part of this book may be reproduced or transmitted in any form or by any means (electronic, photocopying, recording or otherwise) without prior permission of the publisher.

Cover picture: model of Jerusalem in the Second Temple Period, courtesy of Israel Museum, Jerusalem.

Distributed by:
Israel Bookshop Publications
501 Prospect Street
Lakewood, NJ 08701
Tel: (732) 901-3009 / Fax: (732) 901-4012
www.israelbookshoppublications.com
info@israelbookshoppublications.com

Printed in the United States of America

Distributed in Israel by:
Shanky's
Petach Tikva 16
Jerusalem
972-2-538-6936

Distributed in Australia by:
Gold's Book and Gift Company
3-13 William Street
Balaclava 3183
613-9527-8775

Distributed in Europe by:
Lehmanns
Unit E Viking Industrial Park
Rolling Mill Road
Jarrow, Tyne & Wear NE32 3DP
44-191-430-0333

Distributed in South Africa by:
Kollel Bookshop
Northfield Centre
17 Northfield Avenue
Glenhazel 2192
27-11-440-6679

IN HONOR OF MY MOTHER
Mrs. Matti Dubin

whose constant striving for spiritual growth
is an inspiration to her family

Acknowledgments

With heartfelt praise and thanks to the *Ribono shel Olam* for enabling me to complete this project, I offer my deep *hakaras hatov* to His *shlichim* who made this book possible.

Boundless thanks go to my husband, Rabbi Binyomin Greenberg, whose assistance with every aspect of this project makes it truly a joint effort. His thorough research uncovered the text sources that laid the groundwork for this book, and his vast knowledge and teaching skill helped me interpret and understand them. In addition, when questions arose, he communicated them to *rabbanim*. I thank him for the numerous hours he spent reviewing and editing the entire manuscript with a meticulous eye for both grammar and content, providing invaluable input. I am grateful for his technological savvy that guided the design, preparation, and safeguarding of the document along the way. Most of all, it was his constant and much-needed support and encouragement that kept me moving forward to completion. May we be *zocheh* to continue to collaborate in striving to be *mekadesh Shem Shamayim*, and may he be blessed with the *ko'ach* to keep doing all that he does for the *klal* and for his loving and appreciative family.

The enthusiasm of my children energized this project at its every stage, and I thank them for their support and excitement to see it come to fruition.

My dear friend Dr. Carol Rivie Sirken applied her analytical mind, keen eye, sharp wit, and sensitivity to carefully editing the entire manuscript. Her invaluable input and astute comments, delivered with her witty sense of humor, were both technically essential and very enjoyable. I thank her for her countless hours of work that contributed so significantly to the quality of the manuscript.

Mrs. Joan Betesh also read the manuscript, and I thank her for her impressions and comments.

I appreciate the guidance of my close friend, author Deborah Lee Rose, who walked me through the process of submitting the manuscript.

To the Israel Bookshop Publications team, I offer my deep *hakaras hatov* for their professionalism, kindness, and encouragement. Working with them has been a positive, pleasant, and enlightening experience, every step of the way.

Mrs. Liron Delmar, Mrs. Chani Kravetz, and Mrs. Malkie Gendelman coordinated production of the book, and I thank them for their considerable efforts that enabled the project to progress smoothly and seamlessly.

Mrs. Miriam Jakubowicz reviewed and edited every word of the manuscript, investing countless hours of effort and enthusiasm into ensuring accuracy and enhancing readability. I thank her for all of her meticulous input, creativity, and guidance that enabled the excitement and vibrancy of Queen Helene's story to resonate on these pages.

Mrs. Esther Malky Sonenblick proofread the text. Her sharp eye and diligence are very much appreciated.

Zehava Dalia Nadler was responsible for the beautiful cover, and Liron Delmar did an outstanding job with the layout and graphics. I thank them for making the book so aesthetically pleasing.

May this book be a means for an *ilui neshamah* for those righteous souls whose story is told on these pages, and a way to thank them for their contributions to Klal Yisrael. May their lives inspire us to strive for ever higher levels of *kedushah* in our own.

Author's Note

The purpose of this work is twofold: I have tried to illuminate the lives and times of Queen Helene of Adiabene and her family. I have also desired to increase our awe of the Beis Hamikdash by describing the way it enriched our spiritual lives when it was standing. Toward those ends, I have drawn upon Josephus's *Antiquities* and *The Jewish War* as well as Talmudic sources and their commentaries. To identify primary textual sources, I have relied heavily upon citations which appeared in *Otzar Toras Hakorbanos* by Harav Menachem Mekubar, Rabbi Yaakov Meir Strauss's *Three Special Days* and *One Special Prayer,* and *Encylopedia Carta*: *Beis Hamikdash B'Yerushalayim* by Harav Yisrael Ariel. Beautiful pictures in this latter work depicting life during the Second Temple period also served as inspirations for the text.

Below is a listing of the historical characters in this book. While there is no record of any actual interaction between Helene and the great rabbinic figures included in the story, it seems plausible that they could have met. Although the timing of factual events in this story is based on historical records, when the exact year of occurrence is unknown it is estimated. Fictional characters were developed to plausibly support and expand on the historical facts to the best of my ability. I avoided straying too far from the facts when creating a plot in order to focus as much as possible on what we know about Queen Helene and her relatives, in an attempt to create as accurate a picture as possible of this great woman and her family.

Historical Timeline

15 BCE	Helene is born
3 CE	Monobaz is born
4 CE	Herod dies
5 CE	Izates is born
32 CE	Izates and Monobaz undergo *bris milah*
32 CE	Helene and Samacha convert
35 CE	King Monobaz I dies; Izates inherits the throne
36 CE	Izates restores Artabanus to Parthian throne and is granted Nisibis as a reward
38 CE	Death of Artabanus, king of Parthia
40 CE	Vardanes goes to war against Izates; Helene's first period of *nezirus* begins
41 CE	Agrippa I becomes king
46 CE	Helene goes to Yerushalayim
46 CE	Helene builds a palace in Yerushalayim and in Lod
47 CE	Famine in Yerushalayim; Helene procures corn and figs to feed the Jewish people

47 CE	Vardanes is murdered, ending threat to Izates
48 CE	Agrippa II becomes king
48 CE	Helene builds sukkah in Lod
49 CE	Helene contributes Menorah ornament and golden tablet to Beis Hamikdash
49 CE	Monobaz contributes golden vessels for Yom Kippur to Beis Hamikdash
50 CE	Cumanus orders his soldiers to occupy the Beis Hamikdash on Erev Pesach
51 CE	Plot of noblemen of Adiabene and King Abia against Izates is foiled
52 CE	Volgases declares war on Izates but retreats before attacking him
54 CE	Claudius dies, and Nero becomes emperor
60 CE	Izates dies; Helene dies; Monobaz becomes King Monobaz II
61 CE	Monobaz sends troops to Armenia and is beaten at Tigranocerta
63 CE	Monobaz is present when peace is made between Parthia and Rome
67 CE	Monobaz sends assistance to the Jews in their rebellion against Rome
69 CE	Titus's first battle in Yerushalayim takes place opposite tomb of Queen Helene

Historical Background

Adiabene! Such a lyrical name for this small country nestled in the highlands of ancient Assyria! Measuring only about 200 miles from east to west and about 100 miles from north to south, Adiabene was flanked by the Tigris River on the west, Lake Van on the north, and Lake Umla on the east. On a current-day map, Adiabene would include pieces of Kurdish Iraq, Armenia, and northern Iran, perhaps alluding to a history of political significance that outstripped its diminutive size.

Adiabene was a vassal state of the Parthian empire. After defeating the Seleucids, Alexander the Great's successors, the Parthians, conquered most of the Middle East and southwest Asia. They ruled ancient Persia for over four centuries, from 247 BCE until 228 CE, and counterbalanced Rome's strength in the West.[1]

The faith of the majority of Adiabene's population was Zoroastrianism, a pagan religion based on teachings ascribed to the "prophet" Zoroaster and the worship of his deity Ahura Mazda. Nevertheless, the region had a long-standing and significant Jewish presence. One of its chief cities, Nisibis, appears to have housed a large Jewish population, perhaps as far back as the time of the exile of the ten

---

1 Jonah Gabriel Lissner, "Adiabene, Jewish Kingdom of Mesopotamia," [www.kulanu.org/links/Adiabene.php], 2000.

tribes of the northern kingdom of Israel in the year 556 BCE.[2] Nisibis became part of Adiabene in the year 36 CE, when Artabanus, king of Parthia, awarded it to Queen Helene's son, Prince Izates, in return for his loyalty.

The name of the capital city, Arbela, describes its topography; "Ur Bela" means "high city" in the language of the Sumerians. The town is located east of ancient Nineveh (present-day Mosul, in Iraq) and was an important economic center as early as the time of the Assyrians.[3] There was a continuous Jewish presence in Arbela from the first century of the Common Era, at the time of Helene's reign, until the 1950s, when its Jewish population immigrated to Israel.[4]

During this same period in history, about 650 miles to the south and west of Adiabene, the Jewish people in the Land of Israel were experiencing a troubled, tumultuous, and, ultimately, tragic time. While their Roman oppressors continued to consolidate political power in Judea, the spiritual fabric of the nation was being ripped apart through internal challenges to religious life by the Roman-supported Tzedokim (Sadducees), who denied the validity of the Oral Law and the authority of the sages.

Tzadok was a disciple of the sage Antigonus of Socho, who lived during the third century, BCE. He was influenced by the Hellenistic spirit and came to deny the truth of the Oral Law and the authority of the sages to interpret that law and to issue decrees to protect it. Tzedoki philosophy was really just a rationalization for their denial of the Torah. By refusing to adhere to the interpretations of the sages, they robbed the Torah of any precise meaning, and so each person was free

---

2   Pinchas Wollman-Tsamir, ed., *The Graphic History of the Jewish Heritage* (Weehawken, NJ: M.P. Press, Inc., 1982), 205.

3   The reign of the Assyrian Empire spanned approximately from the 24th century BCE to 600 BCE.

4   Dr. Pearl Herzog, "A Light from the Nations," *Family First*, May 16, 2012, 14.

to explain it as he wished. Josephus described the Tzedokim as irreligious Jews.[5]

Nevertheless, in spite of political unrest and the Roman-backed persecution of the masses, the spiritual life of the Jewish people experienced a renaissance with the rise of Hillel and Shammai. These sages succeeded the Torah greats, Shmaya and Avtalyon, as the next of the *zugos*, "pairs" of Jewish leaders, and their authority spanned the reigns of both Herod and Archelaus.

Shammai had previously headed a yeshivah in Yerushalayim and sat on the Sanhedrin as a judge for many years before Hillel arrived in Eretz Yisrael from his native Babylonia. The incident that brought the sage to the Holy Land is recorded in the Gemara.[6] The people came to inquire as to whether the *Korban Pesach* is brought on Shabbos when Erev Pesach falls on Shabbos. The sons of Beseira,[7] the leading scholars of the day, did not know the answer, but once they were informed that Hillel, who studied under Shmaya and Avtalyon, would surely know, they summoned him. Hillel gave convincing proof that the offering should be brought, even on Shabbos. The sons of Beseira, recognizing him to be the superior scholar, stepped aside and appointed Hillel as the *Nasi*. At the same time, Shammai was appointed *Av Beis Din*. The former position, which was always given to a descendant of King David, carried with it a responsibility for political involvement when necessary, while the latter focused solely on the exposition of Jewish law.

Most Torah scholars gathered around Hillel and established a yeshivah, which was known as Beis Hillel. Shammai's yeshivah, called Beis

---

5   Rabbis Nosson Scherman and Meir Zlotowitz, general editors, *History of the Jewish People: The Second Temple Era* (Brooklyn, New York: Mesorah Publications, Ltd., 1982), 55-56.

6   *Pesachim* 66b.

7   Rabbi Yehudah ben Beseira lived in Nisibis, as cited in the Gemara (*Pesachim* 3b), as well as in other places. Earlier, during the first century, Nisibis became part of Adiabene when it was given to Izates by Artabanus.

Shammai, continued to exist. Although the two academies disagreed on many areas of halachah, there was friendship and unity between them.[8] Queen Helene's life was guided by the rabbis of Beis Hillel, and their advice led her to make life-altering decisions, as we will see later. These institutions retained their major role in Jewish life well after the deaths of Hillel in 9 CE[9] at age 120, and Shammai, in 30 CE.

So, in spite of the pall of impending doom, Eretz Yisrael during the first century of the Common Era was alive with vibrant Jewish life. In the academies of Torah learning, students debated the legal issues that were to form the basis of the Mishnah, codified two centuries later by Rabbi Yehudah Hanasi. Day-to-day activities were regulated by the Jewish calendar that dictated not only Shabbos and Yom Tov as we observe them today, but also the offering of *korbanos*, the taking of tithes, the bringing of first fruits, the leaving of gifts in the field for the poor, the presenting of gifts to the *kohen*, and all of the other mitzvos dependent on dwelling in the Land of Israel during the time when the Beis Hamikdash stood.

It was against this backdrop that the royal family of Adiabene lived. While our story opens when Queen Helene is already a grown woman with two adult sons, it really begins in the year 3745 (15 BCE), with the birth of a princess to the king and queen of Adiabene. Surely, no one celebrating the royal baby's birth could have foretold the highly improbable path that her life would take. No one present could have imagined that this child would grow into a woman who would ultimately

---

8 Concerning the fundamentals of Oral Law, there were no differences between the sages Hillel and Shammai. In fact, during their lifetimes, there were only three halachic disputes between them. It was not until after their deaths that there arose many disagreements on specific halachic requirements concerning the legal "fences" erected by the sages to protect the Torah. Once the Sanhedrin was no longer in existence, there was no central authority for deciding these issues. Rabban Yochanan ben Zakkai, who established the yeshivah at Yavneh after the destruction of the Temple, ruled that in most cases the halachah follows the view of Beis Hillel.

9 Matis Kantor, *Codex Judaica* (New York: Zichron Press, 2005), 132.

abandon the culture and royalty into which she had been born to bind her fate to that of the Jewish people!

Who was Queen Helene of Adiabene, also known in Jewish texts as Heleni Hamalkah?

She was a woman whose devotion to her adopted religion is cited numerous times in various *masechtos* in the Talmud Bavli and Yerushalmi. She was a woman who, together with her sons, piqued the interest of the Jewish historian Josephus, as evidenced by the prominence their story is given in his *Antiquities of the Jews*.[10] Indeed, these Talmudic and historical sources give us many insights into the royal family of Adiabene. (See timeline.)

With respect to Helene's ancestry, there is some controversy among *Chazal*. It appears most likely that she was a righteous convert, as were her sons, Izates and Monobaz.[11] It does not appear that Helene's husband, King Monobaz I, who was also her brother, ever converted to Judaism.

In addition to writing about Monobaz and Izates, Josephus also mentions the fact that Izates had five sons, whose names he does not provide. These princes were sent to the Holy Land with their grandmother, Helene, to learn Torah. The Talmud Yerushalmi[12] notes that

---

10 Incidents involving Queen Helene, Izates, and Monobaz are mentioned in the Talmud Bavli (*masechtos Nazir, Yoma*, and *Menachos*), as well as the Yerushalmi (*masechtos Sukkah* and *Nazir*). These citations have been commented upon by numerous sages from the periods of the *Rishonim* as well as *Acharonim*.

11 *Rashi* and *Tosafos* state that she and her family were descendants of the *Chashmona'im*, while others, including *Bereishis Rabbah* and *Sefer Yuchsin*, call her son Monobaz a convert from the ancient kingdom of Hadyav. Rav Mattisyahu Strashon cites the Gemara (*Bava Basra* 11a) to support the view that Monobaz and his mother were indeed converts. The Gemara quotes Monobaz making a declaration from Yerushalayim, "My ancestors amassed wealth…," implying that he was ashamed of his background. Rav Strashon explains that the royal family was of known Roman ancestry, and only some members of the family converted. Rav Shmuel Irons maintains that Rashi did not have access to the sources that would have indicated that Helene and Monobaz were converts.

12 *Sukkah*, chapter 1, halachah 1.

Queen Helene had seven sons, all of whom were Torah scholars. Although Josephus mentions other "kinsmen" involved in the war against the Romans, there is no explicit mention of the other sons. Perhaps Helene's five grandsons were considered the equivalent to her sons, who, when added to Monobaz and Izates, would equal seven. This is the opinion that is adopted for this work.

No mention is made in either the Gemara or Josephus's *Antiquities of the Jews* of Prince Monobaz's marriage or progeny, so no explicit assumptions are made about them in this story. It is possible that Monobaz was married to pagan wives before his conversion and divorced them once he became a Jew. Furthermore, his frequent trips to Eretz Yisrael could have made establishing a family difficult.

Additional questions surround the sukkah that Helene built in Lod. Normative halachah states that a sukkah more than twenty *amos* high (the equivalent of thirty to forty feet) is invalid, consistent with the (majority) opinion of the rabbis in the Gemara. However, the Gemara also brings a *braisa* quoting a dissenting opinion by Rabbi Yehudah, who held that a sukkah can be valid if it is more than twenty *amos* high. Rabbi Yehudah brings as support to his argument an account of the sukkah of Queen Helene in Lod, which was taller than twenty *amos* and which the sages visited without offering critical comment.

Another pertinent fact mentioned in the Gemara is that Queen Helene did nothing without first consulting with the rabbis. The Gemara tries to reconcile this discrepancy of Helene's tall sukkah, given that the halachah is indeed that a sukkah must be less than twenty *amos* high. In this work, we will follow the opinion of Rav Ashi, that the majority of Helene's sukkah was less than twenty *amos* high, excluding a small room, measuring four *amos* by four *amos*, in which she sat for the purpose of upholding the laws of *tznius*. Since a woman is not obligated to sit in a sukkah, no law would have been violated by her dwelling in such a tall structure. We can only speculate on the reason for having the small room constructed in this way.[13]

The royal court included sons of King Monobaz I by other wives as well, but these individuals would ultimately fade into oblivion. The true heroes of this tale are Helene, Izates, and Monobaz. Their *yiras Shamayim* lit up a dark time in our nation's history, producing sparks of holiness whose influence, through citations in multiple *masechtos* of Gemara and commentaries, continues to endure. It is the author's fervent hope that this book will give life to the chapters of our history through which they walked and made such a deep and lasting impression.

Historical Characters

Queen Helene
King Monobaz I
Prince/King Monobaz II
Prince/King Izates
Princess Samacha
Five sons of King Izates (true names unknown)
Chananya
Parthian monarchs
Rabbi Eliezer

Rabban Shimon ben Gamliel
Rabbi Tzadok
Agrippa I
Agrippa II
Emperor Claudius
Fadus (procurator)
Cumanus (procurator)
Felix (procurator)
Emporer Nero
Yonasan, *kohen gadol*

All other characters are fictional.

---

13   *Sukkah* 2b.

Chapter One

"Ready, aim, release!"

The first arrow cut through the heavy air of late summer with a loud whoosh, as if determined to follow a straight trajectory to its target fifty meters in the distance.

"Bull's eye!" the archery instructor pronounced excitedly. "Now, let's put ten more arrows around that one!"

His student readily obliged, making a circle of arrows around the first.

"Good aim, Your Majesty!" the teacher proclaimed. "You have a natural talent."

"Thank you, Xosrov," Prince Izates replied, visibly embarrassed. He was a tall, handsome young man just completing his second decade of life. "I wonder, though, if one can rightly be commended for exercising an ability with which he was born. It seems as if the Power Who gave him that talent deserves the recognition."

"Your Majesty is a philosopher as well as a warrior," Xosrov remarked with a smile. "These are important traits for a future king!"

"Long live King Monobaz!" the prince quickly responded, as if in denial of his destiny. Recovering quickly, Izates smiled. "My esteemed instructor, I give you permission to tell my father of my performance, because it brings him such pleasure and could bring you additional drachmas."

"The former would be my only motivation," the instructor replied. "As you implied, Your Highness, there is no reason for me to be rewarded for having a student who learns so easily!"

Izates chuckled along with the older man, but then he became serious.

"Perhaps you can return ahead of me, Xosrov," the prince requested. "I would like to tarry awhile before setting back for home."

"Your request is my command, Your Majesty," the instructor responded, smiling. He had begun teaching the prince martial arts when Izates was but a young lad of ten. He knew his student and understood his need for solitude.

Xosrov sped off, his stallion kicking up clouds of dust behind him. "Return safely before dark, my prince!" he shouted paternally as he disappeared into the forest.

The summer sun would soon begin to sink behind the craggy mountains of Adiabene, the sky relinquishing its cloudless blue to broad swaths of pink, orange, and burnished gold. Prince Izates reined in his Arabian stallion and paused to take in the breathtaking beauty of his desert homeland. From his vantage point at the crest of the high hill overlooking the royal compound, his view spanned the entire capital city of Arbela as well as the great Tigris River to the west.

The prince looked down upon the busy marketplace, where there was a flurry of activity. While he was too far away to observe the details, he knew that, at this time of the afternoon, the peddlers and merchants would be finalizing their last transactions of the day, carefully pocketing their revenues and packing up their remaining wares in leather sacks, wooden crates, or barrels.

Alleyways surrounded the market plaza like a convoluted maze, with small stone dwellings huddled together along the narrow streets. Encircling the town was a thick wall six meters high, built of pink granite that sparkled in the last rays of the sun. Laundry hung out to dry on cords on terraced patios. Mothers called their children in from the streets for the evening meal. The elderly sat in small courtyards under the shade of broad almond trees.

Beyond this urban environment lay rolling fields of wheat and barley, flanked by lush vineyards and orchards of apple, peach, and nut trees. Vast strawberry fields behind small rural dwellings formed a patchwork of red and green, as the ripe fruit basked in the last rays of the late summer sun. Small figures that looked like children could be seen in the distance. They were bending over scythes, reaching up to pick fruit and piling it into baskets, or pruning vines.[1]

How Prince Izates loved his native land and its people! He liked nothing more than to observe the awesome vitality of nature, together with the collage of human activity interacting with it. But still, many troubling questions coursed through his mind. What purpose was being served by all of these pursuits? To what higher calling was he, as royal scion, intended?

The prince had sought answers in religion but had come up dissatisfied. Adiabene's predominant Zoroastrian faith proposed a single deity representing the forces of good, but evil was beyond its sphere of control. Angels exhibiting less than holy behavior were worshipped. People were expected to behave properly and charitably, but the definition of such behaviors was left largely to the individual to determine. How could such a beautiful, complex world be left to human whim?

Shaking his head, Izates decided to set aside these philosophical concerns for the time being in favor of appreciating the spectacle before him. In just a few minutes the day would end, the disappearance of the sun leaving his beloved nation dark and silent. It was time to turn back.

Upon his arrival, the prince, still deep in reverie, was hoping to slip inside the palace unnoticed, but it was not to be. The king's chief steward spotted him in the courtyard and came swiftly to intercept him.

---

[1] Agricultural crop information is from the Ministry of Interior of the Republic of Iran.

"Your Majesty," he announced, "the king requests an audience with Prince Izates as soon as possible in his chambers. He has been awaiting your return."

"Thank you, Bozan," Izates responded.[2] "Please tell my father that I request just a few minutes to rid myself of the dust of the road and to change my garments."

King Monobaz looked anxious as he sat on his throne awaiting the prince's arrival. He made no secret of favoring Izates over all of his sons, a source of great jealousy to most of his kin. Nevertheless, Monobaz easily rationalized his preference. Helene, Izates's mother, was his favorite wife. While both of her offspring were bright, obedient, and capable, Izates possessed a certain captivating charm, together with the strong physique of the natural warrior. For this reason, he had been chosen by his father to succeed him on the throne when the time would come.

Momentarily, a familiar knock on the door to the throne room brought a broad smile to the king's face. Izates appeared in the entrance, and father and son embraced warmly. Monobaz never tired of admiring the tall, handsome prince. He had fathered the perfect son, he thought with satisfaction.

"Ah," he mused sadly to himself, "precious gifts must be protected." The king gestured for his son to be seated at the long oval table generally reserved for important strategy sessions attended by his advisors.

"Izates, my dear son, now that you have become a man, it is time for you to know that it is you whom I have chosen to succeed me on the throne," King Monobaz said, sighing slightly. "Surely, you are aware that other members of the royal family covet this exalted position. It is for this reason that I have arrived at a difficult but necessary decision, my dear Izates. You must leave Adiabene very soon. My friend and ally,

---

2 See [http://www.iranicaonline.org/articles/personal-names-iranian-iv-parthian] for examples of this and other Parthian names.

King Abennerig of Charax-Spasini, has graciously agreed to grant you refuge and protection in his kingdom. There may be additional benefits for you there, my son, but, most importantly, you must be safe from jealous hearts until the time comes for you to assume the royal mantle."[3]

Izates's face blanched. Although aware of the special relationship he shared with the king, he had always assumed that the line of succession would extend to his older brother, Monobaz. How could he assume the kingship ahead of him? Surely, Monobaz was worthy of becoming king.

The prince quickly shook these thoughts from his mind. His father had made a decision, and it was not possible to object to it. He must hide his true feelings and show his appreciation.

"Exile from my homeland is surely a bitter price to pay for the eventual crown, may it long be in your possession, my dear father, but I humbly submit to your will. While away, I will focus my energies on gaining knowledge and honing the qualities that will enable me to reign with integrity and strength when the time comes."

When Izates finally left the throne room, it was with a heavy heart. Still, he couldn't help feeling a glimmer of anticipation for the time he would spend in Charax-Spasini — and what the future held in store for him.

---

[3] Josephus, *Antiquities of the Jews*, 20:2.

Chapter Two

Izates arrived in the port city of Charax-Spasini to a welcome usually reserved for native sons returning from afar.[1]

"Izates, my son!" King Abennerig exclaimed with obvious pleasure. "Your father has entrusted your welfare into my hands, and I gladly accept the responsibility." He smiled. "It is quite a privilege to host the son of my dear friend, King Monobaz. I have watched you grow over the years into a distinguished young man, Izates. I'm sure you will make a fine king someday!"

"My deepest appreciation to you, Your Highness," Izates replied with deference. "While I miss my homeland, I sense that Charax-Spasini is a place to which I will become fondly attached!"

Izates settled into his new home with relative ease. Only several weeks after his arrival, King Abennerig invited him to join a hunting expedition. Izates reluctantly accepted the invitation. He did not want to offend the monarch, in spite of his own great aversion to the sport.

It was early morning when they started off from the palace, among a group of about a dozen other horsemen. They rode for more than an

---

1   Charax-Spasini was a busy port located on the Persian Gulf, near the current-day Iraqi city of Basra, about 400 miles southeast of Adiabene, [http://en.wikipedia.org/wiki/Charax_Spasinu#cite_ref-ch_1-0]. This city was originally on the coast of the Persian Gulf in what is now Kuwait. It was originally named Alexandria, after Alexander the Great. After being destroyed by floods, it was rebuilt by Antiochus IV (175-164 BCE) and renamed Antiochia.

hour before reaching the forest that was their destination. Many of the other riders had become fatigued and less than clear-headed as a result of the strong ale they had drunk before embarking on the day's excursion.

Nevertheless, those present felt the need to show off to the king their hunting prowess, and a competition ensued to see whose arrow would hit the largest animal. Izates, disgusted by the idea of hunting for sport, had no intention of participating. He rode with the rest of the group, never intending to use the bow and quiver of arrows strapped to his back. The expedition continued for several hours with arrows hitting various small animals and several deer.

"My dear prince," King Abennerig said with some concern, "are you feeling well today? I have heard of your reputation as an expert archer, yet I notice that you are not aiming your bow."

"Yes, Your Majesty," Izates admitted. "I am not feeling quite myself today. I apologize for not contributing more."

"I never impose quotas," the king responded, chuckling. "Today is meant mostly for relaxation."

The prince could feel the tension in his muscles easing, thankful that his lack of participation was not considered offensive to his host. Suddenly, he was startled by a loud voice and perceived a jerky movement. One of the riders, boasting of his great talent, took aim at a figure in the distance, which he supposed to be a moose. In a split second, Izates could tell that this was not an animal, but a man who had dismounted from his horse further along the path! The prince lunged at the horseman, knocking him off his steed just before the second arrow left his hand.

King Abennerig was paralyzed by shock when he realized that the would-be target was none other than his twenty-five-year-old son, Arsak. A tumult ensued, and the culprit was duly castigated and stripped of his hunting gear. The group returned to the palace, humbled by the near-tragedy.

King Abennerig called Izates into his study later that evening.

"Prince Izates, I am forever indebted to you for saving my son's life," he said soberly. "I can see that both your mind and body work quickly and that your character is impeccable. After pondering a proper reward, I came upon a most appropriate one. What better son-in-law could I hope for than you, who have proved your loyalty to me and to the royal family?"

Izates looked down, embarrassed. He felt this recognition to be unwarranted; how could he fail to try to prevent the death of a human being? At the same time, Izates was very pleased with King Abennerig's offer. He had had opportunity to observe the king's daughter, Samacha, and her modest demeanor and the deference and respect she showed her father impressed him.

"I deny the greatness of my act, Your Majesty," Izates protested. "But I accept with great appreciation the offer of your daughter, Samacha, in marriage. If she herself agrees, I pledge to honor and care for her as a devoted husband."

"Excellent! I will speak with Samacha before the day ends."

When King Abennerig gently suggested to his daughter that evening that the time had come for him to give her hand in marriage to an appropriate suitor, Samacha blushed. Then fear gripped her heart. She had been secretly harboring the desire to wed her father's guest, Prince Izates, whom she admired for his refined behavior and kind smile. She had also overheard talk of his kindness toward all people and his loyalty to his family. Whom, then, could her father have in mind?

"My daughter," Abennerig continued, "I can think of no better husband for you than the son of my dear friend King Monobaz of Adiabene, the Prince Izates. Will you accept him in marriage?"

A broad smile lit up the princess's expressive face. "Yes, Father," she replied happily. "I would be honored to become the wife of Prince Izates of Adiabene. He appears to have a kind heart and to be a man with deep thoughts."

"Yes, my dear daughter, I believe you are correct," Abennerig answered after a pause. "Your future husband is quite able in all areas of administration and is politically savvy as well. I can see that he is not only intelligent but also spiritual. Surely his meditations can only make him even more valuable as a future leader. He must be given more opportunity to engage in this important activity. I believe I have a solution to the dilemma, but I would like to propose it to you together at your engagement party."

One week later, King Abennerig held a lavish party in the palace garden for a broad array of Parthian dignitaries, family, and friends, to celebrate the betrothal of Princess Samacha to Prince Izates of Adiabene. As the festivities were drawing to a close, the king took aside his future son-in-law.

"Izates, my son, as a betrothal present, I hereby bestow upon you a prime territory within my realm," the king said. "It should produce sufficient revenue for your sustenance and that of your future family. Together with this comes a loyal and capable administrative staff. This should free you to spend much of your time in study and contemplation, as I have observed is your pleasure."

"Your Highness," Izates replied, "granting your daughter's hand to me in marriage is a gift for which my appreciation is boundless. Your additional generosity leaves me truly overwhelmed with gratitude."

And so it was. Prince Izates married Princess Samacha amid pomp and colorful celebration. The people of Charax-Spasini were jubilant at the alliance between the two territories, as well as their now-official connection to the dashing prince. Prince Izates grew more and more pleased with his wife as he came to know her. She was unlike most young women of his time and place in her ability to share his deep thoughts and interest in the spiritual world.

As his father-in-law had suggested, Prince Izates used his leisure time to explore the sciences and Greek philosophy, but his efforts left him with many questions and few answers. The degree to which these doubts and uncertainties invaded his psyche was limited by the otherwise idyllic nature of his life. Although his mind was receptive to new ideas, he was not actively seeking change.

Charax-Spasini was a bustling city, with ships arriving constantly from such faraway places as Egypt, India, and beyond. While its people identified with their Parthian overseers and shared their religion, Charax-Spasini also housed a small Jewish population. These Jews lived together in their own, largely isolated villages, which provided them with the religious institutions and services they needed for personal as well as communal life. They opened their inns, homes, synagogues, and study halls to their brethren from foreign lands who came to trade at the busy port town. They were able to converse in Pahlavanik, the Parthian language, which bore many similarities to their native Aramaic.

Interaction with the gentile population was limited, except in one sphere. Jewish merchants peddled their wares among the local population and not infrequently struck up animated conversations with their customers. They might have opened with a discussion of the weather or politics, but most often they gravitated toward more spiritual topics. They were not intentionally proselytizing. Rather, their objective was to spread word of the truth of monotheism among a polytheistic people, to abrogate idol worship and to replace it with belief in the one G-d.

Sometimes, listeners were so taken by the principles of the Jewish faith that they craved more than monotheism. For these individuals, nothing less than conversion to Judaism would satisfy their yearning for truth. Although the Torah forbids members of certain nations to join the Jewish people as converts, these restrictions were removed at the time of Sancheriv[2] when it was determined that these forbidden nations could no longer be identified.[3] Such was the setting when the merchant Chananya was summoned to Izates's residence to vend his fine fabrics to Princess Samacha and her friends. Several young women were seated with the princess at a marble table in her drawing room, partaking of sweet dates and figs and exchanging small talk.

"Samacha, what are you wearing for the festival of Sura Anahita? I must say, it is challenging to keep up with all of these holidays!"

"That's exactly the point, Amestris," Samacha admitted, frustration creeping into her voice. "Just between us, I haven't felt drawn to Zoroaster and his cronies since I was a little girl. While the Avesta[4] speaks of one deity, it is a god which has power over good but no power over evil. How could such a god be worshipped? Then there is the angel of the water, the angel of fire, of metal, of earth, and so on and so on. It seems more like a society than something divine."

"Oh, you take it all too seriously, Samacha!" Amestris chided. "Enjoy looking pretty in your different dresses. Then it won't bother you so much."

A knock on the door interrupted the women's conversation. A servant introduced a tall, middle-aged man, dressed in an ankle-length, tan robe tied with a sash at the waist. On his head was wound a white turban, beneath which long, curly side locks could be seen dangling in front of his ears. His beard was long and untrimmed. His appearance was more that of a scholar than a common merchant.

"Ladies, please allow me to introduce myself," the man said in a

---

2   King Sancheriv's invasion of the land of Yehudah occurred in 548 BCE.
3   *Rambam, Kedushah, Issurei Biah* 12:25.
4   The Avesta is the religious book of Zoroastrians and contains a collection of texts.

pleasant voice. "I am Chananya,[5] son of Pesachya of Nisibis, and I have come here to show Princess Samacha my wares, the finest silk fabrics imported from China. May I please display them to Her Highness?"

"Yes, of course, sir," Samacha replied with pleasure. She had heard that the Jewish merchants of nearby Nisibis offered the highest quality and variety of wares, but this was the first time she had received a visit from one of them.

The man's demeanor toward the women was both deferential and modest. He focused his gaze at a point just past them as he spoke. The women hurriedly sat upright in their couches. There was something about the dignified behavior of this man that made them quickly abandon their silly banter.

"Your timing could not have been more fortuitous," Samacha said. "We have just been talking of a festival for which we need to have new gowns made."

The gentleman opened an enormous saddlebag and removed from it more than a dozen samples of fine dyed silk cloth. Gasps of delight escaped the women's lips, as they viewed the exquisite patterns and vivid colors.

"These fabrics are certainly beautiful," Chananya agreed. "How amazing it is to think that they were produced by a lowly worm! How could a tiny creature of such limited intelligence create something of such soft texture, a material unique in its ability to absorb vibrant dyes, and to be of such great value and use? Surely, it did not originate the thought itself! Nor could such great talent be for naught!"

The women were mesmerized. They had never thought about such things before. This was just the reaction Chananya had expected.

"My dear ladies, let me tell you a story," the merchant continued.

"King Solomon was considered by all the people of his kingdom to be surpassed by none in his wisdom. When the queen of Sheba heard

---

5   Josephus, *Antiquities of the Jews*, 20:2.

of this, she sent a message to Yerushalayim stating her desire to test the king's wisdom. On the morning of her anticipated visit, King Solomon was stung on the nose, awakening him from his sleep. The king, who understood the language of all animals, summoned all of the stinging insects of the kingdom to find out which was the culprit. A timid bee came forward and admitted to inflicting the sting but swore that it was an accident. It seems that he mistook the king's nose for a beautiful flower. King Solomon forgave the bee, which promised to help the king in return one day.

"The queen of Sheba arrived later that day, and, after describing her difficult journey, arranged to meet with King Solomon the next afternoon. The purpose of the visit would be to present a challenge to determine if he really was as clever as popularly believed. The next day, the queen revealed eight flowers that looked and smelled exactly the same, but only one was real. She challenged the king to identify the real flower. King Solomon examined each flower closely, but was truly baffled. Then, the bee that had stung him entered and came to the rescue by flying straight to the real flower. King Solomon correctly pointed out the real flower, thus impressing the queen of Sheba with his wisdom."

The women sat forward in their seats, concentrating on Chananya's words.

"One could say that the bee was the hero of the story," Chananya interpreted. "Or, one could look beyond the bee to its Creator. Not only did the Creator form the bee, but He put it in a place where it could help King Solomon. He is a Creator Who actively rules the world, and this supervision is not limited to royalty. It extends down to the simplest individual. Not a finger can be raised without His willing it."

"How different is your religion from ours!" Samacha exclaimed. "The deity of Zoroaster does not control evil. I always wondered how he could be an all-powerful god if his authority is so limited!"

"How true!" Chananya assented. "I can see that Princess Samacha thinks deeply!"

He continued to display his choice fabrics, but it was clear that the princess's mind was elsewhere.

Samacha greeted her husband warmly when he returned home that evening.

"Izates, let me bring you some hot brew and your pipe," Samacha said, excitement in her voice. "After you have rested for awhile, I would like to share with you an interesting experience I had today."

"Surely, my dear," the prince responded. "Your thoughts and activities are always of interest to me."

When Samacha related the story told by Chananya and his discussion of the origin of silk, Izates paled and looked disturbed.

"Have I said anything to upset you, my husband?" Samacha asked worriedly. "I am always ready to defer to your opinion, especially when it comes to matters such as these, where your education is so superior to my own."

"No!" Izates insisted. "I am not reacting negatively to anything you have said. To the contrary, the ideas expressed by the Jewish merchant resonate with me and are strangely similar to those I have recently been considering myself. These concepts are in stark conflict with everything we have been brought up to believe! This is what is robbing me of any inner peace. It is shocking to me to realize that the conclusions I have been reaching are consistent with the religion of the Jews! Samacha, my dear wife and confidante, my heart and mind encourage me to believe in this one all-powerful G-d of the Jewish people. Perhaps you could arrange a meeting between me and the wise merchant you met today. There are a number of questions I would like to pose to him."

"Certainly," Samacha replied. "He is bringing me the fabric I ordered tomorrow. I can ask him then."

Several days later, Chananya paid a visit to Izates at his residence. The crown prince posed many deep and insightful questions to the elderly Jew, questions that could only originate in a heart striving for truth and spiritual purity. It was not until hours later that Izates fell silent, physically and emotionally exhausted by his quest. After recovering somewhat, he spoke softly and slowly, more to himself than to the Jew sitting opposite him.

"My final question is, what next?" Izates said agitatedly. "Is it possible for a Parthian prince to become a member of the Jewish people, or must I remain a gentile in all forms except in my beliefs? I have observed the Jews here. They keep themselves very separate from other citizens. Would they even accept converts?"

"Your observations are accurate, Your Highness," Chananya answered respectfully. "It is possible for gentiles to join the Jewish people as converts, but we do not encourage it.

"I see that you have a pure desire to serve the Creator in the way He established for His Chosen People," Chananya continued. "Nevertheless, there are alternatives for you to serve G-d in the way He has commanded the gentiles. You can study and observe the seven Noachide laws, which were given to all of mankind following the great Flood. This means believing in and worshipping the one true G-d and honoring and respecting His holy Name. It also means maintaining a system of just courts in your land and banning murder, theft, and immoral relationships, as well as the consumption of any limb from a live animal. Observing these commandments would enable you to fulfill your purpose in life as a righteous gentile and would give you the right to live in Eretz Yisrael as a *ger toshav*, a resident non-Jew. This is a privilege not granted to those who worship idols."

He looked at Izates, trying to gauge the prince's reaction. Izates remained silent, so Chananya continued.

"To become a Jew requires fulfilling even stricter requirements.

Any individual desiring to become a member of the Jewish people must first accept that all 613 commandments in the Torah are G-d-given and are binding upon him. Once the potential proselyte has acquired sufficient knowledge to become a practicing Jew, both males and females must immerse in a *mikveh* for the purpose of conversion, and males must be circumcised."

Izates remained silent for a few moments, a faraway, pensive look on his face. Then, suddenly, the prince turned to his guest with piercing eyes.

"Mar Chananya, I would like to begin learning your holy Torah, to become acquainted with its lessons and the commandments contained therein."

Chananya cleared his throat and hesitated before responding.

"Your Highness, Jewish law forbids teaching Torah to a gentile," he said finally. "The only exception is for a gentile who has sincerely committed to abandon the religion of his birth and become a proselyte according to Jewish law. Only then can he begin learning our sacred Torah."

"I understand," Izates declared. "I fully understand what you are saying, and I am ready to make this commitment. I know that you are required to try to dissuade me from joining your people, but my soul craves the closeness to the Alm-ghty that can only be achieved through learning His Torah and observing His commandments."

"But Your Highness," Mar Chananya replied, somewhat taken aback. "Becoming a Jew has many far-reaching implications, especially for a public personage such as you. There is no allowance for partial adherence to the precepts of the Torah. All of the mitzvos would be binding upon you, including observing the Shabbos, refraining from eating forbidden foods, the laws of family purity, laws pertaining to business and warfare, and laws limiting social mingling with gentiles. And once you've become a Jew, there is no turning back!"

"It is indeed reasonable that you require me to think about what you have said," the prince replied, slightly agitated. "Let us meet again tomorrow, sir, and I will be prepared with my answer."

Izates waited for Chananya the next day with nervous anticipation. He asked for his guest to be sent to a secret study located in a private wing of the palace.

Izates rose as soon as Chananya entered the room.

"I understand and accept all that you have said!" Izates declared. "My wife told me that she once heard that every Jewish soul was present at the giving of the Torah on Mount Sinai. She said this includes those not yet born as well as future converts. Could it be that my yearning to learn Torah indicates that perhaps my soul, too, was there at Sinai?"

"Perhaps," Chananya replied hesitantly. "But Prince Izates, are you aware that upon your conversion, you would be 'reborn' as a Jew with no familial connection to your blood relatives? Joining the Jewish people means severing filial ties with your gentile family!"

"That would be difficult," Izates admitted. "But I harbor a dream that, in time, they, too, will see the truth of Torah and seek to follow its laws."

Mar Chananya smiled at the prince in respectful resignation. "Man may dream, but only Hashem knows the future, my dear prince."

"With the Alm-ghty's help, is it not true that anything is possible?"

"You are correct, Your Highness," Chananya replied, clearly in awe of Izates's tenacity. "With Hashem's help, anything is possible."

Immediately following this conversation, Izates began meeting daily with Chananya. Only on Shabbos did their meetings fail to take place. On this holy day, Izates practiced observing the laws and prohibitions of the seventh day. At the same time, he was equally careful to transgress at least one of the mitzvos of Shabbos. In this way, he recognized that G-d gave the gift of Shabbos exclusively to the Jewish people. No gentile may fully share in it.

Izates also came to understand that the foundation of his home, were he to become a Jew, would be built, nurtured, and largely maintained by his wife. He came to appreciate the great breadth of knowledge she would need in order to run their home according to Torah law. He was relieved to learn that her heart likewise drew her to becoming a Jewess.

One late afternoon, Samacha wrapped herself in a white shawl and set out for the Jewish quarter of the city. She stopped before a small house, built into the wall of the Jewish quarter. She knocked tentatively on the wooden door and nervously awaited a response. After a minute or two, she heard voices from inside. A young boy of about six slowly opened the heavy door. He drew back at the sight of Samacha, who, in spite of her modest attire, did not appear to be a Jewess.

"Mama," he called, "someone is here to see you!"

"Invite her in, David," a warm, kindly voice answered. "Please tell her that I will be with her as soon as I finish putting the soup on the fire."

A few moments later, a petite, slender, middle-aged woman emerged. Her graceful beauty was undiminished by the passage of time, and her kind face radiated warmth and encouragement.

"Welcome!" the woman exclaimed. "Please, come in." Although the mistress of the house had been expecting this visitor, she looked curiously at the princess.

"I am Samacha, the wife of Prince Izates of Adiabene," the princess explained. "Your husband has taught us about the one, true G-d. He told me that when I was ready, you would teach me the laws of family purity."

"Greetings, Your Highness!" the woman responded warmly. "My name is Elisheva, and I am so very happy to meet you. My husband has the utmost respect for you and the prince and has instructed me to teach you all of the laws in detail. Make yourself comfortable, and I will pour you a mug of water. Please tell me about yourself."

Elisheva and Samacha chatted for the better part of an hour about their respective lives. Then the dialogue turned to the topic at hand.

"The first thing to remember is that the source of honor and glory for a Jewish woman is her home," Elisheva began. "The laws of family purity are *chukim*, laws for which there is no rational explanation. Nevertheless, we are always encouraged to search for meaning in the laws of Hashem, for this enhances the holiness we can achieve through following them. You will see that the laws of family purity safeguard the basic building blocks of our people, our Jewish homes, and our families."

The two women met several times a week over a period of many months. Samacha learned through these conversations not only the laws of family purity, but about the modesty and piety that defines the Jewish woman. In the process, the two women established a close relationship that would stand the test of time.

Chapter Three

Years passed, and the elderly King Monobaz missed his son so much that he sent for him to return home, in spite of his concerns for his safety.[1] Izates bade farewell to his father-in-law, packed his belongings, and loaded them onto a caravan of wagons drawn by strong mules. In the middle of the pack, where it would be safest, he placed the carriage pulled by Egyptian horses that bore his wife and baby son. Although the prince was looking forward to seeing his father once again, his demeanor was noticeably pensive during the week-long journey to Adiabene. Courtiers assumed that the crown prince was contemplating his future elevation to the throne. In truth, he was thinking about an "elevation" of a different nature altogether.

Following his return home, King Monobaz monopolized Izates's time for days. He reveled in every minute he was able to spend with his favorite son. It was not until the end of Izates's first week home that he enjoyed the luxury of spending time with his mother and brother. How the prince relished the joy of being in Adiabene! In spite of the great kindness and generosity lavished upon him by his father-in-law, Charax-Spasini had never felt like home. Nevertheless, despite the closeness he felt with his family, Izates did not feel ready to share his secret.

A faint sigh of relief escaped Izates as he entered the royal dining room just before the sun began to sink into the western sky. His

---

1   Josephus, *Antiquities of the Jews*, 20:2.

tired gaze took in the enormous room with its long wooden benches arranged around a polished marble table, while the last rays of sunshine reflected off the gilt pillars supporting the vaulted stone ceiling. Even after years of absence from Adiabene, this room evoked many memories. He recalled how he and his brother, Monobaz, had played hide-and-seek among the many deep alcoves and how he had had to sit through interminable state dinners. Strangely, he now looked around this room and felt like an outsider, rather than as a son returning to his childhood home.

It was Friday afternoon, and for the Jews, it would soon be time to greet the Shabbos. Mar Chananya had explained to Izates that Shabbos is the holiest day of the week, a testimony to Hashem's sovereignty as the One Who created the universe in six days. No productive labor could be done on Shabbos. The Jews spend one day each week in prayer, Torah study, festive meals, and rejoicing in this precious gift from Above.

This concept struck a chord in Izates's sensitive soul. To think one could achieve holiness by serving the Creator! Surely, reaching higher and higher levels of holiness was the sole purpose of life. Yet, the gift of Shabbos is only for the Jewish people.[2]

To become a Jew!

Izates closed his eyes, the yearning to join Mar Chananya's people washing over him. Believing in the one G-d came naturally to him. Performing all the mitzvos was likewise a privilege he craved. The only stumbling block was *bris milah*, the sign of the covenant between Hashem and Avraham, the first Jew. This mitzvah was absolutely essential in order for a male to become a member of the Jewish people.

Izates wanted to take this irreversible step, to be a Jew with his whole being, but how could he part ways so starkly with the people he was destined to rule? Beliefs are in the realm of the heart, but *bris milah*

---

[2] In fact, a gentile who observes all the laws of Shabbos is liable to the death penalty.

would physically brand him as inherently different. What would his mother say? Would this represent an affront to his father?

Yet, he reminded himself, the Torah states that Avraham Avinu circumcised himself in the middle of the day, unafraid of the reactions of the gentiles around him. Would his mother understand? Izates stood in the corner of the room, troubled by these conflicting thoughts.

Suddenly, he heard a faint rustling sound as the curtains over the room's far entrance parted, and Queen Helene walked slowly but purposefully toward the enormous table. How regal she was, Izates noted with love and pride. She hadn't noticed him, and he watched as she approached the table. Helene was wearing a long-sleeved robe over a dress, both made of cream-colored silk interwoven with pure gold threads. Her head was covered with an elaborate headdress bedecked with jewels. Necklaces and bracelets of silver graced her neck and narrow wrists, but the most striking and precious of the queen's adornments dangled gracefully from her ears. Each earring consisted of a large pearl set in a round, golden, beveled ring from which hung two pendants. Each of those pendants held a flawless emerald and small pearl set in a golden chain.[3] She had commissioned them specifically to honor the Shabbos and never wore them on a weekday.

Helene removed two small silver candlesticks, two wicks, and a small flask of olive oil from the folds of her robe and placed them on the table. She carefully poured the oil into depressions on top of the candlesticks and then inserted the wicks. She lifted a candle from its sconce on the wall, and touched it to the wicks until they burst into a strong, golden flame. After replacing the candle, she encircled her arms three times around the little lights. The queen then covered her face with her hands and whispered an inaudible prayer, followed by what appeared to

---

3   An earring of this description was found on the site assumed to be the ruins of Queen Helene's palace in Ir David. See "Every Earring Tells a Story," *Mishpacha Magazine* (Libi Astaire, January 31, 2013, 61-67).

be intense supplications. As Izates silently observed, she lifted the veil covering her face. A shiver traveled down his spine. Was he dreaming, or had he just witnessed his mother ushering in the holy Shabbos?

Izates softly whispered, "Mother," so as not to startle the queen. She turned around, surprised, and blushed with the knowledge that her actions had been observed.

Izates swiftly proceeded toward his mother and embraced her, just as he had as a young boy.

"Good Shabbos, Mother!" he whispered into her ear. Helene's face blanched, and she gazed deeply into her son's eyes.

"Izates, my son, you understand what I have just done?"

"Yes, Mother!" Izates answered, trembling. "You have just lit the lights welcoming the Shabbos queen. It appears that Hashem has led both of us to His Torah!" The prince paused, his face suffused with a smile of overwhelming joy. "You see, I, too, have become acquainted with the Jewish customs and laws during my stay in Charax-Spasini, Mother. Samacha introduced me to them after learning of them from the Jewish merchant Mar Chananya, who taught the women of the court the principles of his faith. At my request, she introduced me to Mar Chananya, and we began learning about the Torah together. As you probably know, Mother, Jews must cleave to their Torah teachers, and so I thankfully was able to persuade Mar Chananya to accompany me here."

Helene listened silently, her eyes on her son's face.

"During our trip home, we passed by the ruins of the ancient city of Nineveh," Izates continued. "Mar Chananya told me the story of the Jewish prophet Yonah, who was instructed by Hashem to go to that great city, home to 100,000 people, to convince them to repent for their evil deeds. The people of Nineveh eventually repented, and their city was saved from destruction. If a doomed city like Nineveh can be saved, then surely Hashem desires our repentance and acceptance of His sovereignty. So do my thoughts turn to serving the one G-d."

Izates's eyes shone as he looked into his mother's eyes.

"Mother, please tell me how you came to this same conclusion, even as we were separated by so many miles! What about my brother, Monobaz? Has he, too, accepted the Jewish faith?"

Helene raised her eyes heavenward in silent thanks to the Alm-ghty, Who had so suddenly removed her sense of loneliness and isolation. To be a Jewess was a great privilege in itself — but to know that her son had chosen the same path was a source of unbounded joy. After a few moments, she regained her composure and faced her son.

"My dear Izates, I, too, made the acquaintance of a member of the Jewish faith, who generously shared knowledge of his religion with me. Initially, I just listened, fascinated to learn of the oneness of the Alm-ghty and that He is merciful and just. I admired the beauty of His laws. The Jews treat each other with kindness and respect. They give generously to the poor. The holy Shabbos is a time for prayer and joyous celebration of the day of rest, which hearkens back to the creation of the universe. Gradually, I summoned the courage to ask for explanations of what I was hearing.

"How quickly it became clear to me that Judaism is the only true faith! The Torah answers nagging questions that prevented me from ever fully embracing the faith of Zoroaster in my heart, no matter how carefully I went through the motions! The one true G-d rules not only over the good, but also over evil. There is nothing that is not in His power to do. Life has meaning and purpose that is dictated by the laws of the Torah, not fabricated by men of weak moral constitution. Man can truly achieve holiness through love of Hashem and observance of His Torah, and this holiness is not confined to this ephemeral world. No, it follows us into the World to Come, a world where there is no conflict, but only goodness.

"I began visiting synagogues on Shabbos, disguised, of course, so as not to be recognized," Helene admitted. "I met women there who, like me, were attracted to the beauty of Jewish practices and beliefs. They explained that they had taken upon themselves selected laws and rites but stopped short of identifying totally with the Jewish people. These women are members of a group called 'those who fear G-d.' They tried to convince me of the advantages of this compromise. It avoided family conflict, yet enhanced their lives appreciably. I smiled and nodded, but in my heart, I knew there could be no partial subscription to the Jewish faith. So much of the beauty and holiness I perceived rested on the way every aspect of life is circumscribed by the laws of the Torah through the guidance of its sages."

Helene smiled. "And yes, Izates," she added, "your brother, Monobaz, has abandoned the worship of Zoroaster and now studies the laws of the Torah day and night."

"My brother?"

"Yes, my son," Helene responded softly. "Both of you have discovered the true G-d, and my sense of thankfulness to the Alm-ghty knows no bounds."

The prince remained silent as he gazed into the distance. He finally looked back at his mother.

"Mother, may I ask how our relatives have reacted to your conversion?" Izates asked tentatively.

"They are not pleased," Helene responded delicately. She fingered her long gold necklace nervously as her mind replayed the painful berating she had received from her older sister for her "apostasy."

"You fool!" Cassandra had shouted hysterically, upon hearing of Helene's desire to convert to Judaism. "Not only will you lose all the respect of your subjects, but you threaten the social status of every member of your family with your impulsivity. How can you do this to us? Have you no sense of loyalty? Does our shame mean nothing to you? Do you care nothing for us?"

Helene forced herself to return to the present and responded to

Izates's question dispassionately. "I admit some reactions have been strong. There are those who have ceased to communicate with me altogether. Others have become very distant, but since I am still the queen, their response has been muted by respect for the monarchy."

"I see…" Izates said, avoiding eye contact with his mother.

"I am sorry, my son. I wish I could tell you that all of your relatives are supportive of my desire to live according to the Torah, but alas, this is not true." Helene looked directly into Izates's dark, liquid eyes.

"I see you are troubled, my son. Please tell me what is bothering you."

Izates hesitated, but his mother's kind face and deep, understanding eyes encouraged him to share what he had not yet revealed to anyone.

"Mother, while my heart has yearned to wholeheartedly adopt the faith of the people of Israel, imagining your opposition has held me back. Now, dear Mother, that I see our sympathies are one and the same, I stand prepared, with Hashem's help, to complete the process of my conversion to Judaism with alacrity.

"There is just one issue that steals my peace of mind." The words flowed from Izates's mouth like water rushing through an open floodgate. "For a man to become a full-fledged Jew, immersion in the *mikveh* is insufficient. Only through entry into the covenant of Avraham with circumcision will he be both privileged and obligated to perform the mitzvos. I know there are great risks, Mother, for a king to distinguish himself in such a physical way from the rest of his people. What an affront this could be to our subjects! Nevertheless, I am committed to subjecting myself to *bris milah*, for this is the only way I can fulfill my destiny as a member of Hashem's Chosen People!"

Helene turned pale and began to tremble, overwhelmed by the implications of her son's words. She had already been the target of venomous verbal attacks by members of her family who had heard of her religious leanings. She could ignore them easily enough, since as a woman they would be unlikely to take any action on their threats.

But her son! He was constantly in danger from enemies both within and without.

"No, Izates, this is a step you must not take!" she blurted out with uncharacteristic forcefulness. "Surely, you know how happy and proud you have made me by accepting the Jewish faith. I do not want to dissuade you from believing in the one G-d and His law. But how can a king of a gentile nation perform an act that would inevitably be viewed as odious to his subjects? The people of Adiabene will never agree to be ruled by an openly Jewish monarch! The result could be rebellion, war, death — and the ultimate destruction of our family. My son, putting your life in dire danger would not only diminish your effectiveness as a leader but would inhibit, rather than enhance, your performance of mitzvos."[4]

Izates sighed heavily. "It is very hard for me to accept your words, Mother," he said, "but, out of deference to you, I will let this matter rest for the time being. Nevertheless, I do not know how long I can continue living a masquerade of hypocrisy. One cannot be a half-Jew, but you are correct. Entry into the covenant of Avraham is not just a physical act. It is an act that will transform my soul from that of a gentile to the *neshamah* of a member of Hashem's Chosen People. Nothing less will accomplish this."

Helene stood still as Izates paced back and forth.

"Please consider this, too, dear Mother," he said, turning back to the queen. "I have an illustrious precedent. The sages teach us that Yisro circumcised himself in the desert for the purpose of conversion. Not one of the Bnei Yisrael had a *bris milah* in the desert, because there was no northerly wind, making it dangerous for them to do so. How, then, could Yisro have a *bris*? It was because he had no choice! Those who were born as Jews needed a *bris* to fulfill Hashem's mitzvah, but they were inherently Jews. For one who was not born into the Jewish

---

4   Josephus, *Antiquities of the Jews*, 20:2.

people, the only way to become a Jew is through *bris* and immersion in a *mikveh*."[5]

Helene gazed at her son with both admiration and fear. She nodded, indicating that he could take his leave.

"Good Shabbos, my son."

"Good Shabbos, Mother," Izates responded, smiling wanly. The prince kissed his mother's hand and left the hall.

As much as he wanted to honor his mother's wishes, Izates could not rest with his decision. After several sleepless nights, he decided to consult with Mar Chananya. The merchant was summoned to the royal study, where Izates briefed him on his conversation with his mother. Chananya was silent for a moment as he pondered how to present his response to the prince.

"Your Royal Highness," he said slowly, "after carefully reconsidering this matter, I must agree fully with the queen. When I initially explained to the prince the requirements for a non-Jew to learn Torah, I wanted to be certain that your intentions were sincere, that you were not simply pursuing an academic interest. At that time I did consider the possibility that His Highness would insist upon full conversion to Judaism, but I also knew that achieving the lesser status of the *ger toshav* would represent a great spiritual gain for you personally, and this is the choice I hoped you would make."

Mar Chananya paused. The air was heavy with tension as Izates waited for his next words.

"There is no doubt in my mind that circumcision would be an anathema to Adiabene's populace," he finally said. "Their rage at their ruler for an act that would be viewed as self-mutilation would know no bounds. I must plead with His Royal Highness to desist from taking

---

5   *Sanhedrin* 94.

this step. While you are correct that complete observance of Jewish law requires a *bris milah*, why don't you substitute intensified worship of Hashem for this lapse? The Alm-ghty will surely forgive you for not performing the operation."

Izates's eyes were very dark as he looked steadily at Chananya.

"If you should undergo a *bris milah*," Chananya continued, "I could not subject myself and my family to the personal threat that would result. My only choice would be to leave Adiabene forthwith. Once it became known that I, as His Highness's teacher, encouraged the deed, I would surely find myself in mortal danger."

Izates felt as if a sword had stabbed his heart.

"Your words pain me, Mar Chananya!" he replied. "To think that only this one significant act prevents me from becoming a member of G-d's Chosen People leaves a hollow feeling in my heart. Nonetheless, your persuasions are compelling. Besides, how could I bear it if you left the royal court?"

"Everything will be good, my prince," Chananya reassured his student. "Try not to trouble yourself further with such disturbing thoughts. Your kingdom needs you!"

Chapter Four

As Tammuz turned into Av and then gave way to Elul, the dry hills of Adiabene were relieved of the full intensity of the sun's rays. A visitor approached from the northern region of Eretz Yisrael. Although he was a cloth merchant, Rabbi Eliezer Hagalili's primary occupation was the study of Torah. He was recognized as a leading sage, and his passion for proper observance of the law was well known.

Rabbi Eliezer had heard rumors that Queen Helene had converted to Judaism and that her sons had likewise rejected their religion of birth. Word had also circulated in Eretz Yisrael that the merchant, Chananya, was threatening to leave Adiabene if the men of the royal family would perform the mitzvah of *bris milah*.

The goal of Rabbi Eliezer's long journey to Adiabene was to meet Prince Izates in order to determine if what he heard bore truth and to provide him with halachic guidance. Based on what he understood about the sincerity and honesty of the royal family, Rabbi Eliezer was optimistic that, with G-d's help, his mission would be successful.

The first step was to gain an audience with the prince. Indeed, word had it that the royal court was well disposed toward visitors from Eretz Yisrael. The queen and her family were always thirsty for news from the Holy Land. Hopefully, the prince would be receptive to visitors as well. The actions of the highly visible royal family were closely watched by Jews and gentiles alike, and there must be no confusion about the Torah's requirements for conversion. Rabbi Eliezer spent most of the two-week trip in prayer.

Upon his arrival in Adiabene, Rabbi Eliezer stopped at the home of Daniel Hasocher, a trader whose family had lived in that country for generations. Daniel was the unofficial spiritual head of the Jewish community.

Although weary from his journey, Rabbi Eliezer engaged in conversation right away.

"Tell me," Rabbi Eliezer said, "is it true that the crown prince considers himself a member of our people?"

"Yes, my brother," Daniel responded. "But this is a fact not yet known by the populace and one that must be kept a total secret at present. Prince Izates is quite diligent about following all aspects of Jewish law. Nevertheless, I have been informed by my friend, Chananya, that he has not undergone a *bris milah*. In truth, Prince Izates would become a *ger tzedek* immediately, if not for the precarious political situation. It is only his public position that has prevented him from completing his conversion. He has been pressured to refrain from taking this step out of fear of mass rebellion to the idea of a Jewish king."

"So he is not a Jew," Rabbi Eliezer said thoughtfully.

"Correct, he cannot yet be considered a Jew," Daniel agreed.

Rabbi Eliezer became very agitated, and it was difficult for him to contain his emotion.

"The prince must know the truth!" he cried. "In order for any male to be considered a member of the Jewish people, he must first undergo a *bris milah*. There is no such thing as an uncircumcised Jew. No committed individual should refrain from joining the Jewish nation out of fear of man. G-d, Who never sleeps or rests, will surely watch over any sincere individual who chooses to become a member of His people! The future king must be told the truth."

Daniel nodded. "Of course, you are correct, Rabbi Eliezer. I believe Prince Izates will be open to your words."

"Whom should I see to gain an audience with him?" Rabbi Eliezer asked.

"I can introduce you to Chananya, the Jew who is closest to Prince Izates," Daniel offered. "I would advise you, however, not to mention the purpose of your visit. Chananya's feelings on the subject are strong and are motivated by great anxiety about the possible repercussions to him and to the Jewish community here."

Dusk was giving way to darkness when the two white-robed figures made their way down the narrow winding streets of the Jewish quarter to Chananya's home. A look of surprise came over the merchant's face when he opened the door to see his friend standing alongside a stranger.

"Come in, come in! To what do I owe this nocturnal visit?" Chananya asked.

"Good evening, Chananya!" Daniel responded heartily. "May I introduce you to Rabbi Eliezer Hagalili from Eretz Yisrael? He has traveled to Adiabene to request an audience with Prince Izates. He must discuss an urgent, confidential matter. We seek your assistance in obtaining an appointment with His Highness."

"May I ask what this matter concerns?" Chananya asked nervously.

"I am afraid I am not at liberty to share the topic of the meeting," Rabbi Eliezer said. "But I assure you that it is not prompted by any immediate threat to the Jews either here in Adiabene or in the Holy Land."

"*Baruch Hashem*," Chananya replied, relieved. "Please return here after morning prayers, and I will be glad to accompany you to the palace for an audience with the prince."

The sound of the shofar coming from every synagogue pierced the early morning air in the Jewish quarter. It heralded the start of the month of Elul and aroused the people to do *teshuvah* in preparation for Rosh Hashanah, the upcoming Day of Judgment.

Daniel Hasocher and Rabbi Eliezer traveled with Chananya by carriage to the palace, where Rabbi Eliezer requested an audience with the prince. Rabbi Eliezer unloaded the finest bolts of cloth from his donkey and introduced himself to Bozan, the chief steward, as Eliezer from the Galil, in the northern Land of Israel.

"You are welcome to enter, sir," Bozan replied politely. "However, Prince Izates cannot receive visitors until the completion of his study session, in another hour."

"I am both obliged and honored to wait," Rabbi Eliezer answered with an appreciative smile. *The prince appears to have a fixed time for Torah learning*, he thought to himself. *Perhaps he will be more receptive to my message than I thought.*

Chananya left, so as to give the sage the privacy he had requested.

At the designated time, Bozan returned to usher the guest to the prince's study. Izates was still sitting bent over a large Torah scroll, studying intently. He did not hear the knock on the thick wooden door.

"Your Highness," Bozan said softly. "I sincerely apologize for interrupting your studies, but a visitor has arrived from the Land of Israel who appears to have important information to share with my master. His name is Rabbi Eliezer of the Galil."

Izates nodded. "Please send Rabbi Eliezer in," he said quickly. Guests from the Holy Land were always welcome at the palace. "I will meet privately with our honored guest, so please make certain no one disturbs us."

Rabbi Eliezer was ushered into the room.

"I apologize for interrupting your study session, Your Highness," Rabbi Eliezer said. "I am Eliezer Hagalili, and I come to you with the finest pure wool of Eretz Yisrael. I also offer sewing threads of Egyptian cotton. They are free of linen and consistent with the laws prohibiting the wearing of *shatnez*."

"Many thanks to you, sir," Izates answered with enthusiasm. "It is for this reason that I have determined to accept only cloth from the Holy Land for the royal garments and upholsteries. Here, in Adiabene, we do not have the ability to be so certain of the makeup of textiles imported from elsewhere."

"Your servant is truly impressed with His Royal Highness's knowledge of this law," Rabbi Eliezer responded deferentially. "However, if I may ask the prince's pardon and seek permission to speak further, it is only because I see how very meticulous His Highness is concerning performance of so many of the mitzvos. As Jews, we are all responsible for the spiritual welfare of one another. Part of safeguarding that welfare is ensuring that the definition of a Jew is strictly maintained. As a result of this concern, I will be blunt at the risk of my life, because all who sincerely accept the yoke of Torah desire guidance concerning what is right and true.

"It is clear that Prince Izates of Adiabene considers himself a practicing Jew," Rabbi Eliezer continued. "Word of His Highness's intent to convert has reached the farthest corners of the Parthian Empire and has likewise become known in Eretz Yisrael. Is it not true that, in spite of professing to be loyal to the Torah in its entirety, His Highness has not undergone the mitzvah of *bris milah*?"

Rabbi Eliezer allowed his words to sink in before continuing. "Prince Izates, please consider that you are committing a desecration of Hashem's holy Name by refraining from performing this mitzvah while professing to be loyal to the Torah in its entirety. It is not sufficient to know the laws of the Torah. Every Jew is obligated to practice the Torah's commandments. I adjure His Highness to act in accordance with his convictions!"

Izates's complexion suddenly turned chalk white, and he felt himself growing faint. He sank low into his chair, as if pressed down by a physical force. After a few moments, the prince recovered sufficiently to silently dismiss the merchant with a gesture.

Rabbi Eliezer walked backwards as he exited the chamber, out of respect for the prince. It seemed that his words had made their intended impact. He hurriedly left Adiabene to avoid being questioned about his meeting.

Izates picked up his head weakly.

"Bozan," he said, "please summon my brother, Monobaz, immediately."

The chief steward jumped to attention. "Yes, Your Highness. I know he is waiting to see you."

Moments later, Monobaz hurried into the room with a sense of alarm.

"My dear brother," Izates greeted him quietly, sadness permeating his voice, "come learn with me."

Monobaz sat down at the table, and Izates passed him a large parchment scroll. Together, they began chanting from *Sefer Bereishis*. When they reached the verse that says, *And you shall circumcise the flesh of your foreskin*, each turned his face toward the wall and wept. After some time, they parted silently.

Izates had made his decision. He summoned a *mohel* living in Nisibis and was circumcised. Monobaz, unbeknownst to his brother, engaged a different *mohel* and did the same.

A few days passed before the two brothers met again to study *Sefer Bereishis*. Once again, they arrived at the *pasuk* describing the mitzvah of circumcision. Izates turned to his brother and cryptically asked, "Who are you, my brother?"

Monobaz understood what his brother was implying and responded, "Perhaps you are the same, Izates, but I am not the same as I was."

Unable to contain himself, Izates hugged his brother and cried tears of gladness and relief. Later, out of reach of prying eyes and ears, each revealed to the other details of his circumcision, immersion in the *mikveh*, and official conversion.

The anguish was over. They were both Jews and could now serve Hashem as full-fledged members of the Chosen People. The last vestige of idolatry had been washed away with the purifying waters.[1]

No one was present at the time Izates revealed his secret to his brother. Nonetheless, they spoke in Hebrew to avoid detection, just in case. The court of Adiabene was always bustling. As a matter of national law, potential heirs to the throne could not be left alone in the palace. Servants and messengers were coming and going at every hour of the day and night. Both princes realized how challenging it would be to keep their conversions secret.

Izates and Samacha's baby son, Moshe, was converted to Judaism by being circumcised and immersing in the *mikveh*.[2] Reuven, Yosef, Yehudah, and Yaakov would be born after their mother's conversion, as full-fledged Jews from the womb.

During those days of her sons' recuperation, Helene perceived what had transpired without being explicitly told. Her first thoughts were of her husband, King Monobaz. How would he react if he knew the truth? She thought quickly and proceeded to the king's chambers.

"Helene, my dear," the king greeted her warmly. "I can tell that there is a specific purpose to your visit today, other than to spend time with me."

"Why do you tease me, my husband?" Helene responded, attempting

---

1 *Yalkut Shimoni, Parshas Lech Lecha*, 62.
2 At the age of thirteen, he would validate his conversion by explicitly accepting the Torah by choice.

NEZIRAH ꙮ 57

a smile. "I am always honored to be in the king's presence, but that does not preclude my desire to discuss household developments from time to time."

"Of course," the king replied. "What is on your mind, my most esteemed queen?"

"I did not desire to worry you, my husband, and I am thankful to report that the news is now positive. Both of our sons suddenly developed an illness that affects the skin, and the doctor told me the only cure was for them to be immediately circumcised. The procedure was performed with due haste, and the doctor tells me that they are now cured. We must offer thanks to the Power above."[3]

"Circumcised?" Monobaz questioned incredulously. "The doctor truly saw no other way to save them?"

"No," Helene answered firmly. "There was no other way to save them."

"So be it," the aging king said resignedly.

Fortunately, King Monobaz did not bring up the potentially dire implications of his sons' circumcisions, and the matter was laid to rest.

Helene uttered a silent prayer of thanks that her husband did not suspect the true motive behind the circumcisions. She then retreated into her private quarters to recite Tehillim. Perhaps Hashem, in His great mercy, would prevent the rite from becoming public knowledge just yet. This would at least delay the backlash she fully expected once it did become known. Maybe, with Hashem's help, there would be a way to ultimately avert it.

Chananya understood the true meaning of the royal brothers' "illness" and immediately left the royal court. He was more embarrassed by his opposition to their full conversion than anxious about its potential repercussions.

---

3   *Yalkut Shimoni, Parshas Lech Lecha*, 62.

Now it was time for the queen to finalize her own decision. Helene contacted Rabbi Yitzchak, the head of the *beis din* in Nisibis. It was evening by the time the missive from the queen was delivered to the *dayan*. Rabbi Yitzchak nodded slightly, apparently accepting what he read, and then immediately set out with two of his adult daughters for the royal residence in Adiabene. The gatekeepers were waiting for them and admitted the trio without question. No more than a few minutes later, the queen, escorted by the two young women, exited the palace and entered a covered carriage. Helene was taken to the *mikveh* in Arbela, where she was met by Rabbi Yitzchak; Rabbi Yosef, a rabbi of the Arbela community; and Daniel Hasocher. Helene immersed, shedding her identity as a gentile to become a full-fledged Jewess.

Prior to Rabbi Yitzchak's return to Nisibis, Izates met with the *dayan* to request that a pious, learned Jew be sent to serve the royal court. Rabbi Yitzchak dispatched Rabbi Alexander, a middle-aged scribe, who became a personal *melamed* to Izates's children and a religious advisor to the royal family. His wife, a kindhearted and wise woman, would become the queen's mentor and confidant.

Chapter Five

King Monobaz summoned Izates to the throne room some time after his circumcision.

"It has been so good to be with you, even for a short while, my son," the king greeted him. "Nevertheless, as much as I would like to continue to enjoy your company here, my fears for your welfare stand in the way of my pleasure." He sighed, then continued. "Izates, it is with great sadness that I send you now to your new exile. This time, though, you will reside on land you can call your own.

"My son, you have done well for yourself and have proved yourself worthy of expanding your reign beyond the land given to you by King Abennerig, your father-in-law. I hereby grant you power over the country of Carrae as well, a land whose soil is rich in valuable amomum[1] and history. The ark of Noach rested on this territory after the great Flood. May its remains be a source of Divine protection for both you and your family."

Izates bowed his head in silent acquiescence.

"I know not how much longer I will be in this world, Izates," Monobaz continued. "When I am summoned on High, you will be recalled to your homeland to assume the mantle of kingship. I have no doubt that you will be faithful to your people and to the rich heritage

---

1 Amomum was a substance used in cooking, and as a stimulant, perfume, and medicine.

of Adiabene, and this knowledge gives your old father great peace of mind. For this I thank you, my son."

Izates's parting from his family was an echo of his earlier separation from them. He lived in Carrae for several years, during which time his knowledge of Torah was strengthened by intense study. His physical proximity to the burial site of Noach's ark gave him a constant awareness of the fragility of man in his struggle against the evil inclination.

During this time, his father fell ill and died.[2] King Monobaz I had never questioned his sons' circumcisions or their disinterest in the religion of Zoroaster. The path of succession was much more important to the aged king than differences in philosophy, and so, upon his deathbed, he reiterated his desire that his younger son be crowned king upon his demise.[3]

The day after her husband's death, Helene sent for all the noblemen of the kingdom and governors of the land, requesting that they assemble the following day at the palace. She engaged in intense prayer, beseeching G-d to preserve the kingdom under the leadership of her son and to give her the wisdom to meet the challenges ahead.

The dignitaries arrived by noon the next day, bedecked in their finest clothing, and feeling much honored by the queen's summons. Little did they know how terrified the queen felt at that moment. Helene steadied her voice, quieted her inner trembling, and began to speak slowly and deliberately to the group.

"Respected noblemen, I believe you are not unacquainted with the fact that my husband desired our son, Izates, to succeed him in the government and thought him worthy to do so. However, I have called you

---

2   Monobaz I passed away in the year 35 CE.
3   Henry Zirndorf, *Some Jewish Women* (Philadelphia: The Jewish Publication Society of America, 1892).

together to await your determination on the matter, for happy is he who receives a kingdom, not from a single person only, but from the willing vote of a majority. The purpose of this meeting is to poll the sentiments of those present."

The noblemen approached the throne one by one and paid their homage to the queen, as was their custom. When it was time to voice their opinions, Bagdat, the most senior of the noblemen, spoke first.

"Your Majesty," he began authoritatively. "I confirm the decision of our deceased King Monobaz, may he rest in peace, that Prince Izates inherit the throne. Long live King Izates!"

One by, each of the nobles present cast his assenting vote, promising to submit to the decision of their late king. Then Wahram, one of the local governors, stepped forward.

"Now that Izates has been chosen as king, we must ensure the perpetuation of his reign," he said. "I propose we slay all competing kinsmen immediately to eliminate any jealousy that could threaten our new king's authority."

Helene, who was totally opposed to violence, gasped.

"Thank you, honored officers, for your kindness to myself and to King Izates," she said in a conciliatory tone. "However, I desire to defer the execution of these people until the new king arrives and is given the opportunity to ratify or reject the decision."

"Your Majesty, if you do not approve the rapid execution of these threats to the security of our great King Izates's kingdom, then at least keep them in bonds until the king's return," a particularly vocal member of the group proposed. "This will also provide them protection from potentially violent internecine rivalry."

"Furthermore," another noble piped up, "we advise you, our revered queen, to appoint one of your most respected and trustworthy subjects to serve as acting monarch right away."

"Your advice is well taken," Helene acceded. "Let my elder son,

Monobaz, be appointed interim king. I will apprise him of your opinion concerning the security risk posed by potential rivals to the throne, and he will decide how to proceed."[4]

"Bozan, please summon my son!" she instructed.

Within moments, Prince Monobaz appeared in the state room, looking gaunt and visibly distraught at the fresh news of his father's death, but ready to do his mother's will. Helene temporarily dismissed the assembled officials to have some private words with the prince. Mother and son embraced, tears streaming down their faces. Helene took a few moments to compose herself before she spoke.

"My dear son, I greatly apologize for speaking to you in this way at this difficult time, but, as I have told you many times since you were a young boy, we are royalty, and our first concern is for the people we rule. You know that it was your father's dying wish for your younger brother, Izates, to take over the kingship of Adiabene upon his death. This decision is in no way a reflection of the relative worthiness of my sons. It is simply the decision of your late father, and it in no way diminishes my great love and esteem for you or the regard of your countrymen for you. As a sign of my great trust in you and your affection for your dear brother, I hereby appoint you as regent in his stead, until such time as he shall be physically present to assume his new duties as king. Please lower your head for your mother now, my dear son, so I can crown you as king, and extend your finger for receipt of your father's signet."

"I will do as you wish, Mother," Monobaz replied humbly, "and I ask for your blessing that Hashem grant me the wisdom and His protection to carry out His will."

The queen reassembled the dignitaries and took her official place on the throne, with Monobaz standing to her right.

"My son, Monobaz," Helene announced, "you are hereby enjoined to administer the affairs of Adiabene justly and righteously until the

---

4   Josephus, *Antiquities of the Jews*, 20:2.

arrival of your brother, Izates, who will then take over the reins of kingship. May G-d bless you and grant success to your every endeavor."

Within several minutes, trumpets could be heard blaring long, insistent blasts outside the palace. The sound carried down the mountain to the marketplace below, throwing both merchants and customers into bedlam.

"Surely, King Izates has arrived! Long live the king!" came the excited shouts.

"No, no," others protested. "It is not possible for Izates to have returned to Adiabene so quickly. Maybe there has been a coup and the government was taken over by usurpers!"

A young boy pulled at his mother's long caftan to whisper in her ear. "Will there be a war, Mother?" he asked worriedly.

"No, certainly not, my son," his mother assured him. "The royal family despises violence. Surely, there will be a peaceful transition of power."

"Prince Monobaz has been declared interim king!" another man shouted excitedly.

"I'm not taking any chances," said a petty officer. "I will encourage my family to stay safely in our home to await the outcome. Once I know which king is ultimately in power I will declare my allegiance to one party."

Monobaz's initial reign was short-lived, for Izates returned less than one week later. On the day of his arrival, he made his way ceremoniously through the streets of the capital, riding upon a white Egyptian stallion decorated with garlands of flowers. Following him was a troop of six hundred infantrymen, marching in step, accompanied by a special contingent blowing trumpets. A score of musicians beat rhythmically on a bandir,[5] an engagement gift bestowed upon Izates by his father-in-law, years earlier.

---

5   A small wooden instrument consisting of hide-topped drums.

Behind them came Izates's wife, reclining on a palanquin studded with precious stones that sparkled in the midday sun. Regal as her bearing was, Samacha's gentle features wore a tentative look. She wondered what personal risks were inherent in their new status. The people of Adiabene knew that Izates, the heir apparent, was coming home to claim the throne from his older brother. What would happen, she worried, when they learned that Izates had adopted the Jewish faith? Would they truly accept a Jewish monarch? How would her mother-in-law relate to her now that she was to be the wife of the king?

But, as it happened, Samacha was able to discount most of her fears as unjustified, at least at the present time. As the royal procession wound around the mountain paths toward the palace, the citizens of Adiabene gazed admiringly at their new king and his beautiful wife, reassured by their strong belief that either brother was truly fit to rule their beloved country. It was strange, perhaps, that the reins of power would be so quickly transferred from an older to a younger brother, but politics was of little interest to the largely peasant population. They only cared to have a ruler who was just and honest, who would be strong enough to defend them against outside forces and benevolent enough to spare them from crippling taxes.

Suddenly, as if their collective minds had been made up, a surging groundswell of voices could be heard shouting, "Long live King Izates!" The rhythmic chant grew successively louder: "Long live King Izates, ruler of Adiabene. Long live King Izates!"

The head of the parade had just arrived in front of the arched door of the imposing stone palace. The crowd pushed forward like a wave toward the palace entrance and had to be held back forcefully by armed sentries. Only Izates and his entourage were allowed through the heavy wooden door. After being whisked inside by a liveried honor guard, Izates, his wife, and their attendants were hurried to the throne room, where Queen Helene sat next to her son, Monobaz. Upon seeing her younger son, the queen began to weep uncontrollably. Izates hurried down the long aisle to the thrones and embraced both his mother and brother together, weeping on their shoulders. All three realized that a momentous event was transpiring. The new monarchy would be fundamentally different from the old, for King Izates's rule would be guided by the principles of the Torah. Knowing how to rule in trying situations would require much rabbinic guidance. Would they be able to obtain answers quickly enough? Would their pagan country accept them as Jewish rulers? Would the Parthians and their Roman rivals see them as a small but significant threat to the existing world order?

Helene blessed her two sons. "May both of you, Monobaz and Izates, always support and encourage each other and be blessed with Divine assistance in all your endeavors," she murmured. "Let the Torah guide all of your actions, and do not allow yourselves to be intimidated by any mortal man."

Helene opened her eyes to see Izates's wife and son standing timidly in the background.

"Samacha, my daughter, and Moshe, my beloved grandson, welcome home to take your rightful place in the royal household!" They embraced, and Samacha's intimidation vanished. She smiled, encouraged by the warmth of her mother-in-law's greeting.

Gaining her composure and assuming her standard regal demeanor, Helene turned again to her son.

"Izates," she began, "your father, who loved you more than life itself, intended for you to succeed him. In your absence, your brother has acted as your surrogate, a role which he has assumed with responsibility and honor. I now call upon King Monobaz to resign the government to his younger brother, as per his father's dying request."

A trumpet sounded from the rear of the hall. Monobaz rose, turned to his mother and kissed her on both cheeks, and then stood facing Izates. He placed his hands upon his younger brother's head and pronounced the Priestly Blessing with which Jewish fathers bless their children.

"*May Hashem bless you and safeguard you.*

"*May Hashem illuminate His countenance for you and be gracious to you.*

"*May Hashem turn His countenance to you and establish peace for you.*"

There was silence as Izates stood still, his head bowed.

"Izates, my most honored brother," Monobaz finally said, "I hereby place the reins of the government of Adiabene into your worthy hands. May your tenure be one of longevity, and may your rule be peaceful."

Monobaz kissed his brother, then lifted the crown from his own head and placed it on Izates. He put his father's signet ring on his brother's index finger and gave him the royal sampser ornament.[6] He then quickly left the chamber accompanied by his attendants, who were stunned by the ease and goodwill with which power had been transferred. Izates and Monobaz were thankful for the outward smoothness of the process. At the same time, they were not naïve to the risks facing the new monarchy.

Following the coronation ceremony and accompanying feast, King Izates retreated to the royal study for prayer and to consider the implications of his new role. After several hours, he requested an audience with his brother.

"Monobaz," Izates said, "do you think we will be able to rule unopposed, or are there those who believe they are better suited to run the government?"

"King Izates, my brother," Monobaz replied gently, "although I wish the answer were otherwise, I must be quite frank with you. The dispossessed of our brethren threaten us with nothing less than a coup." He sighed. "The noblemen urged Mother to slay our close relatives immediately upon Father's death," he explained. "Of course, she

---

[6] Josephus refers to this ornament but does not elaborate further as to its description.

firmly opposed that course of action, but I felt impelled to concede to their insistence that they be kept in bonds until your arrival."

"Please take me to them now," Izates said firmly. "I must see them."

Bahram, the keeper of the dungeon, was summoned. He gave the two brothers lit candles and led them down a stone stairwell to a place where no light seemed to penetrate. The heavy metal door was unchained and slowly swung open. The three then descended another stone staircase, where a second door stood bolted. Izates peered through a peephole in the thick door. The sight that greeted him was greatly displeasing to him. In the dark, dank dungeon were about a dozen men, loosely chained together at their wrists. It took several minutes for Izates's eyes to adjust to the darkness before he could discern some vague features. With difficulty, he recognized each of his stepbrothers. Although they had not been raised as a family unit, he was somewhat familiar with them.

The king turned away quickly, visibly shaken. Bahram beckoned for Izates to enter a side room.

"Your Highness," Bahram said, "the queen has ordered that these prisoners be provided with the same food that she herself partakes of, and the cell is cleaned daily. Their chains are removed periodically, and exercise in the adjoining jail yard is provided for them. The period of incarceration was only intended to extend to your arrival, as a protection for the royal family."

"Yes, I understand, Bahram. The treatment you describe is no less than I would have expected from my kind mother. I will inform you when further arrangements for the prisoners are completed."

Izates and Monobaz emerged from the dungeon and returned to the royal study. Izates sat at the large wooden desk that had belonged to his father, his features drawn.

"Would Father desire that his sons wither and die so that I can reign?" he asked Monobaz.

"Yes, dear brother," Monobaz answered firmly. "Our father would have waged a war against his most powerful enemies and, yes, even his own sons, to ensure that you reign, so great was his love for you. You must surely know that your position can only be secure with respect to me. I cannot speak for the loyalty of our half-brothers and our cousins, their cronies."

"Of course, my dear brother," Izates responded. "It would be a crime against G-d to either slay or permanently imprison them. At the same time, I know I cannot trust them to protect our father's dying wish that I succeed him on the throne. Let them live, but far away from here. Make arrangements immediately for the transport of each of our father's blood relatives to our allies Claudius Caesar in Rome or to King Artabanus of Parthia with the explicit instructions that they are to remain there as court hostages for the remainder of their days.[7] I am fully aware that their ability to harm us will remain and that this will necessitate extra vigilance, but let our compassion be a merit for us in Heaven. I cannot kill them."

Celebrations commemorating the coronation of Izates continued for the entire week. The national mood could only be described as ecstatic at the smooth transition of power to the favorite son of their beloved king. The coronation feast, while joyous and colorful, met the highest standards of kashrus. No wine was served, because only wine that is untouched by gentiles is permitted to Jews, lest it be tainted by use for idolatrous purposes. While such celebrations would usually span a full seven days, Izates had announcements posted stating that the parties could continue from Sunday through Thursday, so as not to conflict with preparations for Shabbos.

Helene thanked Hashem that word of her sons' circumcision and full conversion to Judaism had not reached the public ear prior to

---

7   Josephus, *Antiquities of the Jews*, 20:2.

Izates's coronation. However, now that Izates was king, his behavior was scrutinized carefully, and, as was expected, the completeness of his conversion became common knowledge.

So, it was with no small amount of trepidation that the queen entered the great hall of the palace several weeks after Izates's coronation to hold her monthly audience with village representatives.[8] This was a time for special requests to be heard, problems to be aired, and the basic sentiments of the people to be revealed to the court. Helene had come to expect these encounters with the public to be somewhat contentious. She was therefore surprised by the scene that played out before her.

One by one, the village representatives approached the throne, reading similarly worded proclamations declaring feelings of great esteem toward the royal family for the loyalty shown to their new religion and dedication to its laws. Jews were familiar to the people of Adiabene through mercantile commerce, and this opened a small window by which to observe their behavior and customs. These commoners of Adiabene recognized the just and merciful nature of their Jewish minority. Surely, a royal court following the precepts of this upright people would be even more likely to help and protect them from despotic elements that threatened their livelihood and independence.

"*Hodu LaHashem ki tov, ki l'olam chasdo*," she whispered. "Give thanks to Hashem because He is good. His kindness endures forever."

Helene began to relax. No uprising would be instigated by the common folk over the conversion of the royal family of Adiabene, she realized, as a wave of relief swept over her. At that moment of bliss, she tried to avoid thoughts of the court noblemen, whose response, she knew, would be much less positive.

---

8 According to local custom, Helene would continue to hold her title as queen throughout her lifetime. Samacha would remain a princess, even though she was married to the king.

Chapter Six

It was the middle of the night, and King Artabanus's chief steward was forced to set aside all protocol in an effort to save his master. His hand shook as he opened the king's locked bedroom door with the special key entrusted to him, to be used only for emergencies.

Gently shaking the sleeping Artabanus, he whispered urgently, "Awake, my king, I hear an angry mob approaching the palace."

Artabanus jolted awake and stared at his steward as if he were an apparition.

"There has been a coup, Your Highness, and you have been deposed. There is very little time to flee the capital! My staff will gather together the royal family, while Your Highness readies himself for the journey. Carriages are waiting at the palace entrance. We have only minutes! Please hurry!"

Horse-drawn carriages sped away, bearing the royal family only minutes before the mob began hurling rocks at the palace. They fled the capital city of Ctesphon, arriving just before dawn at a villa located deep in the surrounding forest on the outskirts of the capital.[1] Accompanying Artabanus was a small cadre of advisors and officers who remained loyal to their monarch. After settling the king's wives and children in the family quarters, Artabanus held an emergency strategy session. The heavy stone door to the king's meeting chamber

---

1 This occurred in the year 36 CE.

shut with a reverberating finality that sent a shudder through the hearts of those assembled around the large rectangular table.

Artabanus, king of Parthia, sighed wearily before beginning to speak.

"My esteemed advisors, you are, by now, surely aware that a challenge to my authority is spreading like a wildfire throughout the kingdom. I have assembled you here today to consider our options."

"Your Highness," the chief general spoke up, "may I suggest that an aggressive military campaign be immediately waged against the usurpers. It is my humble opinion that we can easily muster the men necessary to quell the rebellion!"

"What would that accomplish?" the defense minister retorted. "You will merely end up with a decimated army, widespread destruction, and a bitter and disheartened populace. The best approach, in my humble opinion, would be mediation."

"Yes, a mediator is what we need," the prime minister agreed. "But whom could we trust who would also be able to carry out our plan?"

"Your Highness," an officer interjected, "there is only one human ruler in the entire world who has both the upright character and the political savvy to carry out this mission. That man is Izates, king of our vassal state, Adiabene."[2]

"Izates!" the foreign minister exclaimed. "But Adiabene is one of the smallest provinces in the empire! How can you expect anyone to listen to him? You are also forgetting that King Izates is a Jew!"

"Silence!" King Artabanus boomed. "I will cast my lot with King Izates of Adiabene. He is a wise man, and he loves peace. His ultimate success is in the hands of G-d, but I know he will never betray me. His reputation for honesty and fairness is sterling."

The king stopped speaking and looked pensive. "Now, let's see if we can convince him to join our cause!" he murmured to himself.

---

2   Josephus, *Antiquities of the Jews*, 20:3.

King Izates rode through the countryside to check on his subjects, as he did from time to time. He turned toward a broad cliff that provided a breathtaking overlook to the rolling fields below. Izates took a deep breath of fresh mountain air before looking downward, but, instead of the familiar scene he expected, he beheld a strange and awesome sight. An army of about one thousand troops was winding its way through the mountain paths. At its head was a grand carriage led by six Egyptian stallions decorated with gold and silver bridles that sparkled in the rays of the late afternoon sun. As the entourage approached, Izates strained to catch a glimpse of the vehicle's occupant, but to no avail.

Gathering his bodyguards around him, the startled king waited until the carriage was within fifty feet of him, and only then did he approach. Izates scrutinized the face of the royal stranger for a familiar feature, but found none.

Izates could not contain his look of consternation when the man dismounted and approached him, bowing a number of times along the way. Izates realized with shock that the man was none other than Artabanus, king of Parthia!

"King Izates!" Artabanus declared beseechingly. "Please do not overlook your servant or reject the plea I am about to make to you, for I have been reduced to a low state. I have been transformed from a king to a commoner." Tears welled up in his eyes, and his demeanor was that of total dejection. "Have pity for my reduced fortune, and know that your care for me is for your benefit, too. As long as those who rebel against me remain unpunished, they are likely to attack other kings as well."

Izates leaped off his horse and faced Artabanus.

"Your Majesty!" he said deferentially. "Be not disturbed by your current calamity and do not consider it irreversible, for Divine salvation occurs in the blink of an eye. As for myself, you will not find a greater friend and assistant. I intend, with G-d's help, to either re-establish you in your position or lose my own."

"Your kindness and deference is greatly appreciated, esteemed King Izates, but I cannot in good conscience take advantage of it," Artabanus demurred.

"But why not, my king?" Izates countered. "Please ride upon my horse, and I will follow by foot. This is the custom of our region when a ruler finds himself in the presence of a king greater than himself."

Izates gestured to his attendants. Four of them stepped forward and lifted Artabanus onto one of the waiting horses. Artabanus winced as if in pain.

"No, no, I cannot continue thus!" Artabanus shouted. "I will dismount immediately unless King Izates agrees to ride his horse ahead of me!"

Acceding to his request, Izates again climbed upon his horse. Followed by Artabanus, the two made their way to the palace in Arbela. The arrival of the two monarchs caused quite a stir. Word of Artabanus's deposition spread in the marketplaces like dry straw on fire. The fact that the beleaguered ex-monarch was seeking the aid of their new king greatly increased Izates's esteem in the eyes of his subjects.

Upon their arrival at the palace, Artabanus briefed Izates for hours on end about his situation and the complicated political maneuvering taking place. Convinced that Artabanus had indeed been wronged, Izates wrote the following letter to the governors of Parthia, the chief instigators of the uprising:

Dear Esteemed Governors,

I am writing to you as the representative of your deposed monarch, the esteemed King Artabanus of Parthia, who has duly considered your complaints and is ready to address them with you once he is re-established upon his rightful throne. Your esteemed king is prepared to forget all that has been so ignominiously done against him and furthermore will accept a mediator between himself and the people of his immense empire in order to address the issues that led to this unfortunate set of circumstances.

Your filial neighbor,
King Izates of Adiabene

To this, the governors replied:

Your words, King Izates, are respected and welcomed by us. Would it only be that we had it in our power to fulfill your request forthwith!

Unfortunately, a decision to restore Artabanus to his kingship is totally out of our hands, since another, King Cinnamus, has been chosen by the people to take his place. Removal of Cinnamus at this point in time would most likely provoke civil war among the provinces, an eventuality we cannot risk.

Respectfully yours,
The Governors of the Great Empire of Parthia

Upon reading this response, Izates felt despondent. He was greatly displeased at the prospect of waging war, and was especially opposed to battling against a potentially enormous army. Thankfully, the stalemate was avoided when King Cinnamus himself quickly resigned his new appointment. Not only did Artabanus's replacement understand the consequence of Izates's message, but he also felt great appreciation toward Artabanus himself, who had raised him. As a result, he wrote to the deposed king directly, inviting him to re-assume his throne. Trusting Cinnamus, who was of a good and kind nature, Artabanus returned home. Cinnamus then removed the diadem from his own head and transferred it to Artabanus, re-establishing him as lawful king.

Thus, the king of Parthia was restored to his kingship with help from Izates, and the deed did not go unrewarded. Artabanus conferred upon Izates great honors and privileges. He was given the right to wear his tiara upright and to sleep in a golden bed, privileges reserved for the kings of Parthia.³

Artabanus also granted Izates a large and fruitful territory ceded from the Armenians. This included, to Izates's great pleasure, the city of Nisibis, a city that had played an important role in Jewish history and continued to host a significant Jewish presence.⁴

Nevertheless, King Izates could not fight a strong feeling of unease at the role into which he had been foisted by Artabanus. He knew that any political machinations that drew attention to him were fraught with dangers, in spite of the potential rewards. He was a Jewish monarch of a gentile country that was part of a pagan empire, and many powerful men felt threatened by him. Oh, if only he could avoid them entirely and focus on taking care of the citizens of Adiabene!

"Please, Hashem, help me to do Your will, and not be influenced by power or prestige!" Izates cried out. "Please help me prevail over my enemies!"

It would not be long before Izates came to realize just how timely his fervent prayer was.

---

3   Josephus, *Antiquities of the Jews*, 20:3.
4   Nisibis was built on the spot where the Macedonians had previously constructed the city of Antioch. Nisibis housed a sizable Jewish population dating back to the exile of the northern tribes in 556 BCE. In fact, this city, which lay along the Mygdonius River, a tributary of the Khabur, is listed in *Sefer Melachim* as one of the places where the ten tribes were deported (*II Melachim* 17:6).

Chapter Seven

When King Artabanus died only two years later,[1] he left his kingdom to his son, Vardanes, who perceived an opportunity to benefit from the relationship the king of Adiabene had shared with his late father. One of Vardanes's first official acts was to send a letter to Izates.

It was a glorious day in early June, and Izates allowed himself a brief break from his administrative work to take in the view of the verdant countryside outside his study window. As his gaze scanned the landscape, the king was stunned to see three horsemen rapidly galloping toward the castle from the mountain path. As they came closer, Izates saw that their uniforms were emblazoned with the insignia of the Parthian Empire. Moments later, he heard a rhythmic knock on his door, indicating the arrival of an official messenger.

Bozan, the chief steward, handed a scroll to the king, announcing tersely, "For His Majesty from King Vardanes."

Izates's brow knit tensely as he carefully read and reread the letter.

"I cannot do this," Izates whispered quietly to himself, momentarily unaware of the presence of his advisors.

Pakur, the chief counselor, looked at Izates with foreboding. "What, Your Highness, is Vardanes requesting of you?"

---

1   This happened in 38 CE; "Parthian Empire," Wikipedia, [en.wikipedia,org/wiki/Parthian_Empire], 11.

"King Vardanes of Parthia, after barely one month in power, wants to go to war against Rome," Izates responded flatly.

"War against Rome!" Husrava, the foreign minister, gasped. "Even Vardanes's father, Artabanus, who was known for his military prowess and political savvy, had never attempted such a brazen act! How could his son, who would surely be viewed as a young upstart, think he could prevail against the Romans?"

"Yes, Husrava, you are quite right," Izates acknowledged. "The strength and good fortune of the Romans greatly surpass that of the new Parthian ruler. Opposing them at this juncture would constitute a suicide mission. I could not agree with you more that Vardanes must be dissuaded from his outrageous proposal.

"Scribe!" Izates called to a man who had been waiting in the background for his instructions. "Please pen the following response to His Majesty, King Vardanes of Parthia."

Most Esteemed King,

I am in receipt of your letter and feel most honored to be considered such a valued ally of the Empire. Rest assured that I only desire to do what is best for Parthia and to assist you in every way possible. I also recognize the close fraternity between myself and your late father.

It is because I have your best interests and those of the Empire in the forefront of my mind that I must implore His Majesty to abandon his proposed plan to rebel against Rome. Their might and good fortune predict that any such effort be doomed to failure. The barbarism of the great armies of the Romans is well known throughout the civilized world. Prevailing against them is impossible, and the consequences of their ire would be devastating to your nation and your authority. I beg you, in your own best interest, to cease from this idea, and to focus instead on building up our internal strength and prosperity.

King Izates of Adiabene

Izates rolled up the parchment and handed it to the waiting courier. "May it be the will of the Alm-ghty that Vardanes agree with my reasoning and desist from aggravating the Roman beasts," he silently prayed.

King Vardanes was lounging on a couch in his private dining room when the courier arrived with the letter from Izates. Slightly soporific after his heavy midday meal, he fumbled lazily with the parchment, seeming to be in no hurry to know its contents. Finally, he began to read from the unfurled parchment. His attendants watched with alarm as an expression of rage overtook the king, turning his face a deep shade of scarlet.

"Who does this young upstart think he is addressing?" Vardanes bellowed. "How dare he tell King Vardanes, ruler of the Parthian Empire, to refrain from waging war on Rome! Izates will see what happens to one who so brazenly defies his king! Izates will pay dearly for his outrageous behavior!"

While awaiting Vardanes's reaction to his letter, Izates spent most of his time in prayer and meditation. Although he had expected a speedy response, the king was startled when his courier returned to the palace after only twenty-four hours. As he read Vardanes's response, his face turned ashen.

Izates struggled to regain control of his racing thoughts. "I have followed the example of Yaakov Avinu," he told himself. "I have prayed to the Alm-ghty. I have tried to appease the enemy with reason, and I have sent tribute. All that is left for me to do is to prepare for war."

"Bozan!" he called to his chief steward. "Summon all senior ministers for an emergency meeting in my study two hours hence."

"Yes, of course, Your Majesty!" Bozan replied obediently, though he was inwardly shocked by the force of his master's sudden command.

The steward left the throne room hurriedly, a look of consternation on his face.

Izates rose from his throne and slowly left the room like a man carrying a heavy burden. He proceeded to the queen's quarters to inform his mother of the foreboding news.

Exactly two hours later, King Izates stood at the head of an enormous marble table, around which were assembled every one of his ministers. He collected his thoughts, cleared his throat, and began to speak to the assembled group.

"Gentlemen," he began, looking each of his advisors in the eye. "King Vardanes is intent on fighting against Rome and has demanded my participation. I have refused him, explaining that such a revolt would be a suicide mission doomed to failure. Vardanes has rejected my reasoning, and he now intends to declare war on Adiabene. We face a difficult choice: We can wait and see if the Parthian monarch makes good on his threat. Or we could attack him first, in the hope of routing his troops by catching him off guard."

"Vardanes is a fool but not foolish enough to waste his resources against little Adiabene!" the foreign minister exploded. "Surely he is just trying to intimidate the king into showing him allegiance! I vote to sit and wait."

"If I may respectfully disagree," said the chief of staff, "a pre-emptive strike could make sense from a military perspective. I agree with the king. Vardanes's troops would likely scatter, if we can truly surprise them."

Izates listened as opinions were voiced on both sides, a grave expression of concern on his face. Finally, he rose and addressed his ministers.

"Thank you, my dear, valued advisors," he said. "Your opinions have been carefully considered. I have concluded that as ill-advised as the threat of the Parthian king may be, we need to take it very seriously. We cannot wait for him to attack us. We must attack first, in the hopes of foiling his plans. I believe the outcome, with G-d's help, will be more positive for our country."

Within forty-eight hours, King Izates left Adiabene to wage a preemptive strike against Vardanes.

Queen Helene stood, as if transfixed, gazing after the king galloping off to battle at the head of his troops.

"*Ribono shel Olam*," she pleaded silently. "Please have mercy on my son. See how faithful he is to Your holy Torah and mitzvos, and preserve his life!"

Chapter Eight

Helene could not shake off the feeling of impending doom that had plagued her since her son left to war.

"Please, Bozan," she urged, "hurry and send a carriage for my dear friend, Miriam. Ask if she could honor me with a visit. I have a pressing issue to discuss with her."

Miriam was a wise and deeply religious woman, a member of the small Jewish community of Adiabene. In recent decades, the overall level of religious observance in the Diaspora suffered from a lack of *chachamim* to advise the people on the proper application of the halachah. Miriam's family was more learned than most, but their distance from the Holy Land resulted in some deficiencies in their knowledge of the fine points of the law. Although the queen viewed Miriam as her consultant on religious issues, Miriam always reminded her that she was far from a final authority.

Helene waited impatiently for Miriam to arrive. When she finally did, she was openly relieved to see her dear friend and relaxed a bit.

"Miriam," she said, "I am in great need of your opinion. My son has gone out to war against an ominous enemy. I have been praying to Hashem night and day on his behalf, but somehow, I do not feel that this is sufficient. I feel a need to take on some additional act of self-sacrifice to accompany my prayers for his safe return from the battlefield, but I am at a loss as to what this act should be."

Miriam was silent for several long minutes before she responded.

"Your Majesty," she began hesitantly. "Our people have a tradition of making personal vows in the face of dangerous circumstances. This act can afford one Divine protection. Perhaps the first person in our history to do so was our forefather, Yaakov, who vowed to Hashem that he would tithe his possessions upon his salvation from Lavan and his safe return to his father's house."

Helene gazed unseeingly into the distance.

"Yes, Miriam," she replied after a few moments. "A vow, to make a vow… While a victory in battle is what we all hope for, it does not come without its spiritual risks. Few achievements can equal the feeling of invigoration at winning in battle. How strong we think we are! How invincible we imagine ourselves to be! What type of vow can save us from these haughty feelings? Perhaps it is the vow that many took upon beholding a *sotah* in her degradation, a vow representing a certain separation from society.

"A *nazir* refrains from eating or drinking any by-product of grapes," the queen continued pensively. "His hair grows unrestrained. He may not come in contact with the dead. Why would anyone accept upon himself such a vow? What could be the spiritual benefit to such behavior? Perhaps the self-discipline required of the *nazir* helps a person avoid the inexorable downward spiral that starts with a sense of personal power, of unrestrained freedom from authority? By experiencing these restrictions, a *nazir* is 'outside' of society, to some extent. He looks different, eats differently, and behaves differently. This separates him from the rest of society, but, at the same time, he remains dependent on it. If he is put in contact with the dead or is fed the produce of grapes, his period of *nezirus* is nullified, and he must start over again. One could learn from this that even the quest for spiritual purity is not totally under the control of the individual."

Helene gazed out her window at the distant, rugged mountains toward the west. Somewhere beyond those mountains, her son waged war against Vardanes. She opened a small scroll with densely scrawled notes. It belonged to her grandson, eight-year-old Moshe, who was studying the laws of the *nazir* with his *melamed*.

"Laws of the *nazir*," Helene read aloud. "A man, woman, or servant can accept the vow of a *nazir*. A *nazir* is forbidden to cut his hair, since hair represents wisdom and letting the hair grow purifies one's wisdom. He may not eat or drink grape products, since wine represents understanding and refraining from drinking wine purifies this. He may not be in contact with the dead, an allusion to the sin of Adam, who brought death into the world by eating of the fruit of the Tree of Knowledge. Avoiding such contact purifies one's knowledge.

"After the completion of the period of *nezirus*, the *nazir* brings three offerings: a lamb between one and two years old for an elevation offering, a lamb under one year old for a sin offering, and a ram for a peace offering. Then the *nazir's* hair is shaved and placed on the fire under the pot containing the cooking peace offering, where it is burnt to ashes. Once this rite is completed, the *nazir* is permitted to do all that was previously forbidden to him."

Helene looked up. "Does this mean that accepting *nezirus* upon oneself is sinful?" she asked, perplexed.

"Well, Your Majesty, your question is a good one," Miriam answered. "Some say that the *nazir* is sinful for withdrawing from the pleasures of wine. There are also those who say that he is not considered a sinner if he successfully completes his period of *nezirus* without becoming defiled. If he does become defiled, however, then the days he spent refraining from wine were done so unnecessarily. Thus there is indeed some risk in assuming this awesome vow."

Helene leaned forward, listening intently.

"Perhaps there is another risk, as well," Miriam posited. "Man engages in a constant struggle between his spiritual, thinking self and his physical self. It can be to a person's benefit to minimize the desires of his physical being in favor of his spiritual existence. This is why the hair of the *nazir* is shaved at the completion of the term of his vow. If it could be fixed and styled, this could revive the spirit of desire for the physical that the *nezirus* held in check. The spirit of Hashem that rests upon the *nazir* who dedicates all of his strength for the sake of Heaven should persist all of his days. Maybe, then, atonement is needed for discontinuing this elevated state."

"Your words speak to my heart, Miriam," Helene admitted. "But the typical thirty-day period of *nezirus* does not seem sufficient for me to achieve the level of spiritual attainment I crave. Seven is a number connoting completion of the physical world. Seven years represent a complete agricultural cycle for the earth, with the land lying fallow during the seventh year. Seven years is a significant period of time."

"It is a very long period of time," her friend said solemnly. "Are you sure you are ready to fulfill this difficult vow for such an extended period?"

"Yes," Helene replied resolutely. "I am ready. Miriam, even though my vow is a personal one and does not require the presence of witnesses for its validity, it is important to me that you hear my declaration. Thank you, my friend, for listening."

Helene closed her eyes and took a deep breath. "I hereby accept upon myself the vow of *nezirus* for seven years, upon the safe return of my son, Izates, from battle. May my vow uplift my soul and be acceptable to Hashem."

"Amen!" Miriam proclaimed. "May Hashem protect King Izates and bring him back safely from war and enable you to fulfill your vow successfully."

The queen sat by the window of her bedchamber saying Tehillim as the sun sank behind the mountains of Adiabene. Billowing clouds of smoky gray, highlighted by deep orange, made the sky look like it was on fire. Her concentration was momentarily disturbed by a small, golden ornament in the shape of a candelabra hanging next to the window. It was a relic from her youth, a gift from her mother, who had showed her how the precious miniature would shine as if on fire when it caught the first and last rays of the sun. Helene's mother told her to always start and end her days with energy and passion, just like the "fire" in the candelabra. The daughter tried to live up to her mother's dictum, and the shining ornament gave her a feeling of hope and peace as she returned to her prayers.

Both the intensity and warmth of that sunset remained imprinted on Helene's consciousness during the days and weeks that followed. Whenever fear born of uncertainty threatened to overcome her, she tried to envision Hashem guarding her embattled son from harm. She prayed, gave solace to the poor and sick among her subjects, and looked forward to the day when she would hear that Izates was safe and returning home to her.

Finally, on a crisp fall day, the much anticipated word arrived. Helene's hands trembled as she took the parchment from the courier and unfurled it hurriedly. Then, she took a deep breath and read:

My dear Mother,
It is with a heart filled with thankfulness to the Alm-ghty and filial love, that I write this letter to you. In spite of great odds against me, Hashem has sent His angels to protect me. As a result, I have been saved from certain destruction and, in a wondrous reversal of circumstances, a glorious victory has been granted me over those who would destroy me. "Many designs lie in the heart of man, but the will of Hashem will always prevail!"

Vardanes has retreated from his ill-conceived attempt against Rome, and I am on my way home to you, dear Mother, bearing spoils of war that will grant testimony to the miracles that have been performed on my behalf.

Your deeply grateful son,
Izates

Helene rolled up the parchment and placed it carefully on the stone shelf by her bed, as tears of happiness streamed down her face. What relief and thankfulness to the Alm-ghty she felt at that moment! Her dear son had survived brutal attacks and was returning victorious from battle!

A mere three days later, the queen was awakened during the dark, still night by a soft knock on her door. She quickly washed her hands and donned her robe.

"Who is there?" she asked, bewildered.

"Mother, it is I, Izates, just returned from the battlefield. Forgive me for not waiting until morning to greet you, but I hoped to see you right away."

Helene pulled open her door.

"Izates! My son, you have returned!" she exclaimed, beaming. "*Baruch Hashem, baruch Hashem*!" she repeated over and over as she embraced him.

"Yes, Mother! It is only through the kindness and mercy of the Merciful One that I have survived, victorious over my enemies."

"May He continue to protect all of us from their hands," Helene prayed. Their eyes met, and Helene felt as if she could see through to her son's soul. "Hashem protects those who love Him, my son. And now that you have returned home safely, I, too, must express love and gratitude in the way I have intended. When you went off to war, I worried that perhaps my past sins would interfere with the constant Divine protection that you needed in order to survive. I prayed day and night for your safe return, but I learned that it has been traditional among the Jewish people for individuals to take a vow upon themselves in times of trouble. I decided to accept upon myself the vow of *nezirus* for a period of seven years, to take effect if you returned safely from battle."

"Seven years!" Izates repeated, shocked. "Mother, are you aware of how difficult and demanding your vow will be? You may not eat any product made with grapes nor even step through a vineyard during this time. Your hair must grow, and you must avoid passing through a cemetery, lest you become impure through contact with the dead. This vow will isolate you from royal society, and, to some extent, from our Jewish brethren as well."

"I am quite aware of the implications of the obligations I have accepted upon myself, my son," Helene responded calmly. "May the discipline now required of me be accepted as a form of *avodah* to Hashem. It is my sincere hope that being a *nezirah* will help me focus on proper thoughts and conduct in order to show the Alm-ghty more fully my gratitude for His great mercy in bringing you home safely from battle."

The king was silent for several minutes. Finally, he looked at his mother.

"Of course I respect your decision, Mother. While I despair of ever reaching the loftiness of your elevated soul, I know that it must influence all those around you for the better."

"Thank you, my son," Helene responded, a glow of happiness spreading over her face. Izates understood.

"May it be His will that you merit to complete your *nezirus* successfully and without mishap," Izates declared.

"Amen!" the queen responded fervently.

Helene turned to Izates.

"My son," she said firmly, "word of my vow will eventually become public, but I ask you to confine knowledge of it to the family for as long as possible. I will, of course, need to inform my maidens, so that they can guard against any food containing grapes or its derivatives being served to me. My coachman will also need to be told to avoid cemeteries during my travels. I will speak to your brother myself, and I ask you to explain my vow to Samacha and the children."

Izates felt a sense of awe as he stood before his saintly mother. He nodded, soundlessly acknowledging her act of profound faith and his love for her. After briefly gazing at her in admiration, he kissed her on both cheeks and left the room.

Helene retreated to her chambers. She then turned toward the direction of the Holy of Holies in Yerushalayim and began to pray.

"L-rd of the universe," she supplicated, "please accept my vow of *nezirus* for a period of seven complete years. Let me fulfill my vow according to the halachah with sincerity and humility, and may my behavior during this time bring me an elevation in my spiritual status, in gratitude for Your miraculous salvation of my dear son, Izates, from battle."

She removed her turban, revealing thick, wavy, black locks, streaked with silver, reaching to her waist. Helene picked up her copper mirror and stared at it for a few moments.

Oh, the vanities of this world! she thought to herself. *How much admiration these tresses brought me so many years ago, and how differently I view them today. What used to give me such joy will one day bring me much greater joy to cast off!*

Helene then walked toward a large wooden box on her dressing table and dropped a large gold coin inside. She could tell by the sound it made that the box would soon be full. She would empty it, giving the proceeds toward the upkeep of the *beis midrash* in the Jewish section of Nisibis.

It was mid-morning, and the queen rang a small bell to summon her maidens, most of whom were orphaned girls Helene had "adopted" and helped raise. Once they became teenagers, she employed them as her personal attendants until she married them off to suitable young men. As each girl entered Helene's chamber, her anxiety at being summoned so suddenly evaporated. The queen was glowing with joy. She looked at each of them, a warm smile spreading across her face.

"Girls, I need your help in preparing for a wonderful event!" Helene exclaimed joyfully. "King Izates has just returned home safely from battle, and tomorrow we will hold a feast of thanksgiving, for family and friends, to thank G-d for protecting him through this dangerous ordeal.

"Artazostre, please ask the chief of provisions to obtain the best cuts of meat from the Jewish butcher, enough for two hundred people," the queen instructed. "Artaynte, please ask Shmuel to prepare dough in sufficient quantity for the loaves that will be served."

Several hours later, when the palace's chief baker, whom the queen had hired from the Jewish quarter of Arbela, completed this task, Helene was notified that the mitzvah of *hafrashas challah* could now be fulfilled. She allowed no one else to perform this mitzvah. At least one of her grandsons was always present to say amen to her blessing, and today she was joined by Yosef.

"Behold, this is designated as *challah*!" Helene declared. She withdrew her hand from the bowl of dough, retaining an egg-sized piece in her palm. She carefully wrapped the dough in a parchment and handed it to Yosef.

"My dear Yosef," she said, "please take this *challah* to the Jewish quarter to present as a gift to the *kohen*, Rabbi Ephraim."

Yosef was well-acquainted with the ritual and knew where Rabbi Ephraim lived. He gingerly handled the parcel and quickly left the kitchen, where the heat from the ovens was beginning to make the air oppressively hot and heavy.

The queen turned to her oldest servant.

"Axzeh," she said, "I would like two cases of the finest wine from the Jewish wine sellers. Make sure to segregate those bottles intended for the family, as no gentile may have contact with them. Also, please make sure that wine is only served to the gentlemen.

"Amytis, here is the guest list," Helene said to another servant. "All of these subjects live at or near the palace, so it should be possible to notify them quickly. Let's extend the invitation for seven o'clock, just after the afternoon prayers.

"Artaynte, you have the loveliest handwriting, my dear. I would like you to draw up invitations on the finest parchment, to be given to the ten horsemen who will read them to the invitees as they make their rounds.

"Thank you, my dear girls," she said gratefully, and a little out of breath. "I will dine with the female guests in my receiving parlor, while the men will be in the dining hall. Please remind the kitchen staff that any leftover food should be transported to the Jewish quarter tonight immediately after the feast, so that Chaim the grocer can distribute it to the poor."

The next evening, approximately one hundred dignitaries and their wives assembled at the palace to take part in the feast of thanksgiving celebrated by their king and his family. The fare was sumptuous, as would be expected at such an event. The guests did not suspect that the subtle changes made to standard recipes were in order to accommodate the laws of kashrus observed by the royal family. For the appetizer, garum[1] was baked with salmon, to avoid the prohibition against eating meat and fish together. Agnum[2] was prepared without white wine, which would have been forbidden to Helene as a *nezirah*. The chicken

---

1 A popular fish sauce, usually served over meat and poultry.
2 Baby goat.

dish, pullum, was praised by all present. Although likewise prepared without its usual wine and fish sauce, the presence of the popular Roman spice laser[3] more than compensated for their absence. All of the meat served was slaughtered according to the laws of *shechitah*, with the food prepared in the constant presence of a *mashgiach*.

Once the guests were duly satiated with the first few courses, King Izates rose from his throne at the head of the vast banquet table. The chief steward silenced all conversation.

"Hear ye, hear ye, His Majesty, King Izates, will now speak!" he bellowed.

Within seconds, there was quiet, as the dignitaries gazed expectantly at their monarch.

"My esteemed guests!" Izates began. "We are gathered here today, not to celebrate a military victory, but to praise the One Alm-ghty G-d for saving us from defeat and certain annihilation. We have just engaged in battle against the powerful Parthian army, a force much better equipped and stronger than we are, politically as well as militarily. Nevertheless, because our cause was just, and due to His great mercy, G-d has saved us from harm and returned us home to a free land. It is for this that we offer our deepest thanks. We must always remember that it is not by our strength, and it is not by our might that we prevail. It is only according to the will of G-d that we prevail. May He, in His great mercy, continue to protect our land and its people from all harm."

After a slight pause, a thunderous applause reverberated throughout the hall, as both Jew and gentile alike paid tribute to the words of their leader.

Izates smiled and raised his arms, exuding confidence and calm reassurance to those present. In his heart, though, he felt a dull ache. He doubted that his political challenges were over and could only hope

---

3   A derivative of the fennel plant.

that he would be worthy of Divine assistance to meet them. For the meantime, though, peace reigned in Adiabene — and for this he was exceedingly thankful.

Chapter Nine

Season followed season, and Helene focused on fulfilling the spiritual needs of her family. She became especially close to Izates's five young sons, who, like their father, had been circumcised, and were being raised as Jews. Their parents called them by their Hebrew names and were able to instill in them a love of Torah and mitzvos, in spite of the pagan environment that surrounded them. Nevertheless, the absence of an appropriate peer group caused Helene great concern. The Jewish community of Adiabene's capital city of Arbela was minuscule, and it was too far to travel to Nisibis on a regular basis. Her response was to redouble her efforts at providing her grandsons with the warm, Jewish atmosphere that a grandmother is so suited to create.

One afternoon, Moshe, the oldest grandson, knocked on the queen's door.

"Enter, my dear child!" Helene exclaimed happily.

The ten-year-old boy sheepishly approached his grandmother and kissed her on both cheeks. She looked admiringly at him. He wore a yarmulke on his head and *tzitzis* with beautiful blue and white threads on the four corners of his cloak. In just a few years, Moshe would reach thirteen, the age of mitzvos, and she knew he wanted very much to live the life of a Jewish man, just like his father.

Moshe pulled a small scroll from his pocket and gave it to Helene. "Grandmama, please read the Torah poem I have composed for you.

I'm practicing the Hebrew my *melamed* is teaching me, and I wanted your opinion of its quality."

Helene perused the poem, suppressing a chuckle.

"Moshe, this is beautiful!" she exclaimed with obvious joy. "The holy tongue is very challenging to master for those of us who are not native speakers. Your words are clear and pure, my dear grandson. You have been given the gift of a sharp mind and creative pen. May you develop your talents to their utmost." She smiled warmly at him. "With Hashem's help, may you someday become a *talmid chacham* who spreads the knowledge of our holy Torah to the masses."

"Amen, Grandmama," Moshe responded, pleased with his grandmother's praise. "I know it takes many years to become a scholar, but I will study hard. Please pray that I become a *talmid chacham*, Grandmama. I know your *tefillos* rise right up to *Shamayim*!"

Helene smiled, filled with gratitude for this child and his siblings.

Yes, I see a future for our family among the Jewish people, she thought.

Helene made periodic excursions to Nisibis. Since the trip comprised a distance of about 150 miles, she would absent herself for several weeks at a time, three times a year, usually during the months of Teves, Iyar, and Elul. She tried to time these visits to coincide with the New Moon, a semi-holiday when special prayers were said in the synagogues. Since Jewish women traditionally refrained from heavier labors on these days, the wives of the sages had more time to spend with her and to address her many questions. These trips satisfied Helene's yearning to be among her co-religionists and to observe their conduct. She particularly liked to watch the way they performed mitzvos with such enthusiasm and joy.

Helene would ride in a common carriage and dress as a simple Jewess on these trips, so as not to attract undue attention to herself. She was all too aware of the controversial nature of her conversion and the resentment it caused some of her countrymen. She had no intention of making waves. On the contrary, her only desire was to live, during these much anticipated days, as if she were born into the people she had so happily joined later in her life.

The queen's first destination was always the home of the great sage Rabbi Yehudah ben Beseira. Rabbi Yehudah held the royal family in high esteem for their wholehearted embracing of the Torah. This relationship was very dear to Helene, especially since Rabbi Yehudah was known for his discerning insight.[1]

"Welcome, Your Majesty!" Rabbi Yehudah's wife embraced Helene warmly. Rebbetzin Rochel was a woman well into her sixth decade, but her face bore a creaseless glow that made her look much younger.

"You must be so tired after your long trip!" she said. "Please come with me. Let's sit in the kitchen, where the hearth will warm you, while I prepare some warm milk." Helene had developed a special friendship with the *rebbetzin*, a woman known both for her wisdom in the ways of the Torah and the kindhearted *chessed* she dispensed so freely.

"How good it is to see you again!" Helene replied, happy to see her friend in good health. "Please tell me all about your children and grandchildren."

Rochel smiled contentedly. "*Baruch Hashem*! They are all following

---

[1] This insight is demonstrated by the following story (*Pesachim* 3b): The *olei regel* who went up from Bavel to Yerushalayim to celebrate Pesach were occasionally joined by an Aramean who posed as a Jew. He ate the *Korban Pesach* in Yerushalayim and then came back to Rabbi Yehudah and boasted, "It is written in your Torah, *A gentile will not eat of it*, but I ate with the best of them." Rabbi Yehudah slyly replied, "And did they give you from the tail?" The gentile answered, "No." Rabbi Yehudah instructed him that next time he partook of the *Korban Pesach*, he should ask for meat from the tail as well.

He followed these instructions, and when he was asked who told him to request meat from the tail, he said, "Rabbi Yehudah ben Beseira." He was found to be a gentile who had entered the Beis Hamikdash unlawfully, and was subsequently put to death. Word was sent back to Rabbi Yehudah ben Beseira: "Peace be to you, Rabbi Yehudah ben Beseira! You are in Netzivin (Nisibis), but your net is spread over Yerushalayim!"

in the ways of Torah and mitzvos. May the Alm-ghty continue to guide and protect them! The boys are progressing well in their learning, and our granddaughter, Shifra, has just become a *kallah*!"

"Mazel tov!" Helene exclaimed. "This is wonderful!" A moment later, her smile faded. "And what do you hear from the Holy Land, my dear friend?" Helene depended upon these trips to keep abreast of both religious and political developments in Eretz Yisrael. She knew that the Roman procurator, Fadus, was instigating trouble for her people, but she had not been made aware of the seriousness of the situation.[2]

Rochel's expression darkened, and she seemed to withdraw into herself momentarily. How loath she was to disclose the series of ignoble acts perpetrated in the Holy Land! Could a recent convert bear the knowledge that, in spite of the perfection of the Torah, there was so much imperfection among the Jewish people? When she again made eye contact with Helene, her face wore a look of sad resoluteness. She must tell the truth! As a *giyores*, Helene had cast her lot with the Jewish people, in both good times and bad. It would be wrong to withhold the facts from her, as painful as they were.

"Our recent history is checkered, Your Majesty," Rochel said, sighing. "Perhaps you heard that Claudius Caesar commanded his then-new procurator, Fadus, to send for the *kohen gadol* and other important citizens of Yerushalayim with an absolutely outrageous demand. He called for the garments of the *kohen gadol* to be placed under Roman control in the tower of Antonia! The Jews quickly responded with a request to send ambassadors to the emperor to keep the holy vestments under their own jurisdiction. The response was positive, but only on condition that they leave their sons as surety! The Jews agreed to do this. What choice did they have?

"Once in Rome, the Jewish ambassadors made their plea to Claudius, who, if you remember, was appointed emperor just three years ago. In

---

2   This took place in the year 44 CE.

that same year, he appointed Agrippa II, son of the late king Agrippa, as king. Agrippa lived with Claudius in Rome and, to his credit, he pleaded on behalf of the Jewish representatives. Miraculously, their request was granted, whereupon the ambassadors were bidden by Claudius to express their thanks to Agrippa for his intervention on their behalf. The holy vestments were to remain under the control of the Jews."

Rochel paused and sighed again.

"But alas," she continued, "the appearance of autonomy was ephemeral. Herod, another brother of the deceased Agrippa, successfully petitioned Claudius for authority over the Temple. The result was that the *kohen gadol*, Cautheras, was deposed and replaced by Joseph, son of Camus.

"I am sure you know, Your Majesty, that the holy role of *kohen gadol* has been tragically corrupted for many years. Selling the position has been a source of revenue to our Roman oppressors for decades. As a result, they have abrogated the lifetime term of a *kohen gadol*, replacing them as many as three times a year! Not a single one of these illegitimate *kohanim gedolim* has lived through a Yom Kippur![3] They may think they can hide from man, but they cannot hide from the Alm-ghty! Even likely death does not serve as a deterrent for these scoundrels! Those who have been 'fortunate' enough to be deposed before Yom Kippur have formed a society of ex-*kohanim gedolim*, which is strong-arming anyone from whom they can extort money or power. They have even formed militias! May Hashem help and protect us!"

Rochel looked at the queen, emotionally exhausted. Helene gazed back at her, stunned and saddened by the devastating words.

"We must not lose hope, Rochel," she spoke in a near-whisper. "Is it not true that the Holy One, blessed be He, is always waiting to accept our *teshuvah*?"

---

3 Only a legitimate *kohen gadol* who performs the *avodah* on the holiest day of the year will merit emerging from the Holy of Holies alive and well.

Chapter Ten

In spite of his aversion to confronting Rome, Izates was drawn into military conflicts with this superpower. Helene's thoughts and prayers were constantly centered on her son. Only when there was a hiatus in these battles did Helene finally permit herself to begin thinking of fulfilling her long-held dream.[1]

Rays of early-morning sunshine streamed through the queen's bedchamber. They slipped through the translucent reed shades, brightening the elaborate design of the carpets, warming the stone walls, and making the high-vaulted ceiling glitter like diamonds. The brilliant rays illuminated the expectant young faces of the maidservants about to attend the queen in her boudoir.

The girls sensed that this was a day of special import. They had been summoned much later than usual that morning, so they assumed that the queen had extended her morning prayers. When they arrived, they could see that she had been reciting Psalms. The parchment scroll lying on the stone table was rolled to the Songs of Ascent, but the queen was absent. She had retreated into an inner chamber for further meditation, and the girls understood that they should wait a few moments for her to appear.

---

1 This occurred around the year 46 CE. There is a difference of opinion as to the exact nature of the conflicts that delayed Helene's visit to Eretz Yisrael, but it appears that there was some reprieve before she left Adiabene.

"Why did Her Majesty prolong her prayers today, and why did she say these particular psalms?" whispered the youngest of the handmaids to her older sister. "It is not her regular custom."

"You are right," her older sister said authoritatively. "I overheard Rabbi Alexander teach Her Majesty that these are the fifteen psalms recited daily by the levites on the steps leading to the Beis Hamikdash. I know that my lady's heart increasingly pines to see Yerushalayim and to bring offerings in the Holy Temple. Perhaps reciting these particular psalms soothes her soul."

Just then, the whoosh of curtains parting could be heard as the queen emerged from her private chamber.

"Artaynte, Artazostre, please be kind enough to accompany me to the gate of the king's throne room. Afterwards, you are both free for the rest of the morning," she said with a smile.

A courier had been sent to King Izates that morning by his mother, requesting an audience with him that afternoon, after he finished his study session with Rabbi Alexander. Izates was curious, as his mother had not revealed the reason for her visit.

A short thump of a leather mallet against the door announced the presence of the queen.

"Thank you, Rabbi Alexander, for your teachings this morning," Izates said. "How I wish the burdens of state would evaporate, so I could sit and learn with you the entire day!"

"You are a diligent student of Torah, Your Highness. May peace continue to reign in Adiabene, and may you merit realizing your wish," Rabbi Alexander blessed the king.

He took leave of Izates through a side exit, just as the large, heavy door to the throne room slowly opened to reveal Queen Helene standing at the entrance. She walked inside, serene as usual.

"Izates, my son," she said. "Thank you for meeting with me on such short notice, in spite of how busy you are with matters of state. The topic I have come to discuss is a weighty one, and I am eager to share my thoughts with you."

Izates looked at his mother, concerned.

"Dear Mother," Izates replied, "it is I who am honored by your visit and your desire to share important issues with me. I always feel a sense of calm and well-being when I am around you, but I see in your eyes a faraway look today. It is as if only your physical being is here with me in this room, while your soul is elsewhere. Has there, Heaven forbid, been a tragedy?"

"Heaven forbid, my son! I apologize if my demeanor does not reflect the inner joy I feel today. In truth, my heart exults at the thought of realizing the dream I have come to share with you this afternoon, but even the realization of dreams comes at times with some sadness and pain."

"Please, Mother, present your request to me forthwith. Surely, it must be an important and worthy desire."

"Yes, it is, my dear son," Helene responded. "And I hope that its fulfillment will bring further glory to your throne. What I request from you, my son, is permission to leave my beloved homeland to travel to the Land of Israel, to dwell near the Holy Temple, to make my lot among our adopted people, and to observe the mitzvos dependent on the Land. I am also nearing the end of my period of *nezirus*, and I desire to fulfill my vow by offering the required sacrifices at the Beis Hamikdash."

Izates sighed and then drew in a deep breath.

"There really is no question here, Mother," he said slowly. "Of course, you must go, but how I will miss you! Where will I go for the advice and inspiration that only you can provide?"

The queen looked lovingly at her son. How much she would miss him as well! She swallowed, knowing that she must not show him her true feelings. He was the king, and his destiny, for the time being, lay in Adiabene, while hers was waiting to unfold in the Holy Land.

"You are fully competent to rule our people," Helene responded reassuringly. "When you need advice, always look to the Torah and its scholars for direction. Pray to Hashem for guidance and protection. You can be sure I will do so, as well. And consult with your wise brother, Monobaz. He will always stand by you and support you in every way he can."

"Surely, Mother, your advice is well taken in every respect," Izates replied. "But you must not travel alone. I will ask Monobaz to accompany you to the Holy Land. He will establish you there and facilitate your introduction to the rabbis of Yerushalayim."

"Do you think it is prudent for Monobaz to be so far from the kingdom?" the queen asked. "It is impossible to predict just when he would return."

Izates paused before responding in a firm voice.

"I will sorely miss my brother's wise advice and warm companionship," he admitted. "But I know that his heart, too, yearns for Yerushalayim. Monobaz belongs with you in the Holy Land. He will serve as ambassador of our small nation. I am certain that he will take every opportunity to make a *kiddush Hashem* through his actions. May his mitzvos be a *zechus* for all of us here." His voice shook with emotion, and he turned away. After a long moment, the king composed himself and turned back to his mother.

"Mother, for many years I tried to understand why my father chose me to succeed him on the throne. Monobaz was always more courageous and capable than I. Thankfully, two events led me to understand why I was in fact chosen. Firstly, I was fortunate, with the help of my dear wife, to come to believe in the one and only G-d. Secondly, I had the opportunity to visit the site of the remains of Noach's ark in Ararat, the place where it settled after the Great Flood. There I contemplated the meaning of world history and its implications for myself, for the role I am personally intended to play while I live and breathe on this earth.

Now everything has become clear to me, Mother. I see that my brother was spared the burden of kingship to enable him to sanctify the Name of the Alm-ghty and to accomplish great deeds in the spiritual realm.

"I understand and accept that *Hakadosh Baruch Hu* has given me an important role to play here in *galus*. The Jewish people are to be a light unto the nations, as our actions testify to the existence of G-d. So, I accept that I myself cannot join you in your holy pilgrimage, as much as my heart yearns to do so. Nevertheless, I can send a part of me with you. Dear Mother, please take my sons, your five grandsons, with you to the Holy Land, where they will learn Torah from the sages, where they will cast their fate with our brethren during these troubled times, and where they will hopefully, with Hashem's help, contribute to the hastening of a salvation for our people."

Izates's eyes clouded over with emotion at the thought of sending his sons so far away. He was silent for a long moment.

"I pray constantly that our Jewish faith will outlive us, Mother," he finally said. "We have a new generation of Jewish children to raise. They must drink in the Torah of the sages and become fully acculturated to the lifestyle of our adopted people. As their father, I hope and dream that they become *talmidei chachamim* and develop fear of Heaven.

"But I am asking you to do more than just accompany them, Mother, and before responding to my request, I beseech you to consider it together with its implications. Samacha and I desire that our sons become like your sons, that they be raised by you, educated through you, cared for by you, and, with Hashem's help, married off by you. You will have the authority of a parent over them, and I enjoin them to honor, obey, and love you as their mother. We yearn for Eretz Yisrael to become their permanent home. Whenever you decide to return home, the boys will be given the option to remain, and we would make appropriate arrangements for them. As much as we will miss them, it is our preference that they not leave the Holy Land to live again in Adiabene."

Izates looked earnestly at his mother, trying to discern her true feelings. Helene gazed at him with moist eyes.

"Izates, you are truly a good father," she said, her voice barely above a whisper. "I am awed that my son has grown to such maturity and moral strength. Of course, I accept with honor, and not a little trepidation, the role you foist upon me. I have always felt so close to my grandchildren! It has made me so happy to see them observing the mitzvos. But this decision must be a very difficult one for you. What about their mother? Does Samacha truly concur with your decision? I would not want to cause her pain or for their departure to harm your *shalom bayis*."

"You can be very proud of your daughter-in-law, Mother. It was actually she who initially brought up the topic to me, when she inferred through your conversations with her that you desired to make the trip to the Holy Land. I would not have had the courage to suggest it to her otherwise."

Helene was silent for a few moments, as she pondered the implications of her son's words. While she had initially viewed her visit to Yerushalayim as a temporary stay, she had come to believe that it could be extended indefinitely. The family would be split as a result, but, in the midst of the chasm there would sprout renewed life that would, in turn, bear fruit. Her grandsons would, with Hashem's help, grow to be Torah scholars, steeped in learning and tradition. They would marry Jewesses and establish homes permeated with Torah and mitzvos. Although she might never again see her beloved son, Izates, he would leave a precious legacy.

"I accept your charge, my son, but we are in need of Heavenly assistance," Helene said after a few moments. "These are difficult times, and even in Eretz Yisrael there is a spirit of impurity that has afflicted many of our people. I will pray daily for my grandsons, that they may grow to be *talmidei chachamim* and *yirei Shamayim*, as I know you and

Samacha will do as well. May Hashem heed our prayers and watch over our children, keeping them safe from any untoward influences."

It seemed to Izates that his mother's excitement over the prospect of traveling to the Holy Land had transformed her into a woman twenty years her junior. Before exiting his chamber, she looked at her son one last time.

"Izates, I know you are wondering why I feel so strongly about going to the Holy Land," she said. "I have heard rumors of the external, as well as internal, struggles currently going on there, and they are discouraging and very frightening. Nonetheless, the *kedushah* of the Land is independent of the actions of those living there. It is this *kedushah* that I desire to imbibe. But I hereby bestow any spiritual benefits I may accrue there to you, my son.

"Izates," Helene continued, her voice faltering, "you need not tell me how much you yourself yearn to ascend to the Holy Land, but alas, you are king, and your subjects need you to rule over them and guide them, to show them what it means to live a life of holiness. Think of Queen Esther, who was brought to serve in the court of Achashveirosh. Remember how Mordechai tells her, 'Maybe it was just for a time like this that you became queen!'[2]

"If we do indeed merit reaching Yerushalayim and the holy Beis Hamikdash, I will be thinking of you when bringing the *korbanos*, separating *terumah* and *ma'aser*, giving *challah* to the *kohen*, and eating the *Korban Pesach*." Helene tried to suppress the tears welling up in her eyes.

"May you offer a *Korban Todah* upon the safe completion of your trip across the desert and your arrival in the holy city of Yerushalayim," Izates blessed his mother.

"Amen, may it be His will!" Helene said, smiling. "Now, enough of our talk! I must begin to prepare for the trip. There is so much to be

---

2   *Esther* 4:14.

done!" A youthful sparkle glowed in her eyes, and she left the room to get to work.

Helene assembled her maidservants the next morning. Her face bore a faraway look as she avoided their questioning gazes. Their relationship with her was more like a mother to her daughters than a mistress to her servants.

"My dear girls," she said, trying to keep her emotions in check, "I have bittersweet news for you. Very soon, I will be leaving you to travel to the Holy Land of Israel, the homeland of my adopted people. I do not know how long I will be away, or, for that matter, whether I will return at all. You see, the Alm-ghty G-d has chosen the Jewish people for a special mission that they can only achieve fully by observing His laws in the Land He chose to grant them. I am no longer young, and so I feel I must not delay. Prince Monobaz will accompany me while King Izates remains here and continues to rule. You will all go to live in Princess Samacha's apartments. I beseech you to serve her with the same love and dedication that you have served me. She is a kind and gentle woman and will not only care for your physical needs, but will guide you as much as you allow her to do so."

There was a stunned silence as the young girls stood still, shocked by the unexpected news. They all loved and respected their queen and could not imagine what life would be like without her.

As Helene approached each girl individually and embraced her, tears could be seen streaming down the cheeks of both monarch and maidservant. She handed each one a small package wrapped in parchment.

"Please, open these when you are alone in your rooms," she requested. "They are personal items of mine that I think you will enjoy owning. I hope it will also help you to remember me!"

The queen gazed for a long moment at each of the girls, as if trying to etch each detail of their faces in her mind. Then she covered her face with a veil, so as not to be seen crying and quickly left the room.

No sooner had Helene exited the chamber than she heard footsteps on the flagstones.

"Your Royal Highness!" exclaimed Azate, who, at thirteen, was the youngest of the girls. "Surely you will take us with you. Who will care for your physical needs in the Holy Land? Who will wind your hair and prepare your garments?"

"My dear child," Helene demurred gently, "I am honored by your loyalty, but you must understand that those who believe in Zoroaster should not reside in the Holy Land. Through our great sins, we find ourselves under the jurisdiction of the Roman pagans there. Nevertheless, Eretz Yisrael is a place intended solely for residence by those who worship the one and only G-d."[3]

"But that is not a problem for me!" Azate spoke up emphatically. "I have observed you, my mistress, since you took on the Jewish religion, and I have carefully considered its merits. I have decided that I, too, desire to join the Jewish people."

Helene looked intently at the girl. "But Azate, as a gentile you can fulfill your spiritual purpose on this earth by accepting the seven Noachide laws incumbent upon every individual. By observing these laws, you can achieve closeness to Hashem and find favor in His eyes. If you totally accept sole belief in Hashem as the one and only G-d, you could assume the status of a *ger toshav*, a resident alien. If it is your desire to accompany me, then becoming a *ger toshav* would be sufficient, and I would be so happy for you to remain with me."

---

3   When the *Yovel* year was observed in Eretz Yisrael, only full-fledged Jews or those who accepted complete monotheism and certain mitzvos were allowed permanent residence in the Holy Land. There is a disagreement among the sages as to whether the *Yovel* was observed during the time of the second Beis Hamikdash. Unfortunately, the absence of Jewish sovereignty during this time resulted in many non-Jews living in Eretz Yisrael, regardless.

"But Your Highness," Azate said respectfully. The young girl raised her eyes to those of her mistress with a determined gaze. "With your permission, my mistress, I would be happy to study the Noachide laws with Rabbi Alexander, but I already feel this will not suffice for me. I want to observe the other mitzvos of the Torah, just as you do, my queen!"

"This is not my decision, dear child. If, after you study, the rabbis find that you accept the entire Torah and are familiar with its laws, you would qualify for conversion."

"And then I could accompany you to the Holy Land?" Azate asked hopefully.

Helene paused as she groped for the right answer.

"I will take you with me regardless of your decision, Azate," Helene answered firmly. "I trust that you have renounced idolatry and believe in the one true G-d, but please think carefully before attempting to join the Jewish people. Study the Torah and its laws. Observe the lifestyle of the Jews and how it differs from that of the Parthians. You are an orphan, Azate, so you have no family with whom to sever a connection, but you have friends. The Torah states, *In their ways, you shall not walk*. This means that joining the activities and entertainment of your pagan acquaintances will be prohibited to you if you become a Jew. Be honest with yourself. Are you strong enough to withstand the possible ridicule of those with whom you have associated until now? Are you ready to leave behind all you have to build your life anew?"

"Yes," Azate insisted, her face wearing a determined look. "Now that I have become acquainted with the Jewish religion through my queen, I see my earlier life as full of falsehood and vanity. I will neither miss the pageantry of the foolish pagan festivals, nor the vacuous time-wasting activities of my former friends. I am looking for meaning in my life, Your Highness, and I see that I can only find that by living a life with values like yours."

"Your words are truly eloquent, Azate, especially for one so young, and I can tell that they come from your heart," Helene responded, unable to suppress a smile of pride in her young charge. "The rabbis will try to dissuade you from converting, as I have, but their wisdom enables them to discern sincere commitment. Oh, my Azate, there is so much to learn! Let's request an audience with Rabbi Alexander. He will then advise you what to do."

Azate agreed and sought out Rabbi Alexander the very next day.

"There is a young woman here to see you," Rochel told her husband.

Rabbi Alexander looked up from his text to see a diminutive figure, dressed demurely in a long caftan and veil. Her eyes were fixed on the floor and her voice was barely audible in her great timidity.

"Rabbi Alexander," the girl whispered. "My name is Azate, and I am a servant of Queen Helene. My mistress has sent me to you to seek guidance on a matter quite important to me."

"Her Royal Highness sent you to me?" Rabbi Alexander replied, surprised. "To what pressing matter do I owe the honor of this visit?"

"I have renounced my religion and desire to become a member of the Jewish people," Azate blurted out, shaking.

"Please tell me, my child," Rabbi Alexander said gently. "Why do you want to join the Jewish people?"

"I no longer believe in the Zoroastrian faith and its multiple powers. I secretly disavowed it many months ago, but it was not until I observed my mistress practicing the ways of the Jews that I came to realize that it is only the Torah that gives us the proper path to follow in life."

"What have you observed the queen do?" Rabbi Alexander questioned her.

"I have observed Her Majesty as she lights the Shabbos candles and refrains from creative work on the seventh day of each week," Azate said. "I have seen her exchange her weekday duties for prayer and beautiful meals accompanied by song and words of Torah, while she spends special time with her grandchildren.

"I have watched her check on the supervision of food preparation in the royal kitchen to be sure it meets all of the requirements of kashrus," Azate continued. "I have learned many of the laws, such as the prohibition of cooking or eating meat and milk together, the requirement to slaughter kosher animals in a specific way, and the importance of eating only food cooked by Jews. By consuming only kosher food in holiness, we can start to correct the sin of eating what was forbidden."[4]

Azate took a deep breath and continued. "Queen Helene has explained to me that acts of charity and loving-kindness are also mandated by the Torah, and that every aspect of life is directed by its laws."

"Your observations are astute and praiseworthy," Rabbi Alexander admitted. "They suggest that your soul has a spiritual sensitivity not commonly found among your people. Are you aware, though, that in order to become Jewish, you must accept that the Torah was given to the Jewish people on Mount Sinai and that all of its commandments are binding? This would include many laws with which you are not currently familiar.

"You would need to sever your association with heathens and their practices completely. As a Jew, you would not be considered related to your birth family but would be as if born anew. Of course, you could only marry another Jew."

"I am aware of the truth of what you tell me, and I also acknowledge the great limitations in my knowledge at the present," Azate said steadily. "Nevertheless, I am committed to correcting my deficiencies through

---

[4] When Adam ate from the Tree of Knowledge, he accused Chava of giving him the fruit. He said, "And I ate," but the words he used implied "and I will eat." Adam understood that the act of eating would again bring him to sinfulness. The mitzvos of kashrus enable us to correct this flaw by elevating our spiritual selves (*Bereishis Rabbah* 19:22).

observing my mistress, Queen Helene, and formal study. My heart is devoted to the one G-d, and I will dedicate my life to His service. I feel that the only way I can accomplish this is by becoming a full-fledged Jewess. I have no relatives, and I would gladly become part of the family of Am Yisrael. I have heard that all Jews consider themselves related to each other, just like the members of a family."

Rabbi Alexander's gaze softened as he recognized the determination in the young girl's voice. "I can see that your sentiments are pure, my child, but you must know that it is sufficient for you to keep the laws of a *ben Noach*. By doing so, you will fulfill your purpose in Creation."

"Yes, this too, Queen Helene told me, Rabbi," Azate responded respectfully. "But now that I know what it is like to observe the Torah, the Noachide laws are not sufficient for me to feel complete and fulfilled."

"Throughout history, the Jewish people has been oppressed and persecuted by the gentile. Do you realize that you are likely to be ostracized by your friends and acquaintances if you become a Jew?"

"I have learned that persecution comes when the Jews do not observe the Torah correctly," Azate replied demurely. "My mistress has told me that we are to view the world as half guilty and half meritorious. It may take only the mitzvos of a single person to tip the scales in favor of merit. It would be my hope that my observance could help in some small way."

"My daughter, like your mistress, the queen, you appear to be a worthy spiritual descendant of Rus the Moabite," Rabbi Alexander said kindly. "Go study the laws pertaining to a Jewish woman with your queen in preparation for conversion. Then, come to me to learn further. If you accompany the queen to the Holy Land, you will meet with a *rav* of the Academy of Beis Hillel. He will determine if you are ready to join the Jewish people as a *giyores*."

Tears of happiness welled up in Azate's eyes. "Thank you, Rabbi Alexander," she said.

"You are welcome," the sage responded sincerely. "May your endeavors be blessed with success!"

Helene was nearing the end of her extensive preparations for her departure. It was on such an afternoon that Izates paid an unexpected visit to the queen's chambers. Lists of provisions and instructions to court staff lay on her worktable, and bound packages of clothing were neatly stacked on the floor. Izates had denied no expense or effort in helping his mother prepare for her trip to the Holy Land.

"I am sorry to disturb you, Mother," the king remarked with a smile. "I see you are quite busy!"

"Yes, indeed, my son," Helene replied. "I am trying to be attentive to details, so that the boys will be comfortable on the long trip."

Izates's expression turned solemn.

"Mother," he said gently. "I just received a courier from Eretz Yisrael, who told me that the oppression of the Jewish people by the Roman procurators is intensifying. How can I send you into such a situation?"

Helene looked intently at her son.

"Izates," she said, softly but firmly. "The purpose of my travel to the Holy Land is to serve Hashem and to unite with my people. Perhaps I must go now, because the Jews of Yerushalayim need my assistance. Surely, there must be something we can do to help. I cannot consider deferring the trip any longer. Please do not try to dissuade me."

"How I admire you, Mother," Izates replied, with deep respect. "Nothing daunts you. Yours is a deep and true *emunah*."

So it was, on Rosh Chodesh Iyar,[5] that Helene, her handmaiden Azate, her son Monobaz, and Izates's five sons set out for the overland trip to Eretz Yisrael. A huge throng gathered outside the palace for the

---

5 While the actual month of Helene's departure is unknown, it is likely that she traveled to the Land of Israel in the year 46 CE.

departure ceremony. King Izates, dressed in a flowing silk robe, stood at a marble podium on an elevated platform to address the crowd.

"May the journey of the royal family be safe and expeditious, in the merit of their faith in the One, All-Powerful, G-d, and their great love for the Land of our forefathers."

Samacha embraced each of her sons, weeping.

"Until now, you have all been princes of Adiabene," she addressed them through her tears. "Now, I pray that you will all become princes of Torah!"

Izates gave a signal, triggering the horsemen to snap the reins. Monobaz and a male attendant traveled in the first carriage with thirteen-year old Moshe, eleven-year-old Reuven, nine-year-old Yosef, eight-year-old Yehudah, and five-year-old Yaakov. Helene and Azate occupied the second carriage, and a third wagon was laden with food, water, clothing, blankets, and other supplies.

Then, surprising most of those present, the king mounted his horse and led the caravan himself on the first leg of their trip. He rode ahead of them the entire first day and stayed with them during the night. Only the next morning did the king take leave of his family to return to the palace.

Izates bestowed blessings upon his sons and brother. Helene blessed Izates and embraced him with great emotion.

"With the help of Hashem, I will constantly pray for your good health, success, and happiness while I am in the holy city of Yerushalayim," she whispered. "Be strong and courageous. May we all merit sanctifying the holy Name of Hashem by our actions and be reunited at a good and propitious time."

The rainy season had ended, and the days would be warm but not sweltering. Nevertheless, the trip would last sixteen days and was long and arduous as they passed through the cloudless desert and over windy mountain paths. The queen had given instructions for the fewest possible number of stops to minimize the length of the trip. She also felt that the more she showed her determination to reach the longed-for destination, the more worthy she would be of Divine help and protection along the way and during her stay. She focused on caring for her grandsons, whose enthusiasm for their future life in the Holy Land sustained them through the tedium of travel and living conditions much more Spartan than the royal comforts to which they were accustomed.

One evening, about halfway through the long trip, Monobaz approached his mother. She was sitting outside her tent, gazing at the crystal-clear, star-studded sky.

"Monobaz," Helene said, more to herself than to her son, "it is so amazing to watch the stars and heavenly bodies, doing the will of their Creator. They are so many and great, but still, what a small portion of the Alm-ghty's universe they represent! It makes me feel so tiny and inconsequential. Yet, it is only man who can increase *kedushah* in the world. Only man can approach Hashem, bringing glory to His Name. How I yearn to be on holy soil, performing the mitzvos that are unique to that place. May I only be worthy..."

"Mother," Monobaz said hesitantly, "when we recite the Shema, we recall Hashem's promise to us that if we observe His commandments and His laws, the Land will be fruitful and produce in abundance. However, if we go astray from Hashem's Torah and worship other gods, then the opposite will occur until, G-d forbid, we will be driven from the Land."

"May it never happen, my son!" Helene answered, a sense of foreboding quickening her heartbeat.

Monobaz continued, forcing himself to express his unpleasant thoughts.

"While there are surely many sages today in Eretz Yisrael who support the Torah through their diligent study, our spiritual condition has suffered greatly as a result of the great oppression and the influence of pagan rulers," he said, sighing. "There are three groups of Jews, each with three different viewpoints as to how to deal with the Roman oppressors. Those who are prepared for outright warfare against the Romans are called the Zealots. Then there are the Moderates, who, while supporting the goals of the Zealots, hope to avoid open confrontation with Rome. The *rabbanim* back this approach. They know there can be no benefit from war against Rome. Finally, there are the Friends of Rome, those loyal to Rome, comprised largely of the Tzedokim." He spoke tersely, his voice masking the strong emotion he felt.

"I want you to know about this, Mother, so you will not be shocked upon our arrival."

"I appreciate your concern, my son. I am aware of the struggles and conflicts that have gripped our beloved homeland. When I hear such distressing news, it saddens and frightens me. But then I think about how Hashem is always waiting for us to repent." Her voice trembled and faded to a whisper. "May we return to Him with all our hearts, and may He accept our *teshuvah*."

"Amen!" Monobaz answered.

After more than two weeks of exhausting travel, the royal family's destination finally came into sight.

"Look, Uncle!" Moshe exclaimed. "What is that smoke rising in the distance?"

Monobaz strained his eyes, scanning the horizon. His heart beat quickly as feelings of awe overcame him.

"Moshe, what you see is the column of smoke rising from the altar of the Beis Hamikdash!" he answered, his voice trembling with emotion. "The fact that the smoke always rises up like a pillar is one of the many miracles that occurs constantly in this most holy of places."

"I know that, Uncle," Yosef piped up. "Rabbi Alexander taught me this, and he also said that the fire on the altar never goes out, even when there is heavy rain!"

"You are correct, Yosef," Monobaz acknowledged. "With Hashem's help, we will witness other miracles in the Beis Hamikdash, as well."

"It looks like a mountain covered with snow!" Reuven exclaimed.

"Yes, my dear nephew," Monobaz agreed. "It appears so from a distance, because the parts of the Holy Temple that are not gilt are exceedingly white."

Helene's vision blurred as she stared spellbound at the miraculous spectacle in the distance. The column of smoke, which rose straight as an arrow aimed at heaven, appeared surreal in the haze of early morning. She could see the surrounding trees swaying in the spring wind, but the column didn't move.

Monobaz noticed that his mother's lips were moving, forming words of silent prayer. He likewise expressed his personal thanks to Hashem for bringing him to the Holy Land as a Jew, and prayed that he merit adding in some small way to its *kedushah*.

Chapter Eleven

In the Holy City, a devout, middle-aged couple prepared for their distinguished guests. Rabbi Alexander had contacted the well-respected family of Amram ben Be'iri, who enthusiastically offered to host Queen Helene, Prince Monobaz, and the boys in their spacious villa until a permanent dwelling could be constructed for them.

Amram was a kindly man in his fifties with a tall, imposing stature and thoughtful countenance, and an ever-present smile. He spent most of his day poring over scrolls of holy writings and discussing matters of halachah with the sages of Beis Hillel. Hashem had blessed Amram ben Be'iri with a bountiful livelihood. At this stage in his life, his involvement with his construction business was minimal. Day-to-day operations of the business were managed by his three sons and four sons-in-law, but, by employing responsible workers, they, too, were able to spend lengthy hours in *batei midrash*.

Rivka ben Be'iri had been born into a prominent family of sages. Her warm, jovial nature was backed by a thorough knowledge of Jewish law as it pertained to all aspects of running a home. The warmth of the ben Be'iris, combined with their high standards of religious observance, had long made their home a favored lodging place for visiting sages from all over the Diaspora, as well as the furthest reaches of Eretz Yisrael.

The ben Be'iris chose to build their home just east of the Tyropean Valley that divided the posh Upper City to the west from the modest

Lower City. Tenaciously loyal to the Perushi rabbis, Amram and his wife eschewed the assimilated lifestyle and the attitudes of the wealthy Tzedokim in favor of a life focused on Torah and mitzvos, and, in particular, acts of *chessed*.

The ben Be'iris were gracious hosts, sensitive to the royal family's status as converts to the Jewish faith. While Rivka prepared for the arrival of her guests, she tried to imagine what they would be like. She expressed her concerns to her husband.

"Amram," Rivka said, "Hashem has given us a unique opportunity in hosting the royal family. In addition to the mitzvah of *hachnasas orchim*, we can also fulfill the mitzvah of showing love to the convert.[1] They are so brave to leave their birthplace and royal privileges to join us here, in Eretz Yisrael, especially during such troubled times! How will they react, and how should we respond?"

"We think similarly, my dear wife," Amram responded, smiling. "This issue has been very much on my mind, so I consulted with one of the *dayanim* of Beis Hillel who is very familiar with the reputation of the royal family. He reassured me that the strength of their *emunah*, coupled with their sharp minds, will enable them to both grasp and accept our situation here. We must give them emotional support and respect and answer their questions as straightforwardly as possible.

"Also," Amram continued, "I think it is most important that we provide them with whatever help we can without yielding to our curiosity about their past. I am certain they will share with us whatever they feel comfortable sharing, my dear wife."

"Yes, of course, Amram," Rivka agreed. "I look forward to getting to know the queen and, with Hashem's help, I'll respond to her questions to the best of my ability."

"That is all you can be expected to do, Rivka," Amram reassured her. "Perhaps our most challenging task will be to protect them from

---

1 *Devarim* 10:19.

exploitation by the Tzedokim," he said thoughtfully. "I'm sure they would relish having the royal family defect to their side. While the queen and prince would never consider allying themselves with the Hellenists, we must still try to prevent any unpleasant confrontations. I am fearful that their idealism makes them especially vulnerable to the persistent ways of those who want us to assimilate into Roman culture."

"And how can we accomplish this without indicting our people?" Rivka asked worriedly.

"I am aware of the potential pitfalls of speaking proactively, Rivka, but I fear that not doing so would be much more dangerous. I will brief the prince as tactfully as I can."

Amram had just returned from the *beis knesses* on a sunny morning several days after his conversation with his wife, when a knock sounded on the door, accompanied by a set of terse trumpet blasts announcing the arrival of a foreign messenger. The foreign-looking man bore a parchment written in Aramaic stating the expected arrival time of the royal guests at two days hence and asking if any further delay would be necessary to accommodate the schedule of the ben Be'iris. It was signed by Prince Monobaz of Adiabene.

Amram took the quill offered him and quickly wrote a reply at the bottom of the parchment. He watched as the messenger mounted his horse and galloped off toward the east. He closed the door as his heartbeat quickened with anticipation. Amram had a feeling that a momentous change in their lives was about to occur.

The royal family arrived at the anticipated time, and what an arrival it was! By the time the caravan had made its way through the Judean hills and reached the walls of Yerushalayim, a crowd of thousands had assembled to observe the pageantry.

In a reversal of their order of travel through the desert, the parade began with six covered wagons led by donkeys, each emblazoned with the royal insignia of Adiabene, which carried provisions and possessions. These were followed by a large carriage pulled by six white stallions, draped with the flag of their homeland. Inside were Monobaz, his five nephews, and a male attendant. Last was the white carriage that carried the queen and Azate. This carriage had a removable cover, which the queen asked be opened for the occasion of her entry into the city. She was so eager to become acquainted with Yerushalayim's physical features, as well as its inhabitants, that only a large parasol of silk protected the queen and Azate from the blazing sun. The vehicle was otherwise open to the elements and to the curious crowd swarming around it. Those who were close enough beheld a slight, dark woman with large black eyes. Her face glowed with kind benevolence and a spiritual fervor that made her seem somewhat other-worldly.

"My lady," Azate gasped, "are you not frightened of all of these people staring at you?" She felt a need to protect her mistress from the unfamiliar surroundings.

"Afraid?" Helene chuckled. "Why should I be? Put yourself in their place, my dear. Would you not be curious and stare at foreigners coming to your city with such fanfare? Surely they must be hopeful that we can somehow help them now that we have arrived. These onlookers are members of the Jewish people — my people. I must try to determine what type of assistance I can provide them."

In the men's carriage, Monobaz, who had studied maps of the Holy City, was busy pointing out the sites to his avid nephews.

"In front of us is the Mount of Olives," he told them, pointing. "From there the coming of Mashiach will be announced. And there, to the west, is the Har Habayis, site of the Beis Hamikdash."

Moshe's eyes grew wide with wonder. "Uncle, I think I can see it now!" he exclaimed. "I see a wall with many gates and a large, majestic building rising in its center!"

Monobaz stared silently in the direction of Moshe's finger. *The Beis Hamikdash!* He was able to see the Beis Hamikdash!

After a few moments, the prince turned to his nephews, looking at each one in turn. "Boys, we are about to enter the holiest city in the world. Always remember what a great privilege it is to live here. Strive to learn Torah diligently, and perform the mitzvos to the very best of your ability. Elevate yourselves spiritually. This is why your dear parents, in their great love for you, sent you here."

Monobaz closed his eyes. "*Ribono shel Olam*," he prayed silently, "please give us the knowledge and strength to help our downtrodden people during this time of trouble."

Surely, the prince's fervent *tefillah* was heard in *Shamayim*. No one could have imagined at the time just how much goodness would come to the holy city of Yerushalayim during their tenure there…

The royal family approached the city from the northeast, entering through Herod's Gate, just north of the Har Habayis. They were accompanied by a vast crowd of curious onlookers and cries of "Long live Queen Helene! Long live Prince Monobaz!" Tales of the royal family's sacrifices for the sake of Torah preceded them, and they received a hero's welcome.

Amram and Rivka remained patiently outside their home as the caravan approached. When it finally came to a stop in front of their house, a tall man with regal bearing, dressed simply in a long robe and white turban, exited the carriage alone and approached the couple with great deference.

"May I humbly introduce myself to the esteemed Mar Amram ben Be'iri?" he began deferentially. "I am Monobaz, prince of Adiabene, making a pilgrimage to Yerushalayim with my mother, Queen Helene, and my nephews. We are here to serve Hashem and His people. We are very grateful to you for taking us in! May we merit bringing blessing to your family and your home, and may we not be a burden."

"Amen," Amram replied. "But surely, the royal family could impose no burden upon us. It is we who are grateful for having the opportunity to host such righteous people as Your Highnesses. We truly feel quite honored to be in your presence, and we are ready to do anything we can to make your stay comfortable and pleasant."

"Then we are well matched!" Monobaz replied with enthusiasm.

Rivka smiled at the boys as they emerged from the carriage. She led them inside and gave each of them a small ceramic bowl filled with assorted nuts and dried fruits. "Please enjoy the fruits of Eretz Yisrael! The almonds, figs, and dates are from local orchards. If you look outside that window, you'll see the pomegranates ripening. G-d willing, they should be ready to pick in just a couple of months."

Yaakov immediately picked a fig from the bowl and admired it for a moment. Then he made a *brachah* aloud and popped it into his mouth.

"This is so delicious!" he enthused. "It's so much sweeter than the figs that grow in Adiabene."

Moshe, speaking for his brothers, stepped forward.

"Thank you so much for your hospitality, Giveret ben Be'iri," he said in Aramaic. "We can see why Eretz Yisrael is praised for its special fruits."

"It is a true pleasure to have Your Royal Highnesses as guests," Rivka responded.

Rivka turned to Helene and Azate. "May I show the queen and her companion to their quarters?"

"With pleasure, Giveret," Helene responded with an appreciative smile. "This young woman is Azate. She aspires to join the Jewish people."

"It is so good to meet you, Azate," Rivka greeted her, taking her hand in hers. "May Hashem grant you success! And Your Highness," she added, looking again at Helene, "I would be honored for you to call me Rivka."

"At your request," Helene replied with a smile. "How wonderful it is to share the name of our holy matriarch, wife of Yitzchak Avinu! I only ask that you dispense with titles when speaking to me, as well."

"Oh, please indulge me, Your Highness, but I do not feel it possible to do so," Rivka said quickly. "Perhaps with the passage of time, I will feel able to fulfill your request, but right now addressing you by title feels more suitable to me."

"Whatever you choose, Rivka," Helene answered with a twinkle in her eye. "But I hope that our relationship will grow quickly so you feel comfortable enough to reciprocate."

Rivka blushed but continued to focus on her role as hostess. She led Helene down a narrow hallway and stopped before a heavy, wooden door. She nervously turned the key in the lock and opened the door, waiting with some trepidation for the queen's reaction.

"Rivka!" Helene exclaimed, with obvious pleasure. "How could you have known?"

Rivka stood still, not sure of the source of the queen's enthusiastic reaction. Helene did indeed seem pleased with the way the rooms had been decorated. Rivka had consulted with a friend whose wealthy family hailed from a region just north of Adiabene in hopes that their taste would please her royal guest.

"The fabrics used in this room are identical to those in my bedchamber in the palace!" Helene revealed, smiling. "Both the colors and the pattern are the same! How amazing! You certainly could not have made me feel more at home!"

The queen embraced her hostess and new friend warmly. "Please do not feel that you need to give us any special treatment, Rivka. Your hospitality and the opportunity to learn from your devout behavior are the greatest of gifts! How can I thank you?"

"If I may ask Her Majesty's forgiveness, there is just one thing I must explain," Rivka offered, visibly uncomfortable.

"Please, Rivka," Helene said encouragingly. "Do not hesitate to tell us whatever we need to know."

"Thank you, Your Highness," Rivka responded, relieved. "You see, anyone coming from outside of Eretz Yisrael is assumed to be *tamei meis*. A week-long process of purification using the ashes of the red heifer is necessary to remove this spiritual impurity. Any food touched by a *tamei* person, which has also come in contact with any one of seven liquids,[2] becomes *tamei* as well. For this reason, I will ask the royal family's forgiveness for seating and serving them separately from members of my family until the purification process is complete. We have adopted the strict interpretation of the law and eat only food that is *tahor*, ritually pure, even though this food is not sanctified as an offering. This is a very temporary situation, and we beg your indulgence."

Helene listened carefully and wondered if this would impact her *nezirus*. She had been scrupulously careful not to come in contact with the dead, but she had had no way to purify herself from previous contact. Surely, the rabbis would guide her…

"Rivka," she said, putting aside the matter of her *nezirus* for now, "I know I can speak for my son in saying that we feel privileged to learn from your adherence to such high standards of observance. We also look forward to the day when we will become ritually pure, in order to bring *korbanos* in the Beis Hamikdash."

The royal group was invited into the dining hall, where upholstered, wooden couches were arranged around circular stone tables of only about twenty inches in diameter.[3] A servant filled small bowls with vegetable stew from a large ceramic pot and then put the pot on the table. The ben Be'iris would eat later from separate fare. Amram invited his guests to wash their hands and then to dip their bread into

---

2   The seven liquids are water, blood, honey, dew, oil, wine, and milk.

3   The Israeli Foreign Ministry, "The Jewish Temples: Jerusalem during the Second Temple Period (516 BCE-70 CE)," [http://www.jewishvirtuallibrary.org/jsource/Archaeology/Jerusalem.html].

the pot. The boys looked confused as their host offered them olive oil, vinegar, and other condiments and demonstrated how to pour them into their bowls from small jugs.[4]

"Don't be frightened, Your Highnesses," Amram chuckled. "Our food may be different from that eaten in Adiabene, but it is not harmful!"

Not quite convinced, the young princes eschewed all but the basic fare. Experimenting with new foods would have to wait for another day.

Helene settled the boys into their rooms for the night and then joined Rivka in the main living area.

"It must be especially difficult for the boys to be so far away from their parents," Rivka remarked.

"Yes, it is," Helene replied. "I love them dearly, as does Monobaz, but what we can provide them is still not equal to a mother's hug or a father's encouragement. We must try our best and ask for Heavenly help and guidance."

"May you have *siyata d'Shmaya* every step of the way," Rivka responded.

"Amen, may it be His will!" Helene replied.

In another part of the house, Monobaz was conversing with Amram in his study.

"My esteemed host," he said, smiling warmly, "how can we ever thank you and your wife for your kind hospitality? We have already learned so much from observing the way you and your family so beautifully and sincerely perform the mitzvos! Our accommodations are most comfortable, and your warm welcome makes us feel like family!"

"As Jews, we are all part of one family," Amram replied. "We are united by our spiritual ancestor, Avraham Avinu."

---

4   Ancient Israelite Cuisine, Wikipedia, [http://en.wikipedia.org/wiki/Ancient_Israelite_cuisine].

Monobaz nodded and smiled. "This brings me to a topic at the forefront of my mind, for which I would appreciate your advice. First, though, I must seek your forgiveness for asking yet an additional favor."

"Please, Your Highness," Amram said, trying to allay the prince's concern. "I consider any way I can serve His Highness to be a true privilege."

"Well, then, I will be straightforward," Monobaz replied. "My mother, Moshe, and I desire to fulfill our obligation to bring a *Korban Hager* as soon as possible. It has been many years since I entered into the covenant of Avraham Avinu, but I still feel deficient as long as I am unable to complete my conversion by bringing the *Korban Olah* of the *ger*. I know my mother concurs with this desire."

"Of course," Amram responded. He was filled with respect for the man beside him. "The *Korban Hager* is reminiscent of the *Korban Olah* that was offered at Har Sinai, where every member of the Jewish nation received a new *neshamah* as they accepted the Torah. So, too, the *ger* receives a new *neshamah* as he joins the Jewish people."[5]

Monobaz was silent for a few moments as he contemplated the words of his friend. His desire to perform this final definitive act of transformation was so great!

"Our family would also like to bring the *Korban Todah* as a sign of our appreciation to the Alm-ghty for bringing us safely across the desert to the Holy Land," he finally said. "While Rabbi Alexander familiarized me with the basic laws concerning this offering, I will surely need your guidance in order to carry out the procedures correctly. I would consider this a great *chessed* on your part, my esteemed host."

Monobaz's eyes shone with excitement.

"We would also like to invite your entire extended family and friends to join us in consuming the *Korban Todah* within the prescribed

---

5   Harav Menachem Mekubar, *Otzar Toras Hakorbanos* (Kiryat Gat: Dani Sefarim, 2011), 149.

time limit," he continued. "We welcome the opportunity to describe the great kindness and wonders Hashem has done for us during our journey and the Divine Hand we have seen in all of the events that led up to it."

"I am glad to oblige on all counts, Your Highness. Surely your story will be an inspiration to all present!"

"There is no way for me to adequately express my appreciation," Monobaz replied, his face suffused with joy and anticipation. "I wish we could go right away, but I know we must wait a week to remove our state of impurity."

"Yes, that is correct," Amram agreed. "Let me explain what must be done. Every person, before bringing a *korban* for the first time, must be purified from the spiritual impurity of *tumas meis* through the process of being sprinkled with the ashes of the *parah adumah*. The entire procedure requires one week, with the sprinkling of the *mei niddah*, the water that contains these ashes, occurring on the third and seventh days. You will need to be extremely careful to avoid any contact with the dead during this time.

"Prince Monobaz, Queen Helene, and the young princes all need to undergo this purification process," Amram continued. "I will contact a *metaher*, someone who is able to perform the sprinkling. I will ask him to come tomorrow, which will be the first day of your week of purification.[6] The *metaher* will return to our home with the *mei niddah* three days hence. After the second sprinkling on the seventh day, you will be able to immerse in a *mikveh* and become ritually pure after nightfall. The following day, you may bring your *Korban Todah*."

Monobaz nodded.

"May the purification process proceed with success!" Amram replied, rising from his chair.

"If I can add an unrelated thought, Amram," Monobaz said as he stood up as well. "While in Adiabene, we heard stories of oppression

---

6   *Rambam, Hilchos Parah Adumah* 11:2.

and strife, but we were unaware of the degree of seriousness of the many troubles that plague the Holy Land. We are ready and willing to help in any way we can."

"This is very generous of you, Your Highness," Amram said. "May Hashem sanction your actions!"

Chapter Twelve

The morning dawned bright and crisp. The sun was just beginning to make its appearance on the horizon when Monobaz, Amram, and Moshe made their way to a small synagogue where the sound of melodic chanting could be heard from outside.

"Have the prayers already begun?" Monobaz asked, puzzled.

"No, we are not late," Amram reassured him. "Any time of day or night, one can find a group of men sitting here and learning Torah. The world would cease to exist if there were even a moment devoid of Torah study."

They entered a low stone building and found empty benches near the rear of the small room. An elderly gentleman walked to the wooden *bimah* and lifted a wooden mallet, banging it to make a single, loud sound. There was complete silence, and then the morning prayers began.

Amram began reciting the morning blessings out loud, hoping that the prince would be able to follow. He quickly determined that his efforts were unnecessary, however, as Monobaz proceeded to recite the prayers fluently and with intense feeling, by heart!

How much time and effort this man has put into learning about Judaism! Amram thought in awe. *If only half our people could feel a similar level of devotion to Hashem and His Torah, surely our troubles would dissipate.*

Following the service, a number of men rose from their seats to retrieve parchment scrolls stored in cabinets along the walls. Soon, the chanting of prayers was replaced by the reading of Scriptures.

"How pleasing this sound is to my ears!" Monobaz told his friend. "But I desire to do more than just listen! I, too, must attend the lectures of the sages and find a *chavrusa*. Perhaps, Amram, you might have some ideas for me?"

"Certainly, Your Highness," Amram replied. "But I must confide that my humble desire has been to claim that privilege for myself!"

The men tarried in the synagogue for a brief hour before setting off on their way home.

"I would suggest we remain longer, but you have a mitzvah to perform," Amram explained. "It is good to show enthusiasm in performing it as early as possible. We can resume our Torah study later."

Amram led Monobaz through serpentine cobblestone alleyways that were already bustling with activity, although it was not yet two hours past sunrise.

"If your mother and nephews are ready, I will summon the *metaher*," Amram said.

"Certainly," Monobaz responded enthusiastically. "We will be ready when the *metaher* arrives."

A few hours later, a middle-aged man approached and greeted Amram ben Be'iri warmly. He was carrying a bowl in one hand and branches of *eizov* (hyssop) in the other. He turned to Monobaz.

"*Shalom aleichem*, Your Royal Highness," he said. "My name is Shmuel, and I have come as a representative of the Beis Hamikdash. I will sprinkle the royal family with the *mei niddah*, the water in which ashes of the *parah adumah* were combined. The *eizov* is a very lowly tree, and dipping it into the water containing these ashes reminds us that humility protects against sin."

"Our thanks to you for coming to us, Mar Shmuel!" Monobaz said respectfully. "My nephews are also waiting to be purified. Come forward, boys, to greet Mar Shmuel!"

As the boys stepped forward, Reuven whispered into Monobaz's ear, "Uncle, doesn't the *metaher* need to be a *kohen*?"

"Not necessarily," Monobaz whispered back. "Any pure Jew is permitted to do the sprinkling."

Moshe, the self-appointed spokesperson of his brothers, stepped forward.

"I am Moshe, son of Izates, king of Adiabene, and I would like to express our appreciation for Mar Shmuel's visit today."

Just then, there was a rustling sound and agitated whispering in the Adiabenean tongue. Monobaz smiled, whispered a few words to the younger boys, and turned to Mar Shmuel.

"My nephews would like to know if one needs to remove one's clothes prior to purification by the *mei niddah*, like one does before immersing in the *mikveh*," he said.

"This is a very good question, Your Highnesses!" Mar Shmuel responded. "The purification of the *mei niddah* requires only that the waters touch some part of the body, not the entire body. You are able to participate dressed as you are."

Mar Shmuel placed the bowl on the table in front of him and tied three branches of *eizov* into a bundle. Then he removed the lid from the bowl, revealing a mixture of water and ashes. He sprinkled Prince Monobaz, Queen Helene, and Moshe. Then he addressed the younger boys.

"Which of you would like to be next?"

"I would," a small voice piped up. It was Yehudah, only eight years old, but already demonstrating leadership qualities beyond his years. The queen glanced appreciatively at Reuven, who had begun to step forward but then quickly returned to his place.

"Please come here, young man," Mar Shmuel directed. Following

Yehudah's lead, his shy brothers, Yosef and Yaakov, stepped forward to receive the *mei niddah*. Finally, Mar Shmuel sprinkled Reuven, whispering to him, "You've set a good example for your brothers. They run to do mitzvos!"

Turning to the group, he continued, "I will return on *Yom Sheini*, which will be the seventh day of your purification. Then you will be able to immerse in the *mikveh* and become ritually pure."

The days passed quickly with the joy of anticipation until the end of the seventh day was upon them. The royal family gave thanks to Hashem that the purification process had gone smoothly. Amram and Rivka shared their joy at reaching this new status. Later that night, Amram requested that the prince meet with him to discuss the next day's plans.

Amram grasped an earthenware pitcher and mug and poured a cup of water for the prince. Monobaz expressed his thanks and recited the *brachah* of *Shehakol*.

"Amen!" Amram answered. He reflected on the greatness of the Alm-ghty, Who created not only the water we drink, but the entire universe, through His word.

"No water anywhere in the world could taste as fresh and clear as the water of Yerushalayim!" the prince commented appreciatively.

"Of course," Amram responded. "It is the holiness that comes from traveling along holy soil!"

"And now that the holy water of the *parah adumah* has cleansed us of spiritual impurity, I look forward to taking the next step," the prince said, looking sober. "How should we proceed, my friend?"

"Now it is time for me to elaborate on a point of halachah that I have not yet explained to His Highness," Amram began. "The Torah does not require even one who has been saved miraculously to bring a *Korban Todah*, but it is a mitzvah to do so."

"But are we not required to perform mitzvos?" Monobaz asked, puzzled.

"Yes, you are correct," Amram acknowledged. "That is why you should make a vow requiring you to bring the *Todah*. By doing this, it will be incumbent upon you to bring the *korban*."

"I am ready to do so," Monobaz answered enthusiastically. "But what about Moshe? Should he not make the vow as well, and is he obligated to bring his own *korban*? And what about my mother? How should the queen behave in this matter?"

"All of these are excellent questions, Your Highness," Amram replied with great admiration. "I will attempt to answer them in order. First, Moshe should indeed make a vow as well, but he can participate in your *Korban Todah* as a partner and does not need to bring his own offering. Each of you will separately perform *semichah* on the animal you bring for the *korban*, and then individually express thanks to Hashem in your own words.[1] The queen is similarly required to bring the *Korban Todah*, although she will not perform *semichah*."[2]

"I see," Monobaz responded thoughtfully. "I will relay all you have said to the queen and to Moshe tomorrow."

"Very good," Amram agreed. "Your Highness, if you desire to make the vow at this time, please repeat after me: '*Harei alai Todah*! Behold, I take upon myself the obligation of bringing a *Korban Todah*!'"[3]

Monobaz stood and declared with joy, "*Harei alai Todah*!"

The prince's eyes met Amram's, and both were brimming with tears of happiness.

"Thank you ever so much, my friend, for guiding us," Monobaz

---

1 Correspondence with Harav Menachem Makover (author of *Otzar Toras Hakorbanos*), February 4, 2014.

2 There is a difference of opinion in the Gemara (*Chagigah* 16b) concerning whether or not women performed *semichah*. According to the opinion of the sages, women did not perform *semichah*, but according to Rabbi Yosi, they were permitted but not required to do so. The mainstream opinion is that women did not do *semichah* (Harav Eliyahu Levine).

3 Eliezer Mordechai Ben-Shem, *Shiurim B'Sefer Vayikra: Tzav-Shemini* (Beitar Ilit, 5770), 133.

said. "May I be so bold as to ask an additional favor?"

"Certainly," Amram answered encouragingly. "It would be an honor to assist you in any way possible."

"I would feel most privileged if you would accompany us to witness the *Korban Tamid* at sunrise," Monobaz requested.

"It would be my sincere pleasure to accompany you, Your Highness," Amram replied. "As an aside, I strongly suspect that the inspiration you will gain from witnessing the morning *Korban Tamid* will infuse your other *korbanos* with added meaning."

He paused a few moments before he continued speaking. "If it meets His Highness's approval, tomorrow morning, with G-d's help, we will first enter the Beis Hamikdash in time for the *Tamid* and afterwards exit to the marketplace to purchase the necessities for the *Korban Hager* and *Korban Todah*. I assume that Moshe will travel with us, and I will hire an additional carriage for the queen to join us later in the morning?"

"No, that will be unnecessary, my friend," Monobaz replied with a smile. "The queen desires to witness the *Korban Tamid* herself and afterwards would be happy to have time for personal prayer on Har Habayis until our return from the marketplace."

"So be it!" Amram declared. "And may the royal family's zealousness for mitzvos be a merit for all of Klal Yisrael!" He thought for a moment, and then continued. "I almost forgot to mention that tomorrow will be a personal holiday for you, Prince Monobaz, so you should postpone all work activities until after the *korban* is totally consumed. The same will apply to the queen and Moshe."

Monobaz nodded, his eyes alight with anticipation.

The early morning sky was still jet black when Queen Helene rose from her bed in the ben Be'iri home and washed her hands. She then descended the steep stairs leading to the cellar to immerse in the *mikveh*, a prerequisite for both men and women prior to ascending the Har Habayis. Upon emerging, she gave thanks to Hashem for sustaining her to this day when she would complete her conversion.

Helene returned to her room and recited Tehillim, recalling the dictum that the time between midnight and sunrise is a special *eis ratzon*. A short time later, she heard a knock on her bedchamber door.

"Mother, shall we leave?" Monobaz called softly, his tone a mixture of eagerness and trepidation.

"Yes, my son," she replied. "I am ready."

The sound of hoof beats against the cobblestones was magnified in the still quiet that clings to the end of the night, as the royal carriage made its way through the narrow streets of the Lower City toward the Har Habayis. Amram followed in a second carriage provided by the prince. Rivka stayed behind to prepare for the meal of thanksgiving.

As they approached the gates to the Har Habayis, Moshe asked Amram, "Who are those people standing guard on the walls?"

"Those are *levi'im*,[4] who serve as guards for the Beis Hamikdash," Amram answered.

"Is there fear of attack?" Monobaz asked with concern.

"No, Your Highness, there is no fear of attack, for it is known that Hashem guards His House, and evildoers are powerless to act against His will. Rather, this is an honor guard whose purpose is to increase respect and awe for this holy place through their presence."[5]

Amram instructed the group to remove their shoes.

"No one is permitted to wear shoes on the Har Habayis," he explained. "You can leave them in storage areas outside the gate."

---

4   The *levi'im* were required to stand guard over the Mishkan and later the Beis Hamikdash every night (*Bamidbar* 18:1-5).
5   *The Artscroll Tanach Series: Tehillim* (Brooklyn, New York: Mesorah Press, 1997), 1594.

Amram accompanied the royal family as they passed through the gate leading to the area of the Har Habayis outside of the Beis Hamikdash. He wondered how they would react to the events they were about to witness.

It was the queen who first noticed a *kohen* standing high up in a tower, gazing toward the east. Then, as if an enormous curtain were parting, the sky exchanged its deep, cobalt blue for broad bands of pink, orange, and burnished gold. It was *neitz hachamah*.

"*Barkai!*" he shouted. "The morning has become light!" Word was passed along to the *kohen* appointed to manage the schedule in the Mikdash. It was now time for the *avodah* to begin.[6]

The air swelled with a thunderous sound as everyone recited, "*Shema Yisrael! Hashem Elokeinu, Hashem Echad!*"

The voices of the *kohanim* in the *Azarah* joined those of the *yisraelim* who had come to bring their personal offerings. The sound of the holy words reverberated everywhere, breaking the silence of the early morning. Helene felt as if she could see them rising straight to Heaven. She remained transfixed as the final tones of the Shema reverberated in the crisp air. She turned to her son, her face glowing.

"Monobaz," she said in a voice that sounded almost other-worldly. "I came to the Holy Land on a pilgrimage of unspecified length, but I now believe that I, as well as the boys, must remain here. Do you understand, my son?"

"Yes, Mother," the prince replied. He gazed with love and awe into the queen's expressive eyes. "I do respect your decision." He looked away, realizing that his mother's words would significantly influence the fate of his family. "May Hashem continue to watch over you and over us," he murmured.

Monobaz and Moshe escorted the queen toward the eastern women's gate that led from the Har Habayis to the *Ezras Nashim*. They

---

6   *Yoma*, mishnah 3:1.

chose this entrance, rather than the women's gates on the north and south sides of the courtyard, because Helene would have the best view of the spectacular Nikanor Gate to the west.[7]

"Thank you, my children." Helene smiled in appreciation. "Please, proceed quickly to the *Ezras Yisrael*. The *avodah* is beginning. I would like you to be as close to the *Mizbe'ach* as permitted."

Amram, Monobaz, and Moshe departed from the *Ezras Nashim*, while Helene was left to observe the proceedings through the open Nikanor Gate.

From their vantage point in the *Ezras Yisrael*, the three were able see two *kohanim* ahead of them ascending the twelve steps that led from the *Ezras Kohanim* to the *Ulam*, the foyer leading to the *Kodesh* section of the *Heichal*. One carried in his hands a basket for the purpose of removing the ashes from the golden altar within. The other held a vessel shaped like a large wine cup to do the same for the Menorah.[8]

The *kohanim* entered via a small gate on the south side of the *Heichal*. Moments later, an extraordinary thing occurred. Without any human intervention, the great door to the *Ulam* opened, emitting a sound like booming thunder. Monobaz could believe, as he had heard told, that it could be heard as far away as the city of Yericho!

Moshe turned to their host.

"Mar Amram, who opened the door?" he asked. "No one seems to be in its vicinity!"

"Prince Moshe, you have indeed witnessed a change in the order of things," Amram said sadly. "It used to be that each of the *kohanim* you see ascending the steps leading to the entrance of the *Ulam* would have grasped a key that could open the two locks to the southern chamber. From there, they would open the gate to the *Heichal* from the inside.

---

[7] Harav Elchanan Eibeschitz, *Habayis Hasheini B'sifarto* (Yerushalayim: Mosad Harav Kook, 1996), 117.
[8] Harav Makover, *Otzar Toras Hakorbanos*, 122.

However, due to our great sins, they have lost this privilege. For about a decade and a half, the door to the *Heichal* has opened by itself. Our sages tell us that this means that, *chas v'chalilah*, if we fail to do proper *teshuvah*, the enemy will be able to enter the Beis Hamikdash easily."

Moshe shuddered visibly and then fell silent. Amram put his arm around the young prince's shoulder and said comfortingly, "Our Torah teaches us that it is never too late to repent. May the merit of your family coming to the Holy Land inspire us all to do *teshuvah* soon."

The three turned their attention once again to the *avodah*. The loud sound of the closing of the *Heichal's* door was followed by absolute silence.

"Is there a reason why the *kohanim* do not communicate with each other during the *avodah*?" Monobaz asked curiously.

"The awe of standing before Hashem demands silence," Amram answered in a whisper.

The *kohen* who had removed the ashes from the golden altar emerged from the *Heichal* and emptied his basket into the *Beis Hadeshen*, the chamber of ashes, a hollowed out area next to the altar. He then poured the remainder into drain holes in the corner of the *Mizbe'ach*. The *avodah* then focused once more on the *Heichal* as the second of the two *kohanim* entered the *Heichal* to prepare the Menorah for lighting.

"There was a time, over three hundred years ago,[9] when the *kohen* performing this task would confront a miracle every day," Amram said. "During the lifetime of Shimon Hatzaddik, the *kohen gadol*, the *ner hama'aravi* remained lit from evening to evening, even though other lights of the Menorah, which had the same amount of oil, would be extinguished by morning. During the *Tamid* offering of the afternoon, the *kohen* would light all of the other lights using the still-lit *ner hama'aravi*. Since the death of Shimon Hatzaddik, the western light sometimes remains lit and sometimes does not."[10]

---

9 Shimon Hatzaddik died in 313 BCE.
10 *Shabbos* 22b.

The *korban* was being prepared in the *Beis Hamitbechayim*, the slaughtering area, north of the altar. The sheep for the *Korban Tamid* was flayed and cut into parts. Six *kohanim* carried the parts to an area next to the *Mizbe'ach*, where they were set down and salted by other *kohanim*. Three other *kohanim* carried the *Minchah* of the *Tamid*, the *Minchah* of the *kohen gadol*, and the wine for the libation. A procession of *kohanim* then brought the parts of the *korban* up to the top of the ramp leading to the *Mizbe'ach*. The *gid hanasheh*, which had been removed from the sheep, was thrown onto the *tapuach*, a pyre shaped like an apple in the center of the altar.

Monobaz listened as the *kohen* recited the *brachah*, "Blessed are You, L-rd G-d, King of the universe, Who has sanctified us with the sanctity of Aharon and commanded us to burn the parts of the *korban* on the fire." Quickly, one after another, the *kohen* threw the parts of the *korban* onto the flame. He then hurried to the top of the *Mizbe'ach*, where he arranged the parts on the fire.[11] After only a short time, they were completely consumed.[12] Monobaz could see intense waves of heat emanating from the large pyre.

Surely, I, too, deserve to be like this animal, he thought. *Just a short time ago, it was healthy and vital — but it's now being incinerated and turned to ashes. This* korban *is granting atonement to Klal Yisrael for all sins committed during the night, just as the afternoon* Korban Tamid *will grant atonement for sins committed during the day. How grateful we must be for* rachamei Shamayim*!*

Monobaz glanced at Moshe, who was watching every step of the *korban* offering and seemed deep in thought. Then a pause in the proceedings caused Monobaz and Moshe to look expectantly at Amram.

"The *kohanim* have entered the *Lishkas Hagazis*, the Chamber of

---

11 To fulfill what is written in *Vayikra* (1:12), *...and the* kohen *will arrange them on the wood that is on the fire, which is on the altar.*
12 Harav Makover, *Otzar Toras Hakorbanos*, 122-123.

Hewn Stone," Amram explained quietly. "There they will recite the Ten Commandments, Shema, and several other prayers before proceeding to the lottery for the offering of the *ketores*. The *kohen* who wins this lottery knows that this is the only time in his life that he will perform the incense offering. Thus it is prescribed by halachah."

"Can you imagine being given a once-in-a-lifetime opportunity and no time to prepare for it!" Moshe exclaimed incredulously.

"Yes," Amram replied. "We never know when we will have our own unique opportunity to serve Hashem. It seems that we must always be ready."

As the *kohanim* began to emerge from the *Lishkas Hagazis*, one of them climbed the ramp to the *Mizbe'ach* and took hot coals from the smaller pyre and placed them in a firepan. As he walked toward the *Heichal* together with the *kohen* who would offer the *ketores* and three other *kohanim*, a loud, brash sound[13] was heard, announcing that the *ketores* service was underway. Everyone in the *Ezras Kohanim* jumped to attention. Four of the *kohanim* had exited the *Heichal* and now stood between the *Ulam* and the *Mizbe'ach*. The *kohen* chosen to offer the *ketores* that day did so alone. No one else was permitted to be present in the *Heichal* during the actual offering of the *ketores*.

As Amram, Monobaz, and Moshe were enveloped by the wondrous aroma of the *ketores*, they watched as scores of *kohanim* assembled on the steps leading to the *Ulam*. They raised their hands above their heads and begin to intone the Priestly Blessing.

May Hashem bless you and safeguard you.

May Hashem illuminate His countenance for you and be gracious to you.

May Hashem turn His countenance to you and establish peace for you.

---

13   This sound came from the *magreifah*, a large, metal disk that was thrown to the ground between the *Heichal* and the *Mizbe'ach* by a *kohen* standing on the steps in front of the *Ulam*.

Monobaz was overcome with emotion. He bowed his head and focused intently on the meaning of the words to fulfill the mitzvah of accepting their blessing upon himself.

The three watched as the *Minchas Tamid* offering of fine flour, as well as the *Minchah* offering of the *kohen gadol*, was consumed on the altar. Monobaz and Moshe stared at the gold and orange flame.

"Our rabbis teach that the *Minchah* offering is a *tikun* for the sin of Adam Harishon," Amram explained. "There are those who say the Tree of Knowledge was actually wheat. As a result of Adam and Chava's sin, some of the great light created on the first day was stored away, reducing the amount of goodness in the world, for light represents good. By offering only the fine portion of the wheat as the *Minchah*, a part of this inner goodness is revealed. This is why every *korban Olah* and *Shelamim* is accompanied by a *Minchah*. Without it, the *korban* is not complete."[14]

Suddenly, trumpet blasts pierced the air, signaling the offering of the wine libation. A *kohen* standing on the southwestern corner of the *Mizbe'ach* poured the wine in his vessel into a cup. Opposite him, another *kohen* waved the baton in his hand, signaling to the *levi'im* standing on the *duchan* to begin singing the song of the day.

In the *Ezras Nashim*, Helene listened to the deep, full voices of the *levi'im* and the lilting strains of their musical instruments. She was transfixed with joy, hope, and thankfulness for the opportunity to be in this holy place and to be a member of this holy people.

Helene remained in her spot, praying, for a long while after the sun rose to its place in the morning sky. She was grateful for the hiatus prior to bringing the *Korban Hager*. She wanted to absorb what she had just experienced.

---

14 *Otzar Toras Hakorbanos*, 59.

Surely, the Alm-ghty does not need these substances in Heaven, she thought. *However, we who are mere mortals, fashioned of the earth, can elevate ourselves through performing His mitzvos. What an opportunity we have!*

By the time the *Tamid* was consumed, the *Azarah* was bathed in radiant sunlight. Helene slowly exited the *Ezras Nashim*. She wanted to find a place where it would be permitted to partake of the light repast she had taken along that morning. Finding herself on the Har Habayis plaza, she beheld a curious sight. Scores of women were purposefully making their way around the Har Habayis, but they were not all moving in the same direction. On closer inspection, Helene could see that those women who were walking from the right side of the courtyard toward the left looked different from those who were coming from the left and walking toward the right. A few women who were walking from the right toward the left greeted those walking in the opposite direction with concern.

"Dear sister, what is your trouble?" a well-dressed, middle-aged woman asked a younger married woman. Her eyes were so full of pain and fear that she looked older than her tender years. "Is there anything I can do to help reduce your pain?"

The younger woman shared a few hushed words with her compassionate compatriot, resulting in a response of "*Hashem yerachem*! May Hashem have mercy!"

Helene spotted a kindly-looking matron making her way toward the *Ezras Nashim* and approached her, seeking an explanation.

"*Giveret*!" Helene greeted the woman. "My name is Helene, and I am newly arrived here from afar. Could you please explain to me what I see here? Why are the women behaving in such a manner?"

"Of course," the woman replied warmly. "My name is Shulamis. You see, the prescribed way to enter the Har Habayis reflects sensitivity to the feelings of those crushed under the heavy burden of their suffering. Those who are troubled enter from the left and proceed toward the right. Everyone else is directed to enter from the right and to proceed toward the left. In this way, it is possible to identify those who are in need of comfort. The same practice is followed by the men. In this way, all entering the Har Habayis to pray are encouraged to pray for others, as well as for their own needs."

Just then, a woman fell prostrate in prayer at the bottom of the steps leading to the *Ezras Nashim*, facing west.

"Why is this woman pouring out her heart over there?" Helene asked, puzzled. "It appears that this spot has significance to her."

"Yes, it does," Shulamis answered. "If one were to draw a straight line from this woman to the other end of the Har Habayis, that line would intersect the *Kodesh Hakadashim*. Our prayers are strengthened by focusing on the holiest place on earth."

"May the *tefillos* of these women be answered positively!" Helene said. "And thank you so much for helping me understand this holy behavior."

The queen took leave of Shulamis, as each exchanged the hope that they would meet again.

Continuing along her circuit, Helene turned the corner leading to the north side of the Har Habayis and gasped. Before her was a long staircase. At the top stood three magnificent, gilded gates, each lintel topped by a unique decoration of hewn, polished stones. Through the leftmost gate, *levi'im* were ascending, clad in their simple but majestic white linen robes. Many of them carried trumpets, harps, lyres, and other musical instruments. The rightmost gate was for non-*levi'im*, while the center gate was designated for women[15] who were streaming through it in droves.[16] Many of these women passing through the gate were accompanied by various animals — lambs, rams, goats, bulls, and turtledoves.

---

15 An additional gate for women was located on the south side.
16 Harav Elchanan Eibeschitz, *Habayis Hasheini B'sifarto*, 117.

Monobaz, too, desired to linger before the site of the *Korban Tamid*, but he, Moshe, and Amram pulled themselves away to attend to the next mitzvah at hand. It was time to obtain the necessities for the *Korban Hager* and the *Korban Todah*. The three exited the *Ezras Yisrael* through the Nikanor Gate and temporarily left the Har Habayis in order to make their purchases. Monobaz was visibly pensive, having been profoundly affected by the scene he had just witnessed.

Amram observed Monobaz with compassion. He could imagine the questions going through the prince's mind.

"You see, Your Highness," he said, "the *korban* addresses the three components of wrongdoing: action, speech, and thought. If one sins, Heaven forbid, and is obligated to bring a sin offering, he will lean his hands upon the animal. This represents the physical act he committed. He will confess his sins out loud, through speech, and then the innards of the *korban*, symbolizing the source of his evil thoughts, will be burned on the *Mizbe'ach* to give him a *kapparah*. The blood that the *kohen* throws on the *Mizbe'ach* is in exchange for our own blood. In witnessing his *korban*, the transgressor should feel in his heart that he is liable for the four types of capital punishment as a result of his sins, but Hashem, in His infinite kindness, is allowing him to offer an animal instead of putting him to death. The fire consuming the *korban* is a fire that consumes the evil inclination."[17]

"Yes, I understand now," Monobaz responded slowly. "How true it is that a friend perceives the thoughts of his fellow."

The three continued to walk toward the marketplace. Amram caught sight of a tall, distinguished, elderly man walking quickly past them. A number of small parchment scrolls were tucked under his arm.

---

17   *Toldos Yitzchak*, as quoted in *Otzar Toras Hakorbanos*, 106.

"*Shalom aleichem*, Rav Shimshon!" Amram greeted the sage. "May I ask if the *rav* has completed checking my *mezuzos*?"

"Yes, *baruch Hashem*," the man responded. A smile spread across his wrinkled face. "They remain in perfect condition, Mar Amram. May you continue to perform the mitzvah of *mezuzah* for many years in a most elevated way!"

Suddenly, as Amram and his two companions turned a corner, the crowded residential streets gave way to a spacious square, teeming with life and activity. Monobaz was struck speechless by what confronted him.

"Welcome to the Cardo marketplace, Your Highness!" Amram announced proudly. "I trust that you will find all of the necessities for your *korbanos* here."

Even at this relatively early hour, the market was crowded and noisy. The voices of merchants peddling their wares combined with the sounds of bleating sheep and goats and the deep grunting of bulls.

"Which types of animals does Your Highness choose to purchase?" Amram asked the prince.

"Please tell me what is preferable for each *korban*," Monobaz answered.

"Certainly, Your Highness," Amram replied. "For the *Korban Hager*, it is best to bring two birds as an *olah* because only these animals are totally burnt on the *Mizbe'ach*. This represents total rebirth, just as the *ger* receives a totally new *neshamah*. Larger animals are also burnt for the *olah*, but their skin is given as a present to the *kohen*. For the *Korban Todah*, bulls are the most expensive; a sheep or a goat is equally acceptable."

"A new *neshamah*," Monobaz repeated, more to himself than his friend. "Please direct me to where I can purchase two birds for Moshe and myself for the *Korban Hager*. For the *Korban Todah*, I would like to purchase two of the finest bulls available — one for Moshe and myself, and one for the queen. Just as Yosef, who withstood the pressures of alien influences, is compared to an ox, this animal represents to me the deep feelings of thanksgiving I feel toward *Hakadosh Baruch Hu* for enabling me, born to a pagan nation in a pagan land, to join the Jewish people and to merit bringing a thanksgiving offering this day in the Holy Land."

The merchant, a small, thin man named Shimon, observed the humility in the prince's eyes and heard the sincerity in his voice. He bowed slightly in deference to Monobaz and then disappeared among the animals in the pen. When he emerged, he was leading two large, impressive bulls with shiny, brown coats and clear, liquid eyes.

"These are two of our finest bulls," Shimon declared. "The sale is not final until they are examined and determined to be free of any disqualifying imperfections. Only a blemish-free animal is worthy of becoming a *korban*."

"They are very handsome creatures," Monobaz agreed. "I would like to purchase them, once it is determined that they are fit to offer as a *korban*." He paid a portion of the price to the seller, and Amram then motioned to a stall adjacent to the bull pen. Inside the stall, a large, strong man was examining the face, neck, and ears of a goat. He looked up and beckoned them inside.

"Amram ben Be'iri, it is good to see you! And whom do I have the pleasure of serving today?"

"Shimon, allow me to introduce Monobaz ben Avraham Avinu, prince of Adiabene, my esteemed houseguest. He has recently arrived in Yerushalayim and is preparing to offer a *Korban Todah*."

"Excellent!" the man said with enthusiasm. "I am honored to make His Highness's acquaintance. We have heard of Queen Helene's acts of *chessed* in her native land and welcome her to Eretz Yisrael. May you merit the performance of many more mitzvos!"

"*Baruch tihiyeh*! May you be blessed!" Monobaz responded warmly.

After taking some time to examine the bulls, Shimon pronounced,

"The animals are perfect specimens! May you merit bringing this *korban* according to the highest standards! I am sending two of my boys to lead the animals to the Beis Hamikdash for you. You will have your hands full just carrying the loaves of bread for the *korbanos*."

"Thank you very much," Amram replied. "I chose not to take any servants with me today, so your offer is especially appreciated!"

As the young men led the bulls down the narrow streets toward the Beis Hamikdash, Amram spoke.

"The *Korban Todah* is unlike any other offering, Your Highness," he said. "It is accompanied by forty loaves of bread, ten of each of four different types. Although leaven is generally forbidden for sacrificial purposes, ten of these loaves are leavened. The remaining thirty are unleavened."

They stopped in front of a store filled with the sweet aroma of baking bread. The sign above the store read, "*Al Taharas Kodesh*," indicating that everything sold was designated for a holy purpose. The walls were lined with boxes of breads, matzos, and wafers.

"We must purchase ten loaves of each of the four types of bread," Amram explained. "In addition to the leavened loaves, there are matzos kneaded in oil, flat matzah wafers smeared with oil, and scalded fine-quality unleavened flour loaves kneaded in oil."

"The leavened loaves are so much larger than the others!" Monobaz commented in surprise.

"Yes, the prince makes a valid observation," Amram agreed. "Each loaf is made from five *se'ah*[18] of flour![19] The ten leavened loaves actually weigh as much as the other thirty loaves combined.[20]

---

18 One *se'ah* is equal to 14.4 liters.

19 *Menachos* 77a, as cited by Yaakov Meir Strauss, *One Special Prayer* (New York: Feldheim, 2005), 86.

20 A *Korban Todah* is brought after a person survives a difficult challenge. The thirty unleavened loaves are brought to the Beis Hamikdash in thanksgiving for the great salvation the individual experienced. The leavened loaves represent the cause of the *nisayon*.

"Now, we must get to work!" Amram announced. "Let's check each loaf carefully to make sure that none are cracked or broken. Only whole, perfect loaves are acceptable for a *korban*. See, this one is split. I'll go back and get another one to replace it."[21]

Amram, Monobaz, and Moshe, carrying the heavy loaves in enormous baskets, proceeded down a narrow street, from which they could see the entrance to the Beis Hamikdash. Amram beckoned the two princes to stop in front of a small building.

"We are approaching the Gate of the Firstborn, where *kadshim kalim*, offerings of a lesser holiness, are brought," he explained. "Let's stop here to immerse in the *mikveh*. It is on a small side street and tends to be less busy than others. Although we immersed this morning, we have since exited the Temple compound, and so we will need to immerse again. You can go first, and I will stay with the loaves outside." Monobaz removed his shoes and entered the small stone building. He was grateful that there was no wait.

When Amram emerged from the *mikveh*, he announced to his friends, "Please come with me to the *Lishkas Hachosamos*, the Chamber of the Receipts, where we will pay for the wine for our *nesachim*. Then, we can present our receipt at the *Lishkas Hashemanim*, the oil chamber, in the *Ezras Nashim*. There we will purchase the *minchas nesachim*, the flour, wine, and oil portion of the offering."

Monobaz and Moshe followed Amram, both thinking about the awesome act they were about to perform. Suddenly, Monobaz was shaken from his reverie when Amram stopped and lightly grasped his arm.

There must have been something within this individual that needed correcting through the challenge. The fact that the thirty loaves are greater in number but equal in weight to the ten leavened loaves teaches that while one must always thank Hashem for the greatness of His salvation, one must also thank Him for the challenge itself, because it is the challenge that causes one to improve and become closer to Him in holiness (Rabbi David Goldberg, Yavneh Seminary, Cleveland, Ohio, recorded *shiur* on *Parshas Tzav*).

21 *Shiurim B'Sefer Vayikra: Tzav-Shemini*, 197.

"Dear prince, I see the queen praying in the far corner of the *Ezras Nashim*. Let us bring her the bull and loaves for her *Korban Todah*."

Helene smiled broadly as she saw the three approaching with the offerings. They bowed respectfully when greeting her.

"Before we proceed further, it is necessary to declare, 'Behold, these are for the *Korban Todah*!'" Amram said.

Monobaz, Moshe, and Helene each made the declaration with much concentration.

"Mother, we will stay with you until the completion of your *korbanos*," Monobaz suggested.

"No, no, my son," she protested. "I see a large group of women approaching. I suspect that my attempts to camouflage my identity have been unmasked. Nevertheless, this, too, is Hashem's will. It will be a merit for me for these holy Jewish women to witness my transformation into a Jewess. Please, depart for the *Ezras Yisrael*. I am in very good company!"

Monobaz and Moshe smiled at the queen.

How convincing she can be! they both thought with a chuckle. They turned to cross through the Nikanor Gate with Amram.

"Since you and Moshe are the ones bringing the *korbanos* today, only you should proceed beyond this point," Amram whispered to his friend. He wished to respect the privacy of the prince at this emotional time. "I will wait here for your return."

Monobaz met Amram's eyes. "How can I ever thank you for everything you have done for me and my family?"

"No, it is I who must thank *you*, dear prince," Amram replied. "It is truly I who am on the receiving end. Please go through the gate now. You are about to complete your process of rebirth as a Jew!"

"Is it our turn now?" Moshe asked a bit nervously.

"Yes, my son," his uncle replied. "It is now our turn."

Together, they passed through the Gate of Nikanor into the *Ezras Yisrael*. They had chosen to dress particularly inconspicuously in order not to draw attention to their identities. They each presented two doves to the *kohen* and stated that they had undergone *bris milah* and *tevilah* for the purpose of conversion. The *kohen* nodded his head when Monobaz showed him the letter stamped with the seal of Rabban Gamliel attesting to this. Both Monobaz and Moshe gazed silently at the *Mizbe'ach* until the birds were totally consumed by fire. They turned to face each other, tears in their eyes. They were now reborn with the *neshamos* of full-fledged Jews. Since embracing would not be proper within the Beis Hamikdash, Monobaz and Moshe suppressed their emotions and turned their attention to the next step in their *avodah*.

Another *kohen* greeted the prince kindly and asked him his name.

"I am Monobaz ben Avraham Avinu," he replied in a low voice. "I have come to offer the *Korban Todah* after having safely crossed the desert with my family. This is my nephew, Moshe, who will participate in the *Korban Todah* with me."

The *kohen* looked knowingly at the two, but said only a warm "*shalom aleichem*." He examined the bull and declared it fit to qualify for a *korban*. He then directed Monobaz and Moshe to the rings where the *korban* would be slaughtered.

"It is now time for you to perform *semichah*," the *kohen* directed.

Monobaz rested both of his hands on the head of the bull, and pressed down with all his weight.

"Alm-ghty G-d! I come here today to offer thanks to You for bringing me and my family across the desert to Yerushalayim. I also offer thanks to You for bringing us under the shadow of Your wings, for allowing us to join Your Chosen People!"

Moshe then did the same, adding his own thoughts. *Thank You, Hashem, for giving me my uncle and grandmother to teach me and guide me in Your holy ways.*

Just then, as if welling up from the depths of the earth, an orchestra consisting of an array of instruments played by identically dressed *levi'im* began a beautiful, stirring melody. Moments later, additional *levi'im* burst out in song:

A psalm of thanksgiving,

Call out to Hashem, everyone on earth. Serve Hashem with gladness. Come before Him with joyous song. Know that Hashem, He is G-d, it is He Who made us and we are His, His people and the sheep of His pasture. Enter His gates with thanksgiving, His courts with praise, give thanks to Him, bless His Name. For Hashem is good, His kindness endures forever, and His faithfulness is from generation to generation.[22]

Monobaz, initially startled by the loud sound, was quickly mesmerized by the music. When it ended, he realized that his cheeks were wet from tears. As he dropped his head in humility and shame, a *kohen* went to his side.

"If only we could all express such deep, pure emotions, surely Hashem would send our salvation immediately! May your *Korban Todah* be a *zechus* for us all."

One *kohen* slaughtered the bull. Another *kohen*, who had been standing ready, collected the blood and rushed it to the altar. He splashed the blood on the northeastern corner and then the southwestern corner of the *Mizbe'ach*, while the remainder of the blood was poured by the *kohen* onto the southern base.[23] The flesh was then taken to an area called the *nanasin*, or low pillars, where the *emurim*, internal parts offered on the *Mizbe'ach*, were removed from the carcass.

The *kohen* explained the procedure to Monobaz, who would offer the *Korban Todah* as a representative of his family, as he led him to the western side of the *Azarah*. At that moment, a procession of more *kohanim* appeared. They were carrying the breast, thigh, *emurim*, and four of the loaves, one of each type, and they piled these high in the arms of the waiting *kohen*. The prince was directed to place his hands

---

22 *The Complete Artscroll Siddur*, 64.
23 *Zevachim* 55a; *Rambam, Hilchos Ma'aseh Hakorbanos* 5:6.

beneath those of this *kohen* and to wave the parts in four directions — north, south, east, and west — and then up and down.

"The waving signifies that we recognize that everything comes from Hashem," the *kohen* explained. "By waving in four directions, we ward off harmful winds, while the up and down motion keeps damaging dews from descending from Heaven.[24]

"Now the *emurim* will be offered on the *Mizbe'ach*, and the breast and thigh will be given to the *kohen* performing the *avodah*. The remainder of the animal belongs to you. Just keep in mind that this meat is *kodesh*. It must be eaten only in Yerushalayim by those who are ritually pure. All of the meat and loaves must be consumed by midnight tonight."

"Thank you, esteemed *kohen*," Monobaz responded with great feeling. "My gracious host, Amram ben Be'iri, has arranged for the hall where the *korban* will be eaten, and we are expecting well over one hundred participants."

The thanksgiving feast was attended by Amram's family and friends, as Monobaz had requested, as well as scores of the poor inhabitants of the Ophel. The meal was simple, since it was extremely important that all of the sacrificial meat and loaves be consumed on time.

Queen Helene presided over her own *seudas hoda'ah* for the women, using the opportunity to tell them of all of the kindness Hashem had shown her until this day.

After the main course was served, Monobaz rose from his seat at the head of the large table. He paused and looked down, as if to collect his thoughts. Then he cleared his throat and began to speak, his face suffused with joy.

"My dear family, friends, neighbors, and compatriots, thank you

---

24   *Menachos* 62a.

for joining our family at this great event. The Torah commands anyone who successfully completes a journey across the desert to offer a *Korban Todah* upon his safe arrival at his destination. We have been delivered of a dangerous trip of sixteen days' duration across the desert from our native Adiabene to the Holy Land of Israel, and for this we give our wholehearted thanks. This trip is an outgrowth of our spiritual journey that began more than fifteen years ago, when our eyes were opened to the oneness of Hashem and the everlasting truth of His Torah. During those years, we encountered great individuals who taught us how to conduct ourselves as Jews. It was explained to us that once we converted to the Jewish faith, we would be severed from our birth families and birth nation and bound to the Jewish people. I can declare truthfully that my family has never felt like orphans, so embraced were we by our adopted brethren.

"But not all of our former countrymen were pleased with our decision. In spite of our continued loyalty to the interests of the Adiabenean people, many in power persuaded other rulers that our conversion represented a traitorous and dangerous act that should result in our deposition and elimination from the political landscape. They waged war against my brother, King Izates, time and time again, but in every war, Hashem saved my dear brother as well as our family from annihilation. The miracles were clear to us. We have seen sudden reversals in the fortunes of our enemies that can only be explained as *hashgachah pratis*.

"Now, it is time for us to show the *Ribono shel Olam* how much we acknowledge His Providence and appreciate His salvation. We gather here today to partake of the *Korban Todah*. May it be the first of many *korbanos* that I and my family merit to bring before Hashem in His holy Beis Hamikdash.

"We are living in troubled times. May our experience strengthen our trust that Hashem is with us always. He is waiting for our *teshuvah*, waiting to see our rededication to His Torah and its commandments.

He is waiting for us to perform good deeds that attest to our love of the Jewish people.

"*Ribono shel Olam*! Just as You have brought us here to celebrate the *Korban Todah*, please continue to protect Your people from those who would seek to destroy them both from without and within. In Your great mercy, strengthen our resolve to remain loyal to Your Torah and its immutable laws and to observe them on our land, forever."

There was a hush as Monobaz left the circle to resume his seat on the dais. The audience was awestruck. In an atmosphere of Roman oppression, official corruption, and internal strife, desperation was a common feeling among many Jews. A convert from a faraway land had inspired them and given them hope.

Chapter Thirteen

Several weeks had passed since the *seudas hoda'ah*. Monobaz had just returned to the ben Be'iri home following morning prayers when he noticed a note on his table.

Dearest son,
Please meet me in the garden, at your earliest convenience, as I have an exciting idea I would like to share with you!
Your loving mother

The prince smiled to himself. Mother was always full of ideas! Intrigued, he walked briskly to the garden.

Helene looked up, her face shining with maternal love and admiration. She thought of her son's eloquent speech at the *seudas hoda'ah*. *May he continue to be blessed!*

"Monobaz!" Helene called happily. "Thank you for coming so quickly. I wanted to speak with you."

"Of course, Mother," the prince responded. "Please, share your thoughts with me!"

"I would like to contribute something personally to the Beis Hamikdash. I have spent many hours contemplating just what type of gift would be meaningful. To me, one of the most inspiring aspects of our experience at the Beis Hamikdash was witnessing the start of the morning *avodah*. It was as if I could imagine the Alm-ghty lifting the curtain of dawn, so to speak, indicating to us that it was time for the recital of the morning Shema and the *Korban Tamid*. The moments that passed until the signal could be given for Shema to be said seemed like an interruption of holiness. Wouldn't it be wonderful if there could be a signal at the very moment the sun begins to rise, so that the *avodah* could begin immediately? Would this not constitute a *kiddush Hashem*?

"A memory from my youth kept coming to mind. Many years ago, your grandmother gave me a golden ornament shaped like a concave mirror, which I hung on my bedroom window. It would catch the first rays of the sun and glitter like a diamond. How I enjoyed watching it sparkle in the early morning sunshine!

"Rivka and I were in the marketplace recently, and I saw similar ornaments shaped like a menorah for sale. She told me the trinket is called a miniature *nivreshes* — a chandelier. Perhaps a much larger golden *nivreshes* could be mounted above the entrance to the *Heichal* in such a way that the rays of the rising sun would shine on it at just the moment of sunrise? The reflection of these rays would be visible for miles around and would signal to everyone in the *Azarah* to immediately begin saying Shema. No longer would there be any interruption in the holiness of this time."

"I can envision what you describe, Mother," Monobaz replied, spellbound by his mother's description. "It is exciting beyond words! Your gift would seemingly be of the highest caliber, but perhaps I should consult with one of the sages to determine for certain that the ornament would be acceptable for the Beis Hamikdash."

"Yes, my son," Helene replied, a bit out of breath from her soliloquy. "Please do, but not quite yet, for there is another gift that I desire to donate that will surely require official approval."

Monobaz looked at his mother questioningly.

"This second gift has special significance to me as a woman," Helene explained. "Before deciding to make my vow of *nezirus*, I studied the Torah's *Parshas Hanazir* with Rabbi Alexander. He explained to me that to fully understand the spiritual feeling that accompanies one who becomes a *nazir*, one must look at *Sotah*, the *parshah* that deals with the fate of the wife suspected of being unfaithful to her husband. The adoption of *nezirus* is an antidote to those passions that can bring a person to the insanity of unfaithfulness. How, I thought, can we save ourselves this pain and disgrace? How can we be reminded of the dangers of the lurking evil inclination?

"Here is my idea," the queen continued. "I would like to commission a large, golden tablet that will be hung on the wall of the *Ezras Nashim*, where the *sotah* is brought before the *kohanim* to undergo her trial. This tablet should contain only the first letters of each word in *Parshas Sotah*, due to the holiness of the words themselves as well as the shame associated with them.[1] The *kohen* will refer to this tablet as he writes the requisite text on parchment, later to be obliterated by the *mayim me'oririm*, the waters of curse. It is my fervent hope that there will never be a time when the *kohen* will need to copy from this tablet. Rather, let its beauty and holiness inspire all of us to preserve the sanctity of our homes and avoid any behavior that could jeopardize the peace and harmony that reign there."

"May it be His will!" Monobaz responded solemnly. "May your unique gifts be a *zechus* for all of Klal Yisrael during these troubled times. I will seek approval for them right away."

The next day, the prince knocked on the door to his mother's chamber.

"Mother," Monobaz said gently. "I am happy to report that I was granted an audience with Rabbi Yechiel, a great Torah scholar. He

---

1 *Yoma* 37a.

has told me that your proposed gifts would not only be acceptable according to halachah, but would be a wonderful asset. By indicating the exact time for the *Tamid* offering, the morning *avodah* would be greatly enhanced, and the tablet is viewed as a gift of the highest order of holiness."

The queen, unable to contain her joy, exclaimed, "How very happy this makes me! Let us proceed to the goldsmith to commission the *nivreshes* and design the tablet. Then we can proceed to a scribe to engrave the tablet!"

"Mother, I also feel a great desire to contribute a gift to the Beis Hamikdash," Monobaz said thoughtfully "I have spoken to a *kohen* who is close to Mar Amram. He tells me that the upkeep of the Mikdash and its vessels has suffered greatly as a result of the devastated economy and infighting among our people. I yearn to bestow a gift that would inspire awe and reflect the holiness of the Temple on the holiest day of the year. I would like to upgrade and refurbish the vessels used in the *avodah* on Yom Kippur by giving them golden handles and bases. The knives used for slaughtering the animals for the various *korbanos* would also be outfitted with golden handles. When I presented the suggestion to the *kohen* in charge of the vessels, it found favor in his eyes. I would like to speak to the goldsmith about these items as well. May they help all of Klal Yisrael to achieve atonement!"

"Come, boys!" Moshe shouted to his brothers. "Uncle Monobaz and Mar Amram are taking us on an outing! We are going to explore the water channel of King Chizkiyahu!"

The younger boys assembled quickly, excited at the prospect of the hike. They set out in a southeasterly direction from the home of the ben Be'iris, with Amram pointing out the sites along the way.

Finally, they stopped in front of a tunnel carved into the earth.

"You are witnessing the results of an enormous construction project, designed by man and completed through the miraculous guidance of the Divine Hand," Amram told them. His voice echoed in the cavernous hole. "King Chizkiyahu, who lived more than six hundred years ago, commissioned the building of this reservoir to divert the Gichon spring to Yerushalayim, where it could be protected. Tunnel diggers chopped at the stone from both ends, knowing that it was not at all guaranteed that they would meet in the middle. Come, see this inscription near their meeting point."

Amram translated the Hebrew inscription into Aramaic for his guests.

The tunnelers lifted the pick-axe each toward his fellow and while three cubits remained, the voice of a man was heard calling his fellow. When they came together, the water flowed from the spring toward the reservoir for 1,200 cubits.[2]

"Does the water from Chizkiyahu's tunnel have anything to do with the Shiloach pool?" Reuven piped up. "I'm told that's where our water comes from today."

"I see, dear prince," Amram said playfully, "that your nephew possesses the dual characteristics of curiosity and cleverness. He must begin learning with an outstanding *melamed!*"

"Yes, Amram, I agree that it is indeed time for my nephews' formal education to begin," Monobaz responded, out of earshot of the boys. "These last several weeks, the boys have had the opportunity to acclimate to their new surroundings. I already see that the younger three are becoming accustomed to the Jewish dialect of Aramaic[3] by listening to it spoken around them, and Moshe and Reuven have sig-

---

2 Partial translation of inscription on stone found in Chizkiyahu's tunnel, discovered by Edward Robinson in 1838.
3 Jewish Aramaic had become quite distinct from the official Aramaic of the Persian Empire by the end of the Second Temple period. See [https://en.wikipedia.org/wiki/Judeo-Aramaic_languages].

nificant background in *Lashon Hakodesh* from their Torah studies in Adiabene. Each of the boys is very motivated and willing to work hard, *baruch Hashem*."

"I would suggest Rav Baruch to teach Moshe and Reuven, and Rav Shimon to teach Yosef, Yehudah, and Yaakov," Amram said thoughtfully. "Both are *talmidei chachamim* who were born in the Diaspora and have some familiarity with your language. Most importantly, they are G-d-fearing men, who are patient and compassionate toward their students."

"I am pleased with your suggestions, my friend," Monobaz answered. "The task of locating appropriate *melamdim* for the boys has weighed heavily on me. I would like to meet them as soon as possible!"

The group made their way back to the Lower City, their spirits elevated by the sunny, comfortable spring weather and their refreshing hike. What a contrast between the open hillside just outside the city walls and the labyrinth of narrow streets within them, Monobaz mused. It was as if the residents of the Holy City were encased within a protective cocoon.

The prince's reverie was broken without warning by a loud whoosh followed by a sharp crack.

"Owwww!" Yosef screamed.

Amram whirled around, instinctively grabbed Yosef's hand and started to run, as a group of about half a dozen well-dressed youths shouted, "Foreigners, go home! Go home! Go home!"

"Follow me!" Amram ordered the group. Monobaz carried Yehudah and Yaakov, and Moshe and Reuven followed quickly. They turned a corner into a back alley and took shelter in a covered alcove.

"Yosef, are you hurt?" Amram and Monobaz bent over the petrified boy.

"Th-th-there w-w-w-was a r-r-rock," the child stuttered in fear. "It missed m-my head b-b-but hit my foot." Yosef's right foot was bruised, but, fortunately, did not appear to be broken. Amram carried him home, where Rivka and Helene, looking worried, calmed the boy and put cool compresses on his foot. The men retreated to Amram's study.

"What was that all about?" Monobaz asked, his brow furrowed.

Amram sighed and didn't answer for a moment.

"I just heard of a rumor this morning that you and your family are Roman spies," he finally said. "It was so clearly preposterous, that I didn't even feel there was any reason to share it with you. There is such intense hatred of the foreign government here that the mere suggestion of collaboration is like throwing a burning ember into a pile of dry straw. It seems that the prohibition against slander has been all but forgotten these days. You must be careful, Your Highness, but don't worry about the youths who tormented us today. I know who they are and how to take care of them. *Baruch Hashem*, no one was badly hurt."

Monobaz nodded, but he sat for a long time staring into the distance.

Chapter Fourteen

The sky was dark, and harsh winds whistled. Although he was safely inside his palace, Izates shivered. He tapped his finger against the parchment he held in his hands, an urgent missive from the governor of Edessa.[1]

With a sigh, he reread the letter.

> To His Royal Highness, King Izates of Adiabene,
> King Vardanes has been assassinated during a hunting expedition, putting his brother, Gotarzes, in power. The Parthian nobility has successfully prevailed upon the Roman emperor, Claudius, to release the hostage prince, Meherdates, to challenge Gotarzes. The king's response is eagerly awaited.[2]

Izates believed that a reign by Gotarzes would be better for his people than that of a Roman puppet monarch, but if Meherdates prevailed without his support, the autonomy of Adiabene could be threatened by an angry Rome.

Izates held no illusions about the personal risk involved in meddling in Roman politics. He thought longingly of his mother, brother,

---

1 Edessa was a vassal state of Parthia; this took place in the year 47 CE.
2 There are various opinions concerning when this conflict occurred. The one adopted here is that it was one of the battles of the ongoing war that led Helene to initially take the vow of a *nezirah*, about seven years prior to her pilgrimage to Eretz Yisrael.

and five sons, all living under Roman domination in the Holy Land. If only he could avoid inevitable conflict with the Roman authorities! Certainly, he needed to tell his wife about the dangers he faced, but what could he say to her? Was he perhaps compelled to ally himself with Rome?

The king retreated to his study to contemplate the matter. He penned a quick letter, sealed it with the royal seal, and sent it with a messenger to the city of Nisibis.

The courier sped to Nisibis, known for its large Jewish presence, and stopped in front of a modest house. A young lad opened the door.

"I am here as a representative of King Izates of Adiabene," the courier announced. "I hereby summon Rabbi Yitzchak, *dayan* of Nisibis, to the palace for a consultation with the king."

Rabbi Yitzchak, as if awaiting the messenger's arrival, wordlessly gathered his *tallis, tefillin*, a small amount of food, and a few personal belongings into a leather sack. He quietly bade his family farewell and climbed onto the back of the courier's horse. The horse raced back to Adiabene at breakneck speed with its two riders, thankfully avoiding any mishap.

Bozan bowed and motioned Rabbi Yitzchak to enter the palace.

"His Majesty is waiting for you," he announced, quickly ushering the rabbi into the king's study.

Izates rose as the elderly rabbi entered. He was clearly troubled.

"Thank you for coming so quickly, Rabbi Yitzchak," he said. "I am in need of your advice."

"What is on His Majesty's mind?" the sage asked, concerned.

"Surely Rabbi Yitzchak has heard about the upheaval in Parthian leadership. I see that I must prepare to go out to war imminently," Izates said, sighing. "I tell you in the utmost confidence that I do not consider a victory at all likely. At the same time, the current political situation gives me no choice but to cast my lot with Gotarzes while feigning support for the Roman candidate. The Romans will ultimately fight against us and my safe return home is not guaranteed, but to refuse involvement would be impossible."

"Tell me, Your Majesty," Rabbi Yitzchak said, "what is your greatest concern about this situation?"

"It is not concern for my own physical well-being that causes me to lie awake at night, Rabbi," the king admitted. "My primary concern is for the welfare of my wife. If I am lost at war, and my remains are not found, she will be unable to remarry. Is there some way I can protect her?"

"I see that the king possesses a Jewish heart as well as a Jewish soul," Rabbi Yitzchak said. He spoke in the fatherly tone that Izates had come to find so comforting. "Of course, these are matters one would rather never contemplate, but there are times when it is inevitable.

"There is a lesser-known halachah that enables a husband about to embark on a dangerous mission to issue a conditional *get* to his wife prior to his departure. A latest date for return would be specified in the document, after which time the *get* would take effect. This means that if you return prior to the date set in the *get*, you are still considered man and wife, but if you do not, your wife is considered to have been divorced retroactively."

"I see," Izates said thoughtfully. "Then this is what I have to do." He fell silent as he pondered the implications of this act. Then he raised his eyes.

"May I ask Rabbi Yitzchak to give me a blessing before he leaves?"

"May His Majesty return safely, a victor in battle," Rabbi Yitzchak responded. "Through his adherence to the Torah, may he merit sanctifying G-d's Name among the nations."

"Amen," Izates responded emotionally. "Thank you, Rabbi Yitzchak. Your words strengthen me to meet the challenge I now face."

"May you meet with success, Your Highness," the sage said, as he took leave of the king.

Samacha gazed out the window at the distant mountains.

It had been more than a week since her husband had left, with little word from the battlefield. As had become her custom, she prayed and recited Tehillim from dawn to dark, beseeching Hashem to once again save her husband from enemies much mightier than he.

Her thoughts wandered to her sons. How she missed her children! Would she ever see them again?

Tears filled her eyes. How were her sons faring in the Holy Land? Where was her husband? Was she destined to become a widow, all alone among a foreign people who disdained her faith?

"No!" she said to herself. "I will not indulge in self-pity. I trust in Hashem! May He Who has guarded my husband to this day continue to watch over him and bring him home to me safely and soon!"

A feeling of peace overtook her, and she returned to her prayers and to *teshuvah*.

A few days later, her prayers were answered.

"A letter for the princess!" a messenger announced.

Samacha's heart lurched, and she unfurled the scroll with trembling hands.

My dearest wife,

With great humility and thankfulness without measure to Hashem, I write to you, my dear Samacha, to tell you that I am alive and well and about to return to you. As we know, every battle is conducted from Above, and it became clear very early on that my involvement in this conflict was unnecessary. My troops were able to extricate themselves from the conflict, while Gotarzes and Meherdates are fighting between themselves. Thankfully, attention is deflected from our little country, and I am able to resign from the conflict.

May we be worthy of His continued salvation, and may we soon be reunited.

Your devoted husband, Izates

Samacha collapsed and began to cry uncontrollable tears of relief. "Thank You, Hashem, for saving my husband! May the Guardian of all converts continue to watch over him always!"

Where was her son? Was he even alive?

Helene had endured separations from Izates in past years, but none had been as painful as this one. Being so far away from him increased her feelings of powerlessness, and communication was exceedingly difficult. She repeated over and over to herself the phrase taught to her by Rabbi Yitzchak, "*Ein od milvado* — There is no other power but His."

"Please, Hashem, have mercy on my son!" she pleaded. "May his acceptance of Your mitzvos serve as a merit for him. Please let him survive and be a light unto the nations!"

How she longed for news that her son was back home, safe and in good health!

A knock startled the queen from her prayers. Yosef burst through the door, crying, and fell into his grandmother's arms.

"What is it, my dear?" Helene asked, alarmed. "Has someone in the street threatened you?"

"It is not me they are threatening — it is Father!" Yosef sobbed loudly. "Some boys on the street said, 'Look, that's the son of Izates the coward! The man who calls himself king of Adiabene just fled the battlefield, when he saw that his cause had no hope. Surely the Romans will finish him off now!'"

Helene's eyes widened, and she tried to stifle a gasp. She must not reveal her fears to her grandson. She quickly composed herself, smiled warmly, and beckoned Yosef to sit near her. She hugged him tightly and stroked his hair.

"Yosef," Helene said softly, "our sages teach us that great merit flows to one who is insulted but who refuses to act in kind. In fact, a *brachah* given by such a person carries great weight in *Shamayim*. Please, my dear Yosef, give your grandmother a *brachah*."

The queen's words touched the boy's heart. He stood up to face Helene and said loudly, "May you be blessed to soon hear that your son, my father, has returned home safely from battle."

"Amen, may it be His will," she replied, her voice shaking.

Yosef fell onto his grandmother's lap, and they both cried.

Several long weeks later, Helene received word of her son's miraculous salvation.

Chapter Fifteen

Late one afternoon, a white-clad messenger knocked on the door of the ben Be'iri home to be greeted by Rivka. Helene could see the messenger from the parlor, where she and Rivka had been chatting.

"Presenting a letter from the *beis din* of Beis Hillel for Queen Helene!" he announced.

Helene stepped forward to receive the letter and thanked its bearer. She unfurled the scroll and read its contents, her hands trembling in anticipation and awe.

To Her Royal Highness, Queen Helene of Adiabene,
We respectfully request an audience with the Queen today at five in the afternoon to discuss her vow of nezirus *and any other matters for which she may seek advice.*

Helene shook her head in disbelief as she read and reread the short missive.

"I, a mere foreign-born proselyte, will have the privilege to meet with the great scholars of Beis Hillel," she marveled. "How caring are the Jewish people! How great is the Alm-ghty, Who sends His messengers to care about great and small alike!"

She quickly penned a reply and requested that it be sent with the waiting messenger. A few hours later, a knock on the door to her room startled Helene from her recitation of Tehillim.

"I apologize for disturbing, Mother," Monobaz told his mother, "but the carriage is outside waiting to take you to your meeting with the *beis din* of Beis Hillel."

"Thank you, my son," Helene replied with some trepidation. "Azate will accompany us. It is my hope that she will be accepted as a righteous convert."

The royal horses trotted through streets paved with large, flat stones, leading the unobtrusive carriage bearing the queen, the prince, and Azate. They rode past pushcarts laden with cloth, pottery, metal scraps, and other goods peddled by merchants hoping to turn some profit during these bleak economic times. Customers were dressed as shabbily as the peddlers, and the subdued monotones of their conversations were a sharp contrast to the activity of the marketplace. Many people walked with slumped shoulders, as if weighed down by heavy loads.

Azate's heart was filled with compassion for these unfortunate people, only intensifying her determination to achieve her goal. Gripping a letter from Rabbi Alexander, she prayed silently during the short trip. Azate understood how much depended on her audience with Beis Hillel. She would surely be tested for her knowledge of Jewish law, as well as her beliefs, and she beseeched Hashem that her great desire to become a full-fledged Jewess would be fulfilled.

The queen was also deep in thought.

I came here to be one with them, not to rule over them or remain aloof from them, Helene mused. *But how can I help my poor, downtrodden people? There must be a way!*

She was shaken from her musings when the carriage came to an abrupt halt on a narrow street. The driver had stopped before a modest stone building whose most elaborate feature was a domed roof. The sing-song of Torah study was carried by the warm breeze through the open windows.

"How can I approach such a holy place?" the queen whispered to her son. "Surely, matters much weightier than mine are debated in this hall."

"The Torah teaches, *And you shall love the convert*," Monobaz countered. "The scholars will welcome the opportunity to fulfill this mitzvah by listening to what weighs heavily on your heart, dear Mother."

Azate turned pale and began to tremble. Helene took her by the arm as they exited the carriage and whispered in her ear, "Remember that Hashem supports those who falter and straightens those who are bent over. He will help you through this ordeal, my child."

The door opened slowly, revealing a tall, thin young man with penetrating dark eyes and a full black beard. He seemed to be expecting them.

"Please enter, most honored guests!" he announced. "I am Nechemia, *shamash* to Rabban Shimon ben Gamliel. The Nasi awaits your arrival. Please follow me!"

Nechemia took a long, lit candle from an alcove and led Queen Helene, Monobaz, and Azate through a dark corridor surrounding the *beis midrash*, so they would not disturb the scholars learning there. At the end of the hall was another door, which was slightly ajar. Light emanating from the room cast a beam into the hallway, illuminating their way as they approached.

Where there is Torah, there is light, Helene mused.

Monobaz and Helene, followed by Azate, entered a tiny vaulted room lit by beeswax candles in sconces. A small table was in the middle of the stone floor, and nooks carved into the walls held carefully rolled parchment scrolls protected by tubes made of animal skins. One of these scrolls lay unfurled on Rabban Shimon's desk, where the sage sat hunched over a text he was composing with pen and ink.

"Esteemed Nasi," Nechemia announced, "I introduce Queen Helene and Prince Monobaz of Adiabene."

Rabban Shimon ben Gamliel rose, a smile appearing on his worn face.

"The reputations of the queen and prince precede your coming to the Holy Land. The people are greatly impressed that the Parthian kingdom of Adiabene has Jewish rulers!

"I recognize that it is with great dedication to the Torah that the queen and prince stand here before me today," Rabban Shimon ben Gamliel declared. "In spite of our preoccupation with our own political situation, we are keenly aware of the challenges you faced in your conversion and subsequent decision to visit the Holy Land. Your renouncement of paganism has caused a great *kiddush Hashem* in the world. Just as the Alm-ghty provides extra protection for the convert, may He continue to watch over you and give you strength and success in your endeavors."

"Many thanks, esteemed Nasi," Monobaz responded, overwhelmed by Rabban Shimon's words. "I believe I speak for my dear mother as well as for myself in saying that we feel quite undeserving of the Nasi's generous sentiments. If I could be so forward, I ask for a blessing that the queen and I merit contributing to Jewish society in the Holy Land."

"Your desire is a pure one, dear prince," Rabban Shimon responded, gazing at Monobaz. "Just like the *ketores* offering,[1] all of us must discover the role the Alm-ghty meant for us to fulfill. May the strength of your characters and the magnificence of your royalty inspire the Jewish people in the Holy Land during these dark, troubled days."

"Amen," Monobaz and Helene said quietly.

After a few moments of silence, Rabban Shimon nodded at Azate. "I assume there is a special reason this young woman has accompanied the queen and prince."

---

1 The *ketores* offering is comprised of eleven spices that are combined in specific proportions. If even one spice is left out, the one making the *ketores* is liable to the death penalty. If an extra spice is added, the entire mixture is invalidated. Two of the spices seem to have no independent function of their own, but they are just as important as the other spices. Carshina lye is used to bleach the onycha, which makes it pleasing. Similarly, Cyprus wine is used so that the onycha can be soaked in it, to make it strong and pungent.

"Thank you, esteemed Nasi," Helene responded. "I have weighty issues for which I seek the advice of Beis Hillel today, but before discussing them, my maidservant has come seeking to join the Jewish people as a righteous convert."

Azate stepped forward, bowed slightly to the sage, and handed the Nasi the letter Rabbi Alexander had given her prior to her departure from Adiabene. Rabban Shimon read the scroll carefully, his brow furrowed in concentration. When he finally looked up, a warm smile appeared on his face.

"I have utmost respect for Rabbi Alexander," he said. "He recommends that you be accepted as a righteous convert. I will ask you just two questions. What would you do if forced to perform an act of idolatry?"

"I would give up my life," Azate replied.

"And why is it that you desire to join the Jewish people?"

"I believe that the only way to truly serve Hashem is by observing His Torah," the girl said with conviction.

"I see," Rabban Shimon said gently. "Your sincerity is evident in your voice, my child. Rabbi Alexander writes that he has tried to dissuade you three times from converting to the Jewish faith, and you have remained steadfast in your resolve to become a Jewess. I hereby accept you as a righteous convert obligated to observe all of the mitzvos of the Torah. Once you immerse in the *mikveh*, you will emerge as a new person — a Jewish woman. This will necessitate giving you a proper Jewish name. Have you thought about choosing one?"

"Yes, esteemed Nasi!" Azate was overcome with emotion. "I would like to be called Chava. My queen suggested this name, because Chava was the mother of all life. She feels that inherent in this name is a prayer that I merit to build my own family with my future husband."

"Well chosen," Rabban Shimon responded. "You shall be known heretofore as Chava bas Sarah Imeinu."

"Thank you, esteemed Nasi," Chava answered, regaining her composure. "It will be the goal of my life to serve Hashem as a true *bas Yisrael*. May I ask the great Rabban for a *brachah*?"

"May you, Chava bas Sarah Imeinu, be blessed with a long life and a husband who will dedicate himself to Torah study," Rabban Shimon ben Gamliel intoned.

"Amen!" the queen and Chava responded. Tears of joy streamed down both of their faces. Helene longed to hug the girl, but she would have to wait for later. This was not the time or place.

"And now, Your Majesty," Rabban Shimon addressed Helene. "Please tell me about your vow of *nezirus*."

"Seven years ago," the queen began, "when my son, Izates, left for war, I prayed to Hashem to protect him and vowed to become a *nezirah* for seven years upon his safe return from battle. Thanks to the kindness of Hashem, my son returned to me unscathed, and I immediately began my *nezirus*. Since that time, I have foregone consuming wine, grapes, or any fruit of the vine. I have refrained from cutting my hair, and I have not been exposed to the dead. I pledged seven years of *nezirus* and have merited completing them without mishap, *baruch Hashem*. The desire to fulfill my vow was indeed a major impetus behind my decision to travel to Eretz Yisrael, where I could offer the sacrifices of the *nezirah* and officially complete my obligation. Please, honored Nasi, direct me how to proceed. It is my utmost desire to fulfill my vow to Hashem properly."

"Her Majesty speaks with the modesty and sincerity of a true Jewish woman," Rabban Shimon ben Gamliel responded. "It is true that the sin offering of the *nazir* would normally be brought at this time, notwithstanding one complication. Although the Torah allows a vow of *nezirus* to be assumed outside of Eretz Yisrael, Beis Hillel holds that, in our days, *nezirus* can only be carried out in Eretz Yisrael due to rabbinic ordinance.² This is because burial practices of the gentiles make it impossible to avoid becoming *tamei meis* anywhere except in the Holy Land. The rabbis have therefore determined that any period of *nezirus* served outside of Eretz Yisrael is null and void.

"Although Your Majesty has observed *nezirus* for a full seven years in your home country, now that you have come to Eretz Yisrael, you must start your term as a *nezirah* from the beginning. Beis Shammai rules that the new term lasts only thirty days, but our understanding of the halachah requires the repetition of the full period of the original pledge."³

Helene was pensive. It was not the prospect of continuing her *nezirus* for another seven years that daunted her. She was saddened by the thought that she had not properly fulfilled her vow during the seven years she had spent as a *nezirah* in Adiabene. Pushing aside these thoughts, she stood tall and straight.

"I accept wholeheartedly the decision of the rabbis and hereby restart my seven-year vow of *nezirus*. May Hashem remove from me any impediment to completing my obligation successfully!"

"May it be His will!" the Nasi responded. He paused, then said, "I would like to share a thought with you, Your Highness, as you set out to fulfill your vow."

Helene nodded and lowered her eyes.

"The *nazir* holds a status even more exalted than the *kohen hedyot*," Rabban Shimon said. "While the latter is permitted to become *tamei* for a close relative, the *nazir*, like the *kohen gadol*, may not come in contact with any dead. This is because the *kohen hedyot's* position is dependent on his family — he was born to a father who was a *kohen*. The *kohen gadol*, however, is chosen to fulfill his role. Since his status is not family derived, he does not have the dispensation to become defiled for family.

---

2 According to the *Keren Orah*. Other sources disagree.
3 *Nazir*, mishnah 3:6.

"The *nazir* also achieves his position as a result of his own actions," Rabban Shimon continued. "He strives to reach greater heights in *kedushah*, just like one who chooses the faith of Avraham Avinu. A *ger* lacks parents and family traditions that have been handed down through generations. Every step he takes in his new life is a difficult climb upward. So, Your Highness, you, too, are held in great esteem both as a *nezirah* and as a *giyores*. May your willingness to stand alone enable you to achieve the pinnacle of service to Hashem!"[4]

Helene swallowed and looked up. With tears in her eyes, she uttered a barely audible, "May it be His will."

---

[4] Rav Eliyahu Schlesinger quoting the *Avnei Nezer* in Rabbi A. Leib Scheinbaum, "*Peninim al HaTorah: Parshas Emor*," *Yated Ne'eman Magazine*, 16 Iyar 5773/April 26, 2013, 39.

Chaper Sixteen

An elaborate carriage, drawn by two white mares, made its way down the street. In the rear of the carriage rode a woman flanked by two attendants. She wore a robe of imported silk and elaborate jewelry of gold and silver, and she was smiling smugly to herself. She was a woman on a mission — one very important to her.

Salome Miriamne, wife of the wealthy merchant Onias ben Hyrkanus, flicked away an imagined speck of dust and peered out the window. Her heart beat quickly in anticipation of her meeting with the queen. She had been chosen by her influential husband and his cronies to introduce Helene to the society of followers of Tzadok.[1] The more power their faction acquired, the stronger their cause would be. And once the queen was won over, surely her son would follow suit…

Sunshine glowed brightly through the lattice of the windows in Helene's room. The warm weather of Sivan made it a perfect day to explore the city, she thought with a smile.

A knock on her door announced a visitor.

"Pardon me, Your Royal Highness," a servant announced hesitantly.

---

1 Followers of Tzadok, a Jew who lived over a century earlier, were known as Tzedokim. They denied the Oral Law and claimed that they were more loyal to the Written Law. In truth, these Jews did not live their lives according to the Torah.

"Giveret Salome Miriamne from the Upper City requests an audience with the queen. Shall I invite her in?"

"Certainly," Helene responded, intrigued.

She deferred her plans for an outing, instead seating herself in the ben Be'iris' parlor. Rivka had told her that she would be tending to some family matters that day and would likely return home in the late afternoon.

The front door was opened, and a tall, imposing figure entered. She walked with an air of confidence that bespoke her high position in Yerushalayim's social hierarchy. Her fashion of dress was distinctively Roman. Her long, loose-fitting stola was draped over a half-sleeved under-tunic, identifying her as a married woman. A palla[2] was draped dramatically over her left shoulder, under her right arm, and over the left.[3] While not immodest, her appearance was difficult to reconcile with that of the Jewish matrons Helene saw each day in the Ophel. Helene felt suddenly uncomfortable.

Giveret Miriamne curtsied slowly and deliberately before introducing herself.

"Your Highness, my name is Salome Miriamne, wife of Onias ben Hyrkanus, international importer of marble and other fine stones," she said in a slightly affected accent. "It is my great pleasure to welcome the queen of Adiabene to the beautiful city of Yerushalayim."

"Thank you," Helene responded warmly. "You are so kind. Please, do sit down."

Salome Miriamne perched herself delicately on a chair near Helene.

"I assume that the queen is seeking a suitable site for her palace, and I would like to be of service," she said.

"Yes, I am anxious to be in my own home. Only then will I truly feel like a resident of the Holy City. In fact, my son, Prince Monobaz, is

---

2   The stola is a long tunic, and the palla is a type of shawl.
3   *Roman Clothing*, Part II. Vroma.org. Retrieved on 2012-07-25.

planning to bid on a parcel of land later today. It is in the heart of the Ophel, not far from here."

"The Ophel!" Salome Miriamne gasped. "Only the poorest of the poor live there. Why would the queen desire to live in such a dismal place?"

"It is for that very reason that it is so attractive to me," Helene responded. "The residents of the Upper City do not need my assistance, but with the help of Hashem, I hope to be able to do something to comfort the downtrodden residents of the Ophel. I also believe that the presence of a palace inhabited by those desiring to help could give the people encouragement during these very troubled times."

"Your Highness," Salome Miriamne said quickly, "this decision has implications that extend far beyond your kindhearted desire to do good deeds. The Jews of the Ophel are Perushim.[4] They live by laws dictated by elderly rabbis rather than by the Torah! We, in the Upper City, follow the sage Tzadok, who exposed the rabbis for promulgating their own personal interpretations of the halachah, to the great detriment of the people. Only the followers of Tzadok follow the halachah to the strict letter of the Written Law!"

Helene's eyes narrowed. Who was this woman to fabricate such nonsense?

"I beg to differ," the queen said calmly. "Just as Hashem gave the Written Torah to our people at Har Sinai, He gave them the Oral Torah. One cannot exist without the other, and only by adhering to both can we hope to do His will. I came to the Holy Land to absorb its *kedushah*, and to be influenced by the wisdom of its great rabbis. Living close to those who are loyal to them is my greatest wish."

"Then, so be it!" Salome Miriamne declared flippantly. "I am frankly surprised that a woman from such a cosmopolitan background as Her Majesty's could be influenced by such parochial views, but I

---

4   Pharisees.

accept them in deference to the queen. Please do let me know if your mind changes once you actually live among the lower classes. I am sure the palace could be converted to a public building, and we could find a perfect site for the queen in my neighborhood." She smiled disarmingly. "Please, at least come to visit for a few days. I think Her Highness will find our guest quarters quite comfortable."

"No doubt," Helene said definitively, "but I am afraid that I must decline your kind invitation. Our ways are too different for such a visit to be profitable for either of us. I thank you, Giveret, for honoring me with your kind visit."

Helene escorted Salome Miriamne to the door. She appreciated the opportunity to perform the mitzvah of accompanying a guest when she had female visitors. As the horses leading Salome Miriamne's carriage departed, the rhythmic "klop, klop" of their hooves pounding the ground sounded ominous to the queen.

"What is happening to the Jewish people?" she wondered. She closed her eyes and began to pray. "Let us combat our Roman oppressors by renewing our loyalty to Hashem! Let us not succumb to their evil ways!"

Little did she know how necessary her prayers were…

Salome Miriamne was visibly agitated as her carriage made its way back to the Upper City.

"I cannot accept the fact that the royal family of Adiabene so openly supports the Perushim!" she fumed. "The queen and her sons have their own gripes against Rome and could threaten our status if King Izates goes to war against them. If Helene refuses to join us, we must try to gain her loyalty in another way. Surely, her grandsons are vulnerable. They must miss the honor and attention paid them as princes in their homeland." She paused, and her eyes gleamed. "What if they were offered that — and more?"

She smiled as her mind worked feverishly to construct a foolproof plan. She didn't notice the worried glance her attendants exchanged. Who knew what the dire consequences of their mistress's wrath could be?

Helene and Rivka sat quietly, admiring the new spring blooms in the ben Be'iri garden. The air was warm and comfortable, but the queen was clearly disturbed.

"Rivka," she said. "Salome Miriamne's visit yesterday has left me feeling very unsettled. She is a determined woman, and she is unlikely to accept my refusal to ally myself with the Tzedokim. I don't know if she's acting independently. I fear she could try something underhanded in order to accomplish her goals."

"What do you think she might do?" Rivka asked, wide-eyed.

The queen was silent for a moment, as if trying to decide whether or not to verbalize her fears.

"I am not certain, Rivka," she finally said. "But I'm worried she might somehow try to ensnare my grandsons."

Rivka paused and then nodded.

"Yes, she might indeed try to do that. How will you protect them?"

"As little as I desire to cast aspersions on any member of our people, I feel the need to warn them," Helene replied sadly. She took a deep breath. "But enough of this political talk on such a beautiful day!" She smiled at Rivka. "Salome Miriamne's visit has also made me think about my role in the new palace. If I am truly to become part of the Ophel community, I must become acquainted with its populace. I would like to demonstrate to the neighbors that my home is being built among them so that we can help them and be good neighbors. I would rather not wait until the palace is complete to get to know them. Do you have any ideas?"

"Your Highness's goals are lofty indeed," Rivka commented. "As a start, I can introduce you to an elderly friend of mine who would appreciate an occasional visit and words of encouragement from the queen."

"Oh, please do, Rivka!" Helene said excitedly. "This is just the opportunity I welcome."

"Please tell me about Savta Dina," Helene said, panting slightly.

She was following Rivka through the winding cobblestone streets of the Ophel to a narrow alleyway.

"Certainly," Rivka obliged. "Savta Dina was born into a family of *talmidei chachamim*. Her husband was also a great scholar, who passed away many years ago, before they were blessed with children. The title 'Savta' is well earned, though. When Savta Dina was younger, she cared for many young children in the neighborhood when their mothers were ill or giving birth. She kept up a connection with these mothers, and they would visit her often. Their children called her Savta. Unfortunately, Savta Dina has few friends still living in Yerushalayim, leaving her quite lonely. Although her eyes no longer see in the physical sense, I think this has only deepened her insight into the metaphysical world. Savta Dina seems to be surrounded by an aura of Divine inspiration. You can ask her any questions you'd like. I think you will be impressed by her answers!"

The alley opened into a courtyard surrounded by four small houses. Rivka headed to one of the houses and bent down to pass through its low door, apologizing to the queen for the inconvenience.

Inside, a single oil lamp provided very little illumination in what looked like a tiny cave. In a hushed voice, Rivka explained that she and her husband had repeatedly tried to send workers to make improvements to the dwelling, but Savta Dina rebuffed them time and time again. She simply considered it an unnecessary use of funds. Against one wall was a narrow mattress, on the other wall a fireplace and makeshift kitchen. The small skylight was so dusty that it allowed virtually no light to enter. It took a few minutes before the eyes of both women became accustomed to the dark. They could discern a small figure sitting in a chair at the corner of the room, apparently sleeping.

"Savta Dina," Rivka whispered gently.

She placed a basket of warm pita bread on the woman's lap, so that she could enjoy both the aroma and the warmth of the fresh bread.

"It is Rivka ben Be'iri, and I have brought a special friend with me to visit. She is Queen Helene of Adiabene. Surely, you have heard of her recent arrival in Yerushalayim?"

"Ah, Rivka," Savta Dina said, stirring. "I am always so happy to hear your lovely voice, and a new visitor is surely welcome."

A warm smile spread across her face, a face whose features retained their beauty and purity even after decades of toil and poverty.

"I would rise in honor of Your Royal Highness, but my legs no longer have the strength to support me," Savta Dina said matter-of-factly. "I must beg your forgiveness."

"Oh no," Helene protested. "It is I who must rise before you! The Torah teaches that everyone is obligated to rise before the aged, in honor of the wisdom they have accumulated in their lifetime."

Savta Dina smiled. Rivka prepared tea, and the three women conversed animatedly. Suddenly, Savta Dina turned her head in the direction of Helene's voice and addressed her.

"Tell me, Queen Helene, what are your impressions of the Holy City?"

Helene gazed at Dina's kind, wrinkled face. There was something about the wise and pure demeanor of this woman that made her feel intimidated.

"I hear the holiness of the sages studying," Helene finally said. "I see the holiness of the little children running through the streets with their *tzitzis* flying in the breeze. I see holiness in Rivka and her family and those like them, living their lives according to the Torah out of love for the *Ribono shel Olam*. I feel the holiness and constancy of the Beis Hamikdash wherever I go."

Helene fell silent. No one said anything. Savta Dina seemed to be waiting for her to continue.

"But…but I also feel tension in the air," Helene said hesitantly. "I feel deep resentment and even hatred of the Romans, but fear enters my heart when I hear heated discussions about how to throw off their heavy yoke. What will become of us? There is factionalism in the city, with many refusing to greet one another in a civil manner as a result. Of biggest concern to me are the Tzedokim and their growing influence. I fear lest my grandsons be exposed to them."

"As indeed you should be!" The force of Savta Dina's voice surprised both Helene and Rivka. The lines in her face deepened. "Let your grandsons spend their days in the *beis haknesses* and *beis midrash*, learning with Perushim loyal to the Torah! I caution you, dear queen, to be on your guard. Winning over your precious grandsons would be a true coup for the Tzedokim. These people crave political advantage to compensate for the spiritual advantage they so sorely lack!"

Helene paled. It was frightening to hear her concerns validated in this way.

"What do you suggest I do?" Helene asked, dread creeping into her voice.

"First and foremost, you must pray for the spiritual welfare of the boys daily," Savta Dina advised. "Ultimately, all salvation is in the hands of the *Ribono shel Olam*. We must learn to be patient, but we must never stop beseeching Him to help us."

Savta Dina shifted the basket on her lap and breathed slowly and deeply.

"Next, we must look to our holy rabbis to guide us," she said. "There are zealous ones among us who think they know the will of Hashem, but they may be very wrong. Only those steeped in the Torah of Moshe Rabbeinu are worthy of our obedience and loyalty."

"Thank you for your wise words," Helene replied. "But still, I am so afraid for their safety."

"Dear queen, we must make a *kiddush Hashem* by upholding the Torah and supporting our sages," the elderly woman insisted. "They will tell us if any further action is required."

"Savta," Rivka spoke up, "I heard recently from a visitor that there is a *rav* who is assembling a group of young *talmidei chachamim*. They want to develop strategies to combat the influence of the Tzedokim and their Roman cronies. Those standing behind this *rav* are moderates in their political views, not Zealots. They truly represent the majority of the people, who just want to live their lives in peace. Could this be an answer for us?"

"Perhaps, perhaps," Savta Dina replied pensively. "But we must pray. We must pray…" Her voice trailed into a whisper, and silence enveloped the room.

Helene and Rivka waited a few minutes, but it seemed that the elderly woman had fallen asleep. They stood up, but Savta Dina held up a hand.

"Please wait, my dear ladies," she said.

Helene and Rivka looked down at her and waited.

"May you be blessed with good health, success, and peace of spirit, and may all of your children and grandchildren walk in the ways of our holy Torah!" she said warmly. "And thank you again for the pita."

"What can I do for her?" Helene asked Rivka, upon exiting the house.

"Savta Dina's spiritual strivings dwarf her meager material needs," Rivka explained. "Visit her, and discuss Torah, mitzvos, and your various activities here with her. Your visits will surely make her very happy, but you are probably the one who will gain the most!"

The queen's visits to Savta Dina's abode became regular weekly occurrences that both women looked forward to immensely. The queen relished the opportunity to absorb Savta Dina's wisdom and warmth. The elderly woman spoke to her of the *halachos* of the Jewish woman in the home, providing Helene great encouragement in her observance of mitzvos. In turn, Helene enlightened Savta with the goings-on of the outside world. But always, Helene would uneasily recall their first conversation together.

"Please," she constantly prayed, "spare my grandchildren from any spiritual harm!"

Chapter Seventeen

The bright Tammuz sun made the granite cobblestones of the Ophel glitter like diamonds and baked the walls of the small mud huts scattered among only slightly larger stone dwellings. Monobaz was pondering the irony of streets that looked like they were paved with precious gems in this poverty-stricken neighborhood, when his serious expression gave way to a smile.

"While I cannot renovate the entire Ophel, I can give its residents a place of beauty to relieve some of the drabness," he murmured to himself.

His step quickened as he approached Amram's home, a rolled parchment under his arm. Monobaz proceeded to the garden, where he encountered the queen sitting on a stone bench under a fig tree.

The prince waited until the queen looked up from the Tehillim she was reciting. The startled expression on her face was quickly replaced by a smile at the welcome sight of her son.

"Greetings, Mother! I see you are enjoying this glorious day Hashem has made for us!"

"Yes, Monobaz," she replied. "May His Name be blessed! You seem excited about something. Is there something special underway?"

"I always felt you could read my thoughts, dear Mother!" the prince remarked, smiling. He stepped forward. "I hereby present to you a blueprint of your future home. I have had the good fortune to purchase a large, empty tract of land in the Ophel. The seller questioned why I would be building a palace in one of the poorest neighborhoods of Yerushalayim, but I merely told him that I was following my mother's instructions."

Monobaz unfurled the long parchment to reveal a detailed sketch of a large, palatial structure.

"What a beautiful building!" Helene gasped. "I see that it does resemble our palace in Adiabene, but there are some significant differences."

"Yes, Mother," the prince agreed. "The palace will be built with thick walls of limestone. The main building will consist of two large stories. The halls will be long and spacious with high ceilings, just like in Adiabene, and I've made sure to allocate space for a large dining hall on the ground floor where meals will be served to poor travelers and others in need, as you requested."

Monobaz sat down beside his mother and pointed to a smaller structure.

"This building will include water installations and *mikva'os*,"[1] he explained. "The architect has designed an underground cistern. A shaft will lead from an opening on the eastern side of the northern building's courtyard to a bell-shaped cavity below ground level. Water will be collected from the roofs of the palace and from the courtyard through a network of channels and pipes. It should hold enough for our needs, even during the dry summer months."[2]

Helene nodded approvingly.

"I have consulted with local halachic authorities on every aspect of

---

1   See R. Steven Notley and Jeffrey P. Garcia, "Queen Helena's Jerusalem Palace — In a Parking Lot?" *Biblical Archeology Review*, May/June 2014, 35-37.
2   Israel Ministry of Foreign Affairs, [http://www.mfa.gov.il/MFA/History/Early+History+-+Archaeology/Jerusalem+-+The+Upper+City+during+the+Second+Templ.htm], "Jerusalem – The Upper City during the Second Temple Period," November 20, 2000.

the construction," Monobaz said. "The *mikva'os* will be built according to the strictest halachic standards, and the kitchen will be designed to facilitate observance of the most intricate laws of kashrus. The courtyard will be encircled by a wall that will serve as an *eruv*, so that you can carry within it on the Shabbos. The architect is ready to commence with the building as soon as you have placed your royal seal upon the contract."

Helene scrutinized the heavy parchment, her eyes quickly scanning the outline of the structures and then focusing on rooms in the eastern wing. There, she saw the outline of enormous storehouses, much bigger than those needed for the family and their periodic guests. There was also a large hall located in that wing with a small entrance accessible from the exterior. A smile spread across her face, and she looked up at her son.

"There is no greater joy for a mother than seeing her children exhibit a giving nature," Helene said happily. "How can I adequately thank you, my son, for the time, careful thought, and effort you have devoted to this project! Clearly, my palace will be comfortable and spacious and — most importantly — enable us to properly observe the *halachos* relating to purity and kashrus. But the fact that you anticipated my desire to feed the poor in a respectable way gives me additional joy. May we merit to see the completion of the project and to perform many mitzvos in the new palace!"

Monobaz gazed at the queen with a twinkle in his eye and an almost childlike smile on his face.

"Mother," he said, unable to hide his excitement, "behind the house is enough land to plant extensive gardens. I've also purchased a pomegranate orchard and a small plot to plant a vineyard in the north, in Gush Chalav, near Beit El. It is far from the palace, so that you will not need to go to any trouble to avoid the grapes. With Hashem's help, the boys and I will cultivate the land and reap the fruits by which Eretz

Yisrael is praised. By the time your *nezirus* is completed, it should, G-d willing, be producing enough grapes for us to begin to fill a wine cellar! I dream of bringing Izates a bottle of wine from the Holy Land to use for Kiddush."

"How I have yearned to perform the mitzvos dependent on the Land! Now, with Hashem's help and your foresight, I will be able to fulfill them! Thank you, my son!"

Monobaz smiled triumphantly, pleased to have brought his mother such joy. He kissed her hand and stood up, anxious for her to give final approval to the architect.

"Just a few more moments of your time, Monobaz," the queen said. "There is something I would like to share with you before you leave."

"Of course, Mother." Monobaz sat down again. "You look troubled. What has happened?"

"It is not so much what has happened as it is what *could* happen that disturbs me." Helene sighed. "I am worried about the Tzedokim. I realize that we are vulnerable to their machinations, both as prominent people here in Yerushalayim and because of our disaffection with Rome.

"I am very concerned about the boys," Helene said. "I must speak to them and warn them to avoid all involvement with those they do not know well and to report to us any suspicious overtures these individuals may make."

"You are right, Mother," Monobaz agreed. "I am most concerned about Reuven's safety. His hatred of the Romans is virulent, and I fear he could be lured into the Zealot camp."

"*Chas v'chalilah!*" the queen responded. "Rivka told me there is a group of *talmidei chachamim* who are working with the rabbis to undermine the Tzedokim. Do you think we should tell Reuven about them?"

"He is aware of them, Mother," Monobaz said. "I have discussed with him the relative merits of joining such a group. For now, Reuven has decided to remain within the four walls of the *beis midrash*.

Eventually, he is likely to take some action in this regard, but I trust his judgment. He is a level-headed young man."

Helene nodded.

"We must constantly pray for the physical and spiritual well-being of Izates's children," Helene said, more to herself than to Monobaz. She fingered the Tehillim in her hands and sighed. "May Hashem protect him, and all of us!"

"Yes, Mother. May it be His will!"

Monobaz returned to Adiabene at the end of the month of Tammuz. He had spent nearly three months helping his mother and nephews get settled in the Holy Land, and his brother now needed his help and support back home. Monobaz would spend the next fourteen years shuttling back and forth between his country of birth and the land of his adopted people, spending as much time as possible in the Holy Land, where his heart always remained.

During his absence, the palace rose steadily from the ground, stone by stone, as the months passed. Speculation about how the grand home would ultimately look and the nature of its occupants had been a favorite topic of conversation in the Ophel since the construction project began. Some worried that the presence of such a mansion would divert the government's attention away from the majority of the neighborhood's very needy residents. Most residents looked forward with great anticipation to living near a royal family, and especially one that had chosen to dwell close to them. Surely, it could only bode well for them.

Finally, in the month of Nisan of the following year, the palace was ready for occupancy. The day the royal family left their home was bittersweet for the ben Be'iris. They had gained so much from their close relationship to Helene and her family, and it was so difficult to part! Nevertheless, they were happy that the queen would live not far from their home. They were proud that her palace would be not only a home to the royal family, but also a center for *chessed* and support for the rabbis who were valiantly upholding the Torah against the ongoing threat from the Tzedokim.

Rivka and Amram looked at each other when a knock sounded on the door separating the guest quarters from the main house.

"I will answer it, Rivka," Amram said, standing up.

At the threshold stood Helene and Monobaz, who was back for another visit. Each of them was holding a parcel.

"Please come in, Your Highnesses!" Amram declared warmly. "Mazel tov on the completion of the palace!"

Rivka gestured for Helene to sit with her in the parlor. Once the men had retreated to the study, Helene hugged Rivka, unsuccessfully trying to hold back tears of gratitude and sadness.

"You are like a sister to me, Rivka," Helene whispered, trying to regain her composure. "You understand my thoughts and dreams like no one I have previously met. Your warmth, kindness, and encouragement make me feel that I truly belong here. I cannot imagine what it would have been like had I not been delivered into your welcoming arms, nor could I ever sufficiently thank you for all you have done for me and my family."

Helene swallowed hard and brushed a few tears away.

"You taught me by your example how to live as a Jewish woman, how to perform the mitzvos, how to view life. I could never begin to repay you, Rivka, for nourishing my soul and caring so generously for my physical needs. Here, please take this gift as a token of my love and appreciation."

Helene placed the small parcel into Rivka's hands.

"But Your Majesty," Rivka protested. "It is I who must thank you for honoring me, a common Jewish woman, with your companionship. I have often thought that there are other homes that would have been more appropriate for a guest of your stature, and I thanked Hashem for sending you to us. Your stay with us has been a gift of the greatest magnitude. How could I accept a present from Your Highness?"

"Please, Rivka, take it," Helene urged. "I chose it especially for you."

Slowly, Rivka opened the linen sack. Inside was a package wrapped in a long bolt of embroidered white silk. Rivka gasped as she unrolled the beautiful fabric. She was even more unprepared for what lay within. Two tall silver candlesticks, each decorated with the elaborate trademark of famed Yerushalmi silversmiths, shone brightly in her lap.

As Rivka gazed, speechless, at the splendor before her, Helene quietly spoke.

"These are a copy of the candlesticks that my dear son, King Izates, imported to Adiabene for me when we first became Jews," she explained. "The silk shawl will give you privacy when you pray after kindling the candles. May they bring light and blessing to you and your husband, and, through your righteousness, to all of Klal Yisrael."

The women embraced again silently. A bond of understanding had been forged between them that made words unnecessary.

In the study, Monobaz handed Amram a large leather sack. Amram's face lit up upon uncovering the contents. He withdrew parchment scrolls, one after the other, until he realized, with delight, that they corresponded to each of the holy books of the Prophets! To own these texts was considered a rare luxury that only a few of the wealthiest Jews enjoyed. Studying them generally necessitated sharing a handwritten copy with many others or copying the texts by hand.

"Dear prince!" Amram exclaimed. "What a wonderful gift! I feel so unworthy of your generosity!"

"It is merely a small token of appreciation for my *chavrusa*," Monobaz responded with a smile. "In exchange for all that you have taught me, it is only fitting that your learning be made more convenient! I could never sufficiently express my thanks to you, my friend."

As Helene and Monobaz left the ben Be'iri house and boarded the carriage that would take them to their new palace, Amram and Rivka watched quietly. They both murmured a silent prayer of thanks to the Alm-ghty for sending them these exemplary individuals, who lit up their lives during these dark times.

Chapter Eighteen

The sound of knocking startled Rivka. She hurriedly wiped her hands, wondering who could be at the door.

She pulled it open curiously and beheld a courier, dressed in elaborate livery, bearing a letter from Queen Helene requesting the presence of her dear friend that afternoon.

When Rivka arrived at the palace, she was surprised to be ushered into the kitchen, rather than being escorted to the queen's sitting room, as she had been during previous visits. The enormous kitchen was actually a building unto itself, connected to the main palace by a short, covered hallway. Rivka was amazed at the volume of food being prepared by various cooks and assistants. Enormous pots were cooking above burning firewood, and meat was being roasted on long spits. Rivka was aware of the queen's efforts to feed the poor, but she had never appreciated the extent of the operation.

"Rivka!" Helene exclaimed happily. "Thank you so much for coming!"

Helene wore a long white apron over her simple linen dress. Her hands were covered with finely ground white flour, and her face was radiant.

"I apologize for the frenzy here today," she explained. "One of our good neighbors is marrying off her daughter on Friday, and the wedding feast will also serve as the Friday night Shabbos meal. I have asked the palace baker to wait for me before baking the bread. Now I am ready to perform the mitzvah of separating *challah* from the dough, and I would like you to be here the first time I say this *brachah* in the Holy Land. Although I have performed this mitzvah many times in Adiabene, the requirements are more stringent here in Eretz Yisrael, so I would like you to make sure I am doing it correctly."

Rivka happily obliged. She watched the queen, amazed at a vitality that made her seem many years younger than a woman in her seventh decade. Helene inserted her hand into a large bowl, which held twenty-four strands of dough. She covered the dough with a cloth and recited the *brachah*.

"Amen!" Rivka responded enthusiastically, and smiles spread over both of their faces.

The queen grasped one complete strand in her right hand, instead of the small, token amount she had separated in Adiabene,[1] and declared with deep feeling, "*Harei zo challah* — Behold, this is *challah!*"

She quickly wrapped the dough in a linen cloth and handed it to her nine-year-old grandson, who had been observing the ritual with rapt interest.

"Yehudah, please take this dough to our neighbor, Mar Yechezkel the *kohen*," Helene instructed. "Tell him that we humbly present to him this gift of *challah* with our thanks for his service to Hashem in the Beis Hamikdash."

"Certainly, Grandmama," the boy replied. He left the kitchen, pleased with his assignment.

Helene and Rivka braided the remaining strands of dough and then placed them on the bottom of a large, stone-lined oven.[2] Helene

---

[1] One strand represented 1/24 of the dough, as required in the Holy Land; see *Sefer Hachinuch*, mitzvah 385.

[2] Called a furn by the Romans, this oven was commonly used in Jewish homes. "Ancient Israelite Cuisine," Wikipedia, [http://en.wikipedia.org/wiki/Ancient_Israelite_cuisine].

watched as the baker's assistant lit the fire. In Adiabene, Monobaz had faithfully performed this task to ensure that the bread would fulfill the requirement of being baked by a Jew. Here in Yerushalayim, only Jews faithful to the Torah worked in the kitchen, so the baking could be done without her constant presence. Quickly, the room filled with the heavenly aroma of baking bread.

"Challah in honor of *Shabbos Kodesh*!" Helene declared.

Rivka echoed her words, and the two friends exchanged smiles of joy.

The bounty that nourished the inhabitants of Eretz Yisrael that summer was ephemeral.

As the month of Elul passed, making way for the Yamim Nora'im of Tishrei, the populace prayed fervently for another year of plenty. Sukkos was celebrated with great thankfulness and joy, and intense supplications could be heard rising toward Heaven on Hoshana Rabbah, when the Jewish people are judged for rain. As thousands of *olei regel* witnessed the *hakafah* circuits around the *Mizbe'ach* on that solemn day, everyone's thoughts and *tefillos* were focused on the great need for rain.

The prayer for rain was recited on the following day, Shemini Atzeres, accompanied by the declaration that Hashem is "the One Who causes the wind to blow and rain to fall." Several weeks later, the request for dew and rain was said in the *Shemoneh Esrei* prayer on the seventh of Cheshvan, but to no avail.

People everywhere could be seen scanning the cloudless sky for signs of rain, but there were none. The ground became increasingly parched, and the fall harvest was almost non-existent. The severe drought scorched the Judean hills and turned the fertile Galil into a desert, bringing famine and starvation to the land.[3] Farmers were

---

3   Henry Zirndorf, *Some Jewish Women*, 98.

hardest hit, but the impact spread quickly to the cities, where food was scarce and, in some places, nearly unobtainable. The wealthy could import grain from abroad at inflated prices, but most of the populace was reduced to levels of nourishment below subsistence.

Helene continued to serve hundreds of meals per day to the needy. She had dried and preserved food during the times of plenty and now kept it in underground storehouses beneath the palace. Nevertheless, this was not sufficient to meet the growing demand of the hungry populace. They swarmed around the palace, their eyes beseeching and their hands outstretched.

Chava hurriedly rushed to shut the curtains, attempting to shield the queen from the distressing scene, but Helene would have none of this.

"My child, will these people be any less hungry if I hide from them?" she asked rhetorically, her eyes moist with tears.

"See how low the sun has dropped in the sky," she added, sighing. "Let us pray the afternoon service and beseech Hashem for mercy and salvation."

"Yes, Your Highness," Chava said quietly. "Please excuse me while I go to pray in my room."

She left the chamber and closed the door gently behind her. Helene rose and faced north, toward the Beis Hamikdash. She prayed with great intensity and then put her face in her hands.

"Are we not to view ourselves as messengers of Hashem, created to perform His will?" she said to herself. "Surely, there must be something more we can do to lessen their hunger." After sitting deep in thought for over an hour, the queen suddenly rose. She sat down at her desk and began to write.

To King Izates,

I write to you, my dearest son, with deep sadness to inform you of a severe famine with which the Alm-ghty has afflicted His people in the Holy Land. Stores of fruits and grains have been exhausted, and those dependent on the output of their fields are starving. There is no governmental method in place to provide for these poor, wretched souls, so we must do our share.

I beseech you, as king of Adiabene, to authorize the release of sufficient funds from our family's personal coffers to finance the importation of food from Alexandria to assuage the hunger of our people.

I suggest that your brother, Monobaz, supervise this effort, in recognition of the great burden you bear due to the affairs of state.

I believe that it would greatly please our Creator for you to act in such a manner.

With great love and respect,
Your mother

Helene signed her name to the document and affixed the royal seal. Then she rang a brass bell. Within moments, the chief butler knocked on the door.

"Please hurry, Gershon!" Helene ordered. "Send a courier to King Izates with this letter, and have him wait for a reply before returning!"

The courier sped away at breakneck speed toward Adiabene, aware that every hour could mean lives saved. He arrived at the palace in a mere ten days, triggering shock and alarm at the royal court.

"The royal courier of Queen Helene is here to see the king!" boomed the chief butler.

Izates looked up, startled. Had something happened to his family?

As he carefully read his mother's anguished letter, sadness spread over his face.

"I must speak to my brother," the king said, almost to himself. "Bozan, please summon Prince Monobaz to the throne room, and let him know that the meeting could last several hours."

A few minutes later, Monobaz entered the room, a worried expression on his face.

"What has happened?" he asked in alarm.

"Mother writes that people in Eretz Yisrael are starving as a result of severe drought. Shipping raw grain is impractical, since it is perishable, and by the time it would reach the populace and be processed, they would all be dead of starvation. Surely, there must be a plentiful, high-energy food that requires little preparation."

"I saw the signs of imminent famine during my stay in Eretz Yisrael for the Sukkos holiday," Monobaz replied solemnly. "I hoped that our prayers and *teshuvah* would evoke Divine mercy to reverse the situation, but it seems that we are not yet worthy of salvation. There must be something we can do to help!"

He thought for a few moments, and then a half-smile eased some of the wrinkles in his furrowed brow.

"I seem to remember Rabbi Alexander teaching me that dates are considered comparable to grain foods in certain halachic applications, due to the sense of satiety they provide. Surely, dates can help revive the famished people!"

"This could indeed be the answer we seek," Izates agreed. "I ask you, my dear brother, to serve as the administrator of the rescue effort."

"I humbly accept the role out of my desire to do whatever possible to help you and our people," Monobaz responded.

"I will put Vahumana, the minister of the royal treasury, under your jurisdiction to implement the plan," Izates said. "Of course, shipping the food will take time, and time is of the essence."

"I understand fully," Monobaz replied.

"Vahumana," Monobaz instructed, "please contact Murashu and Sons[4] in Bavel immediately and have them contract to purchase corn

---

4   There has been found (on clay tablets) a fully documented mention of a Jewish family "Murashu and Sons" – International Bank, Insurance, Conveyancing, Loans, Personal

from Egypt, dried figs and dates from Cyprus, and other foods as they are available. Instruct them to debit our account for the full amount. Bring to their attention the fact that this unusual order is signed by myself and is being carried out with the full faith and credit of the royal family of Adiabene."

"B-b-but Your Highness," Vahumana stammered, shocked. "This will only further convince the noblemen of your disloyalty to our country! I fear it will put you in grave danger!"

Although he was fully aware of the potentially negative political consequences that could result from his actions, Monobaz was undeterred.

"The money that will be used to pay for this food is from my family's personal funds, not funds segregated for the maintenance of the kingdom," he said.

As anticipated, word of the expenditures circulated quickly, and the prince's explanation fell on deaf ears. Grumbling grew louder and louder from the extended royal family. Helene's sister Cassandra and her husband, Varazduxt, became self-appointed spokesmen for the nobility.

A messenger was dispatched to the palace. With a sinking heart, Monobaz unfurled the scroll.

To Monobaz, our nephew,

We will be blunt in our expression of horror at your recent activities. Surely you are aware that your fathers augmented the royal treasury and added to that of their forefathers, but you have squandered their wealth. Your irresponsible actions not only threaten our inheritance, but

---

and Real Estate. The head office was in Nippur, and it had "branches everywhere." The Murashus were exiles from Yerushalayim who had arrived in Babylonia after the destruction of the first Beis Hamikdash. For about 150 years, the firm enjoyed the full confidence of its clients.

reduce respect for the monarchy, causing all of us great shame. Do not expect your impulsive actions to be without negative consequence! It is your brother's welfare that you jeopardize by your rash acts! We call for a cessation of your plundering of our family assets and restitution of every last lira you have taken from us.

We cannot guarantee your safety if you fail to heed our warning.

Your Uncle Varazduxt and Aunt Cassandra

The prince smiled wryly, unruffled by their anger. He quickly summoned his devoted scribe.

"Mena, please transcribe these words, and send them back posthaste," he requested.

My dear Uncle and Aunt,

I write in the attempt to correct your misunderstanding and to explain how my deeds are indeed beneficial to the family. You see, my ancestors built treasure houses below, and I do so above,[5] as the holy King David said, "Truth must first spring forth from the earth, and then righteousness will look down from Heaven."[6] My ancestors amassed wealth in a place vulnerable to plunder, but I amass in a place invulnerable to plunder, as it is written in the holy writings, "Right and order are the foundation of Thy throne."[7] My ancestors collected things that do not bear fruit, but what I have amassed does bear fruit, as it says, "Say the righteous one is good, because the fruit of their deeds they do eat."[8] They amassed treasures of money, and I amass treasures of souls, as it says, "The fruit of the righteous is the tree of life, and a wise man acquires souls."[9] They gathered wealth for others, but I do so for myself, as it says,

---

5 *Bava Basra* 11a.

6 *Tehillim* 85:12, based on interpretation of *Rashi* and *Radak* as cited in *The Artscroll Tanach Series, Tehillim*, 1067.

7 *Tehillim* 89:15.

8 *Yeshayahu* 3:10.

9 *Mishlei* 11:30, as translated in the Stone edition of Tanach.

"And for you it will be considered righteousness."[10] They amassed for this world, and I amass for the next world, as it says, "Your righteousness will walk before you, and the glory of G-d will gather you in."[11]

Respectfully,
Your nephew, Prince Monobaz II

The letter did not garner a response, and the prince's relief efforts continued unabated. The importation of food was conducted in an unusually expeditious manner. The starving populace viewed Queen Helene and her family as benevolent messengers of the Alm-ghty, Who shows mercy toward His people.

As the sun began to rise in the eastern sky near Yaffo, Meir prepared for another day at sea. He was hopeful that he'd be able to catch enough fish to sustain his family for the coming week. Fish were a precious commodity, and only the wealthy could afford to purchase them.

Suddenly, Dovid, his twelve-year-old son, began to jump up and down on the dock.

"Look, Father, look!" He pointed excitedly toward the point where the Mediterranean Sea met the horizon. "There are huge ships — and lots of them!"

Meir squinted into the distance and saw a fleet of merchant ships in full sail. In all of his years of fishing in the usually quiet waters of Yaffo, he had never seen a fleet that size. Meir and his son gazed at the flotilla, mesmerized by the slow, graceful procession. As it approached the shore, dozens of stevedores on the wharf began bustling around frantically and gesticulating to scores of wagon drivers.

"Please, let's see what's happening, Father!" Dovid begged. "What

---

10   *Devarim* 24:13.
11   *Yeshayahu* 58, as quoted in *Bava Basra* 11a.

could the shipment be? It appears to be enough food to feed the whole country!"

"Yes, Dovid, I believe it is just that." Meir had tears in his eyes as he watched the incredible scene unfold. "I have heard that Queen Helene of Adiabene personally took responsibility to send enough food to stave off starvation until the new crops can be harvested. May they be plentiful and of good quality!"

Over the next two days, donkey-drawn caravans of wagons carrying burlap sacks of corn, dates, and dried figs could be seen winding around the hills and valleys. A cheering populace greeted the drivers with cups of wine, stored from earlier years of plenty.

Helene appointed impeccably honest officers to distribute the food to the hungry people in each major population center in the country, while she personally assisted in the distribution of provisions in Yerushalayim. Hordes of men, women, and children, weakened by lack of food, lined up before the queen.

Helene sighed as she gazed upon faces filled with suffering. How she wished she could relieve the pain of her people! As she gave out food packages, she blinked back tears at the sight of small children scurrying to gather figs that dropped from the baskets. Yet, the grateful relief on the faces of the recipients heartened her.

"*Ribono shel Olam*!" she murmured. "Have mercy on Your chosen nation! Give them the food they need to have strength in order to perform Your mitzvos! Forgive us our transgressions!"

A young woman holding the hand of a little girl stood before Helene. As the woman shyly accepted a bundle, she whispered her thanks. Her daughter tugged gently at her skirt, and the woman nodded. The child took a few steps forward, curtsied, and spoke in a voice mature beyond her years.

"Your Majesty, I thank you on behalf of the residents of Yerushalayim for saving our lives."

Indeed, it was not long before the name Helene Hamalkah was praised on the lips of the populace in all quarters of the Holy City — and beyond.

It was a cold, dreary morning. The earth that had refrained from giving forth her produce now lay frozen and still. Tu B'Shevat had just passed, and with it countless prayers for bountiful crops.

A carriage pulled up in front of the palace, and a young man dressed in the simple linen robe of the Perushim emerged. He spoke briefly to the guard, who immediately walked to the carriage and opened its door to help its occupant exit. The tall, stately man who appeared was none other than the Nasi, Rabban Shimon ben Gamliel, paying an unprecedented visit to the queen. He was promptly ushered inside.

"Your Majesty, Queen Helene," Rabban Shimon began respectfully. "I have come on behalf of Klal Yisrael to thank you and the royal family for your efforts in alleviating the famine that afflicts the Holy Land. Your actions bring to mind an earlier epoch in our history, more than one thousand years ago, when another famine devastated our land and its people. At that time, Elimelech, a great and wealthy Jew, did not act as you did. He turned his back on his brethren and left the country, taking his wealth and his family with him. Hashem punished him severely for his lack of compassion, and he lost nearly everything: his animals, his wealth, his life, and his sons.

"But his wife, who was not in favor of that fateful decision to leave the Holy Land, survived. So did her gentile daughters-in-law. Surely, Your Majesty has become acquainted with the story of Rus. She was a woman who, like yourself, was of royal lineage. She turned her back on a comfortable life of pleasure and insisted on accompanying her destitute mother-in-law back to her homeland as a full-fledged Jewess. In Eretz Yisrael, she both bestowed and received kindness and merited to become the great-grandmother of Dovid Hamelech!"

Helene and Monobaz listened silently.

"Your acts of kindness are in keeping with those of Rus, your spiritual ancestress, Your Majesty," Rabban Shimon continued. "May the Alm-ghty consider your *chessed* to be a *tikun* of that earlier sin committed by Elimelech, when he abdicated his responsibility toward his people."

Rabban Shimon smiled. "Did you ever wonder why converts are called a son or daughter of Avraham Avinu? It is because Avraham's name means 'the father of a great multitude of nations.' But that is not your only connection to our first forefather, whose defining character trait was *chessed*. You are truly worthy, Queen Helene and Prince Monobaz, of your holy appellation — son and daughter of Avraham Avinu.

"Just as this famine exemplifies the great spiritual, political, and physical quagmire that has besieged our people, so, too, may your great kindness be a *zechus* for our full redemption, speedily, and in our days."

Chapter Nineteen

Monobaz rose when it was still dark and dressed quickly.[1] His joy at the opportunity to celebrate the upcoming Yom Tov in Eretz Yisrael with his mother and nephews was tempered by a pang of regret that his brother and sister-in-law could not join them. How grateful he was to Izates for allowing, and even encouraging him to make frequent, lengthy trips to the Holy Land, especially for the Yamim Tovim.

Monobaz knocked on seventeen-year-old Moshe's bedroom door. Moshe awoke, startled. What was going on?

In a flash, he remembered that today was the fourteenth of Nisan. Moshe immediately sat up, recited *Modeh Ani* with exuberance, and washed *netilas yadayim* from the metal basin beside his bed. Then he opened the door a crack.

"A good Erev Yom Tov, Uncle!" Moshe called out. "I will be ready in just a few minutes."

"Very good," Monobaz replied. "The first *minyan* will start promptly at dawn, and we do not want to be late."

Before leaving the palace, Monobaz lifted a torch from a sconce in the foyer to light their way along the dark streets that were already streaming with men and boys on their way to the synagogues. Prayers had to be said as early as possible on this special, busy day. As they

---

1 This occurred in the year 50 CE.

walked, Monobaz and Moshe engaged in a lively discussion of the laws concerning the disposal of *chametz*, the *Korban Pesach*, and the Seder. The prayers that day were infused with a special joy, as the community anticipated the offering of the *Korban Pesach* later that day and the celebration of the Seder at nightfall.

As they left the synagogue, Monobaz and Moshe enjoyed the smell of freshly baked matzah coming from the bakeries and homes of the Ophel. The prince stopped at one of these commercial establishments to arrange for the delivery of one thousand matzos to the palace later that day. This order was intended to feed the poorest residents of the Ophel, who would pick up their matzos at the soup kitchen.

As they made their way home, Monobaz and Moshe continued to engage in a lively discussion about the *halachos* of Erev Pesach. The prince was pleased with his nephew's level of understanding of the relevant laws. So engrossed was the pair in their discussion that they were surprised at how quickly they arrived back at the palace.

Unlike other members of the family, neither Monobaz nor Moshe would be eating breakfast that day. As firstborn sons, both would be fasting. Although converts were not obligated to fast on Erev Pesach, both had chosen to take on the custom voluntarily.[2]

Reuven and Yosef were waiting outside and excitedly confronted the two as they approached.

"Dear Uncle," Reuven said respectfully, "Yosef and I are now both over the age of bar mitzvah. May we please come with you to the Beis Hamikdash?"

Monobaz smiled, pleased that his nephews were so eager to witness the performance of this annual mitzvah.

"Reuven and Yosef, my dear nephews, your desires are pure, and

---

2   Due to the Talmudic disagreement over this obligation, Rav Yosef Shalom Elyashiv *zt"l* recommended that firstborn converts participate in a *siyum* so as to obviate the need to fast.

may they be a *zechus* to you! But do you know that in recent years there have been over one million animals brought to the Beis Hamikdash each Erev Pesach to be offered as the *Korban Pesach*? It is an open miracle that there is always room in the *Azarah* for those bringing the *korban*, let alone room for additional spectators. I regret that only Moshe may accompany me, so he can help me carry the *Korban Pesach* and the *Korban Chagigah* home for roasting. But you can be sure that I'll share the details of our experience with you at the Seder tonight!"

"I understand, Uncle," Reuven acquiesced, but Yosef looked especially disappointed.

Monobaz hugged Yosef and whispered into his ear, "When I return, you will be my special assistant in distributing the *Korban Pesach* at the Seder."

Monobaz and Moshe prepared to begin traversing the short distance to the Beis Hamikdash long before midday. Prior to leaving the palace, they descended to the kitchen to bid farewell to the queen. She was actively involved in the supervision of the cooking of Yom Tov meals, not only for their family, but for the scores of poor who would partake of the Seder in the special quarters prepared for them.

"Mother," Monobaz called loudly, trying to make himself heard above the din of clanging pots and shouting servants. "We are leaving for the Beis Hamikdash now."

Helene looked up, smiling.

"I see that enthusiastic ones hurry to do mitzvos!" she exclaimed proudly. "May you have the merit to offer the *Korban Pesach* according to all of its laws!"

"Amen!" Monobaz responded. "And may you merit completing the preparations for the Yom Tov smoothly and expeditiously!"

"May it be His will!" Helene said joyfully.

She removed her apron and left the kitchen with them.

"Goodbye, Uncle! Goodbye, Moshe!" the other boys chorused.

"May you merit performing the mitzvos in the most complete and honorable way!"

Helene and her grandsons waved as they watched the prince and Moshe lead two somewhat reluctant young sheep, tethered by leather straps. One would be offered as the *Korban Chagigah* and the other as the *Korban Pesach*. The *Korban Chagigah* would be used to feed the large group of people that would assemble at the palace for the Seder. The *Korban Pesach* would be consumed only after everyone had achieved satiety.[3]

"May you be blessed!" Monobaz and Moshe shouted back. Their voices blended with the din created by the sea of people and sheep moving slowly through the streets of the Ophel toward the Har Habayis.

"Look, Moshe!" Monobaz shouted. He pointed at the crowded stone dwellings they were passing. "All of the houses have towels hanging from their doors! The residents are opening their homes to guests."[4]

"And look, Uncle!" Moshe replied. "The weather is so warm, but it looks as if there is snow on the hills surrounding Yerushalayim! Surely it is due to the multitudes of sheep being brought to the city by the *olei regel*. There are so many of them, that all we see is their wool. Now I know why there were so many workers fixing the roads the day after Purim!"

"Yes, Moshe," Monobaz responded, somewhat distracted. "It seems as if the whole world is converging on Yerushalayim to offer *korbanos*."

The pure whiteness of the vast number of sheep had engendered an uncomfortable feeling in his heart.

---

3   *Pesachim* 70a.
4   It was forbidden by Jewish law to charge a fee to feed or lodge anyone who came to Yerushalayim for Pesach, Shavuos, or Sukkos. Instead, residents would hang a towel on their door as a sign that vacancies still existed within. The towel was only removed when the house was so full that no more guests could be accepted. While it is stated in the Gemara (*Chagigah* 17a) that *olei regel* were required to stay over in Yerushalayim only one night after bringing their *Korban Pesach*, it is assumed here that the *olei regel* chose to remain for the entire Yom Tov.

So many of our people are bringing the Korban Pesach *with a pure heart*, he mused. *But so many others seek to sabotage the* avodah *of the Beis Hamikdash through imposing their self-serving political agenda. May the Alm-ghty accept the service of His true servants and forgive us for our personal and national sins. And may He protect my brother's sons from the evil that surrounds them.*

Monobaz continued to stare into the distance, mesmerized by the living "snow" before his eyes. As their journey progressed, they were joined by more people and livestock, until they finally arrived at the Chuldah Gate. Now the cacophony of human voices and bleating animals reached a crescendo.

Before passing through to the Har Habayis, Monobaz and Moshe immersed themselves in one of the many *mikva'os* available to the *olei regel*. Then they dressed and removed their shoes. There was little conversation as the pair slowly made their way to the *Azarah*. Suddenly, a middle-aged man broke out in a heartfelt melody.

"Mah ashiv laHashem, kol tagmulohi alai… How can I repay Hashem for all of the kindness He has bestowed upon me?"[5] His deep voice was joined by another voice and then another, until the sweet, lilting melody filled the courtyard.

The *olei regel* were so tightly packed together that it was nearly impossible to see more than a few *tefachim*[6] ahead, making the anticipation of what they were soon to witness even greater.

"Moshe, you are gifted at mathematics," Monobaz said to his nephew. "Mar Amram told me that, just a few years ago, King Agrippa watched the people bringing their *Korban Pesach*. He reported that the animals numbered twice the number of Jews who left Egypt![7] Tell me, if

---

5 These words from *Tehillim* 116 would be sung by the *levi'im* during the offering of the *Korban Pesach* and again that evening at the Seder as part of the Hallel prayer.

6 A measure of length equal to approximately three or four inches.

7 *Pesachim* 64b.

there are 1.2 million sheep that must be slaughtered and offered before sunset, how many need to be slaughtered each hour?"

Moshe furrowed his brow in concentration.

"Well, Uncle," he said slowly, "on a weekday other than Friday, the *afternoon Korban Tamid* is slaughtered at seven and a half hours and offered at eight and a half hours into the day, about two and a half hours past noon.[8] That leaves about three and a half hours until sunset, so that would mean over 340,000 per hour! I never thought about it this way before. It's incredible to think that anyone's hands could move so quickly, let alone those of so many *kohanim* working together!"

"That's right, Moshe," Monobaz agreed. "A person depending on his own physical abilities could not possibly accomplish the task. Hashem provides Divine assistance every Erev Pesach to enable us all to fulfill the mitzvah!"

"What time is it, Uncle?" Moshe asked. He was beginning to feel disoriented among the huge crowds.

"One hour before noon," the prince responded, gazing at the sundial hanging on a nearby building. "We have time to offer the *Korban Chagigah* and hopefully to still be included in the first of the three shifts for the *Korban Pesach*."

As the two made their way from the *Ezras Nashim* to the *Ezras Yisrael*, they were spellbound by the scene they confronted. At the center of frenetic activity was the majestic *Mizbe'ach*, its stones sparkling white after being freshly plastered in honor of the *chag*.[9] Thousands of *kohanim* were working at breakneck speed, slaughtering animals, carrying the blood, applying it to the base of the *Mizbe'ach*, flaying and cutting up the meat. Other *kohanim* hurried up and down the main ramp of the altar.[10] As Moshe observed the scene, he turned to his uncle, a puzzled look on his face.

---

8   *Pesachim*, mishnah 5:1.
9   *Middos*, mishnah 3:4.
10 Yaakov Meir Strauss, *Three Special Days* (New York: Feldheim, 2003), 151.

"Why are some of the *kohanim* eating meat while standing among their brethren, who are performing the *avodah*?" he asked.

"I can understand your bafflement, Moshe," Monobaz answered, "but these *kohanim* are performing their task, just as the others are. They are required to eat the sacrificial meat within a certain period of time. They may not sit, because only kings from the House of David are permitted to sit in the *Azarah*."[11]

One of the *kohanim* beckoned Monobaz and Moshe to come forward to offer the *Korban Chagigah*. Monobaz leaned his hands on the lamb's head and thanked Hashem for bringing him to Yerushalayim to offer *korbanos* in honor of Pesach. Moshe looked on, astonished, when his uncle then checked his knife, recited the blessing over *shechitah* and slaughtered the lamb with a firm stroke. Although he knew that it was preferable for the one bringing a *korban* to slaughter it, he had no idea that his uncle had learned how to perform *shechitah*. Restraining himself from blurting out questions, Moshe merely flashed a quick smile of admiration at his uncle, since any speech unrelated to the *avodah* was forbidden in the Mikdash.

After all steps of the *Korban Chagigah* were completed, Monobaz and Moshe exited the Beis Hamikdash, carrying the meat of the *Korban Chagigah* that would be their meal that night and still leading the lamb that would become the *Korban Pesach*.

"Uncle, please tell me, who taught you how to do *shechitah*?" Moshe asked, the words tumbling out quickly.

"Last Pesach, I decided that, with G-d's help, I wanted to *shecht* my own *korbanos* this year. I approached Reb Ovadiah, the only *shochet* in Arbela, and asked him to teach me the *halachos* and the method of *shechitah*, which he so graciously and patiently did. I didn't want to tell anyone, lest I did not feel prepared to go through with it, so you are the first to know, Moshe."

---

11 *Yoma* 96b.

"Mazel tov, Uncle, on your great accomplishment! May I be *zocheh* to walk in your footsteps."

"The footsteps you take will be your own, my dear nephew," Monobaz quipped. "Just remember that you're never too old to learn new things."

Suddenly, the people around them began to look upward, and a collective "Aaahh" could be heard gaining volume.

"It must be the end of the fifth hour," Moshe observed, his voice tense. "See, Uncle, the second of the two loaves has been removed from the roof of the Temple portico. It is now forbidden to own *chametz*."

Monobaz nodded. "Let us find some shade to rest awhile. It will be another three and a half hours before the afternoon *Tamid* is offered. Then it will be time to await our turn to offer the *Korban Pesach*. We must conserve our strength."

"Yes, Uncle," Moshe replied. "I have not had a moment to think of feeling hunger, but I know that there is still a lot to accomplish today."

When it was time to pass once again from the plaza of the Har Habayis to the *Ezras Nashim* through the men's gate, Moshe contemplated what was occurring inside the walls of the Beis Hamikdash.

As many men as are here today, there are at least ten times the number present in Yerushalayim to celebrate Pesach! he thought incredulously.[12]

"Please follow me, Moshe!" Monobaz shouted above the din. "Let's stay here. It's much too crowded inside!"

Before long, the heavenly fragrance of the *ketores* wafted into the *Ezras Nashim*, and those present knew that the afternoon *Tamid* was nearing an end.

"*Tekiah! Teruah! Tekiah!*"

The blast of the shofar startled the crowd. The *levi'im* began to sing the first section of the *shir shel yom* for *Yom Sheini*. This was

---

12   The *chaburos*, or groups, that would assemble to eat the *Korban Pesach* that night included at least ten people, only one of whom needed to offer the *korban*.

punctuated by two sets of trumpet blasts, introducing the two other sections of the *mizmor*.[13] As if spontaneously, the doors leading to the *Azarah* opened, and the first shift to offer the *Korban Pesach* flowed into the Mikdash, like tributaries of a flowing river. Monobaz and Moshe were part of the throng.

Suddenly, a booming sound caused everyone to snap to attention.

"Who pushes the doors so that they all close at the same time, Uncle?" Moshe asked, wide-eyed.

"Mar Amram told me that no one stands at the doors," Monobaz answered. "The doors close without human intervention — it is none other than the Alm-ghty Himself Who causes the doors to close! This is only one of the miracles you will witness today. Look, the *avodah* is beginning. Come, we must join in to recite Hallel."

Adding their voices to the masses filling the *Azarah*, they sang and sang. Their spirits were carried higher and higher by the lilting sound of the repeated chanting of the songs of praise to Hashem.

"Look over there, Uncle!" Moshe gestured excitedly.

Their eyes were riveted to the eastern wall, where over one hundred *kohanim* and *levi'im* garbed in white linen robes stood on the three steps of the *duchan*. The ground in front of them was graced by a choir of young boys adding their sweet voices to those of the adults singing the Hallel, over and over, as the *korbanos* continued to be offered. The trumpets, flutes, lyres and harps created a sound so pure, so holy, that one could almost feel his soul soaring up to *Shamayim*. Those assembled joined in spontaneously.

There was little time to reflect before Monobaz realized that his turn had come. He trembled as he came forward to offer his *Korban Pesach*. His face took on a look of intense concentration, as he focused on fulfilling the mitzvah consistent with the will of Hashem. Like the sin offering, any foreign thoughts while offering the *korban* would render it invalid, carrying a punishment of *kares*.

---

13   *Tamid*, mishnah 7:3.

The long trumpet blasts of "*Tekiah!*" followed by the staccato blasts of "*Teruah!*" and a final "*Tekiah!*" brought everyone's attention to the frenetic activity of the *avodah*. The *kohanim* stood in no fewer than 126 lines.[14] Some of them held gold vessels, while others held silver vessels.

The *kohen* slaughtering the animal would fill a silver or golden cup with blood before quickly passing the animal back to its owner. The *kohanim* would then pass these cups from hand to hand down a long row, for a mitzvah performed by many gives more honor to Hashem than one performed by few. This continued until the full cup reached the *kohen* at the end of the line standing near the altar. He would have the privilege of pouring the blood at the base of the *Mizbe'ach*. This process was repeated, as the *kohen* received cup after cup filled with blood.[15]

Moshe could see beads of perspiration form on his uncle's forehead as he again prepared himself to perform the *shechitah*.[16] He watched carefully as his uncle crouched in front of a *kohen* and slaughtered his sheep. Monobaz watched as the blood sped down the row of *kohanim*, until he felt Moshe tap on his shoulder. Now he had to quickly prepare the *korban* to be sacrificed.

"Look, Uncle," Moshe pointed excitedly. "I see a pair of hooks along the southern corner of the *Azarah*!"

"Very good," Monobaz replied with a smile. "Let us head there to perform the flaying."

They were fortunate to find unused hooks protruding from the walls of the *Azarah*, where they could remove the lamb's skin. Others would need to flay the lamb on thin, smooth poles held on the shoulders of two men.

The two of them cleaned and removed certain internal parts of the

---

14   Yaakov Meir Strauss, *Three Special Days*, 195.
15   *Yalkut Me'am Loez, Shemos A*, 151.
16   It was preferable, although not required, for the owner of the *korban* to perform the slaughtering.

animal[17] and placed them on a special tray. They gave it to a waiting *kohen*, who offered them on the *Mizbe'ach*, one *Korban Pesach* at a time.[18]

The offering of the *Korban Pesach* was now complete, and all that remained was for Monobaz and Moshe to wrap the skin around the lamb's carcass and tie it to a pole that they would hoist onto their shoulders. Moshe buckled briefly under the combined weight of the animal and the meat of the *Korban Chagigah* that the two carried in large sacks on their backs.[19]

Suddenly, Moshe's eyes widened. He turned to Monobaz, startled.

"Look over there, Uncle! Who are those menacing-looking people?"

As Monobaz looked up, his face tensed. Roman soldiers had stationed themselves around the Temple courtyard and in its halls. He was not alone in his feeling of discomfort. The ominous presence of the soldiers visibly put the *olei regel* on edge and marred the otherwise festive mood that usually accompanied the bringing of the *Korban Pesach*. A low murmur gradually gained volume, as angry words of protest were hurled at the foreign troops.

"Ignore them," one man murmured. "We know that to provoke them would be unwise. May Hashem protect all who come to serve Him during the festival, and may there be no violence to sadden our holy days."

Monobaz and Moshe silently exited the Har Habayis, trying to forget the scene they had just witnessed. Before long, they were making their way along the streets of the Ophel. Now that the *chag* was so near, preparations had reached a high pitch.

---

17 Called *emurim*, these comprised the kidneys, liver, tail, and their associated fats.
18 *Kitzur Hilchos Pesach*, Pesachim 58a.
19 The *Korban Pesach* would be roasted whole that evening and served at the Seder, after the meat of the festival offering was consumed. No bone could be broken in the process of roasting or eating the *korban*. The identity of the sheep, once worshipped by the Egyptians, must be recognizable to all. The holiness of the *Korban Pesach* required that it be eaten when one was satiated, as a remembrance of the great miracles Hashem performed for His people in Egypt.

Inside the palace, too, the atmosphere was frenetic. Not only was the royal household readying itself for the *chag*, but the many guests who had been taken in as lodgers were preparing for their own Sedarim as well. Yehudah and Yaakov were the first to spot the prince and Moshe approaching.

"Reuven, Yosef, they're back!" they shouted excitedly. Their older brothers were busy looking out for poor *olei regel* to invite for the *chag*.

"Yes, they're here!" Reuven cheered. "Come, let us greet them!"

The four boys walked as quickly as they could toward their uncle and Moshe, intercepting them about a quarter of a *mil*[20] down the road. Helene had instructed them never to run, unless it was to do a mitzvah. They were sons of the King of kings, and must behave at all times with decorum.

The boys quickly took positions on either side of the pole and helped support the *Korban Pesach* the rest of the way home. As soon as they arrived at the palace, Monobaz and Moshe stoked the large oven in the courtyard used exclusively for the Pesach holiday. Minutes later, the *Korban Pesach* was placed inside the oven on a spit with those internal organs that had not been offered on the *Mizbe'ach* piled at its end. There it would remain until all the parts were completely roasted. Then it would be taken into the palace carefully, so that no bone would be broken, to be stored until it was needed for the Seder that night.

Queen Helene smiled as she surveyed the massive soup kitchen hall, where the neighborhood poor would celebrate the Seder. Low, round tables were set for five massive *chaburos* of one hundred people each. Partitions comprised of large pottery vessels separated each group from the other, as required by halachah.[21] She closed her eyes and imagined the sight and sounds of five hundred celebrants retelling the story of the Exodus from Egypt.

---

20   A *mil* is equivalent to about 0.7 miles.
21   *Pesachim*, mishnah 7:13.

Tonight, these indigent Jews will feel like kings, she mused, before bustling off to ensure that her guests had everything they needed. She checked with the laundrywomen to see that each family had been given linens and water, and with the kitchen staff to make sure they would have enough matzah and *maror*. The sun was sinking low in the sky before the queen returned to her chambers to dress prior to lighting the Yom Tov candles.

The telling of the story of the Exodus from Egypt took on a special poignancy that evening, as the royal family sat down to their Seder with Amram, Rivka, and their family. The palace staff made up the other members of their *chaburah*. Monobaz recited Kiddush with great intensity, and all present, besides for the queen, drank the first of the four cups.[22] No one looked at Helene while drinking, not wanting to add to the pain that refraining from this mitzvah caused the queen.

Before long, it was time for nine-year-old Yaakov to stand and recite the Four Questions.

"*How is this night different from all other nights?*

For on all other nights we eat both chametz *and matzah, while on this night, only matzah.*

For on all other nights, we eat all types of vegetables, while on this night, we eat maror.

For on all other nights we do not dip our vegetables even once, but on this night, we dip them twice.

For on all other nights we eat meat that is roasted or baked, but on this night, only roasted meat."[23]

---

22 Since drinking the four cups of wine on Pesach is a rabbinic requirement, and the vow of *nezirus* is a Torah obligation, a *nazir* may not drink the four cups of wine. There is a disagreement between the Rivan, Rabbi Yehudah ben Nasan, son-in-law of Rashi, and *Tosafos* as to whether this exemption applies when the first night of Pesach falls on Shabbos, in which case reciting Kiddush is a Torah obligation. The Rivan says the *nazir* is obligated in Kiddush on wine, while *Tosafos* says that the part of Kiddush that is on wine is *d'Rabbanan*, and so the *nazir* would not need to drink (*Nazir* 4a).

23 Today, we substitute the question: "For on all other nights we sit among those who

Before Monobaz could answer, Reuven stood up, looking disturbed.

"Uncle and esteemed guests," he began. "I respectfully request to ask yet another question.

"On all other nights, the Har Habayis and the Beis Hamikdash are sanctified for the service of Hashem by the Jews. Why is it that on this night, pagan Roman troops invade our holy precincts?"

Reuven sat down, deflated. A sensitive lad, the import of his question seemed to sap him of his strength. Silence overcame the *chaburah* for several moments, while Monobaz sat deep in thought. Finally, he looked at Reuven and addressed him as if there were no others in the room.

"Yours is a valid question, my son," Monobaz said. "But not all questions can be answered by us, because we are mere mortals. Nevertheless, I will share with you some of my own thoughts.

"*Hakadosh Baruch Hu* gave us the mitzvos for all time, to sanctify ourselves and bring us close to Him through their performance. He took us out of Mitzrayim, and we are no longer slaves. Yes, we are physically subjugated to the Romans, but our spirits are free. This is what we mean when we say in Shema that we love Hashem '*b'chol me'odecha.*' With every measure that Hashem metes out to you, every circumstance in which He places you, your goal is to love Him and serve Him using the unique abilities He gave you.[24] So, try to rid yourself of your anger, Reuven, and understand that everything He does is for our ultimate good."

Reuven remained silent, thinking about what his uncle had just said.

The Seder proceeded until its climax just prior to midnight, when the *Korban Pesach* was distributed to the assembled group and consumed. There was an expectant pause.

"Come, boys," Monobaz called to his nephews. "Follow me!"

---

are leaning and those who are sitting."

24 Harav Shimon Schwab, *Sefer Iyun Tefillah* (Brooklyn, New York: Mesorah Publications, Ltd., 2002), 242-243.

Together with the other members of the *chaburah*, they rose from their seats and exited the palace. The cool spring night air was refreshing. They walked quickly around the building, where a tall ladder rested. One by one, the group climbed the ladder until they reached the high, flat roof. Monobaz began to sing a traditional melody, and the group joined in.

Monobaz smiled at Amram and then grasped Yosef, Yehudah, and Yaakov's hands. He danced with them in a circle, beckoning the others to join. As their feet stomped rhythmically against the hard granite, their spirits soared with joy and thanks to the *Ribono shel Olam*.

From their high vantage point, they could see hundreds of men and boys standing on rooftops throughout the Ophel, singing and dancing, just as they were. In the distance was the Beis Hamikdash, its stones shining in the light of the full moon.

"May we always prove ourselves worthy of Hashem's mercy and salvation," Monobaz whispered to himself.

Pesach continued, its days infused with an atmosphere of quiet tension.

On the fourth day of the festival, the sun shone brightly as Monobaz, accompanied by Amram and his nephews, made his way to the Beis Hamikdash to offer the *shalmei simchah*. As soon as they passed through the Chuldah Gate, Yehudah pointed excitedly to some tablets.

"Uncle, are those made of real gold?" he shouted above the din of the other *olei regel*.

Monobaz stopped as long as he could to admire the tablets, before the crowd pushed them further along.

"Yes, Yehudah, those are genuine gold tiles from the *Heichal*," Monobaz answered. "They have been temporarily peeled from the walls and put on display for the *olei regel* to see.²⁵ Isn't it wonderful that even though we're never allowed inside the *Heichal*, part of the *Heichal* is being brought to us!"

The group proceeded through the Eastern Gate, which brought them to the *Ezras Nashim*. From there, they passed through the Nikanor Gate to the *Azarah* of the Beis Hamikdash, where an even more spectacular sight awaited them. One group of *kohanim* was standing before the *Ulam* carrying the Menorah, and another group carried the *Shulchan*.

"Are we permitted to get any closer?" Moshe asked his uncle. "I thought only *kohanim* could stand between the *Mizbe'ach* and the *Ulam*."

"You are correct, Moshe," Monobaz replied. "In most cases, this is true, but the sages made an exception so that the masses can better appreciate the wonders of the Beis Hamikdash, thus glorifying the Name of Hashem."

Just then, the *kohanim* carrying the *Shulchan* announced to those assembled, "Behold, Israel, the constant miracles of the Alm-ghty! This *lechem hapanim* has remained on these open shelves since last Shabbos, and they are still as fresh as they were when they were baked! Behold, but do not touch the holy *Shulchan*, lest it become *tamei*!"²⁶

The crowd recoiled slightly at the stern warning but then gasped in awe as they saw the fresh loaves, together with the *Shulchan* and the exquisite Menorah. After a short while, the *kohanim* retreated behind the curtain covering the entrance of the *Heichal*, but the spectacle still had not come to an end. Other *kohanim* emerged, bearing additional vessels used in the Beis Hamikdash.

In all, ninety-three vessels were displayed to the awestruck onlookers. The boys watched wide-eyed, trying to take in everything at once.

---

25   *Pesachim* 57a.
26   Rambam, *M'tamei Mishkav U'moshav* 11:11, as quoted in Israel Ariel, *Carta's Encyclopedia of the Beis Hamikdash B'Yerushalayim* (Carta: Yerushalayim, 2005), 247.

They fired questions at their uncle, wanting to identify each item and its use. Toward the end of the presentation, the vessels used in the Yom Kippur *avodah* were brought forth.

"Uncle, didn't you donate golden handles and bases for these vessels?" Yosef asked.

"Yes," Monobaz replied. "May their use bring atonement for us and for all of Klal Yisrael!"

After offering his *shalmei simchah* with great joy, Monobaz and the boys left the precincts of the Beis Hamikdash, elated by their experience.

As they descended the Har Habayis, they could hear a low rumble of conversation that was gradually turning into a roar. Rumor had it that an abominable act of desecration had been committed by one of the soldiers within the holy sanctuary of the Beis Hamikdash. Outrage spread from one Jew to another like a bonfire.

"Cumanus, you pig!" a group of young men shouted at the Roman procurator in charge of the Holy Land. "No human soldiers would agree to serve you, so you resorted to hiring beasts!"

"Such idiocy betrays your Emperor!"

As if their shouts were the cue he was waiting for, the procurator commanded his soldiers to encircle the northern side of the Har Habayis, in the vicinity of the Antonia Fortress.[27]

"The *olei regel* are likely to stampede!" Amram shouted. "They will be afraid that the troops will storm the Temple. I don't think Cumanus would be so foolish as to do such a thing, but this could still lead to a riot. Let's pray that there will be no casualties. Hurry, follow me!"

Monobaz quickly grabbed Yaakov's hand and slipped into a side street leading toward the palace. The other boys followed right behind them. As they ran through the still deserted streets, an old man sat weeping in front of a small house.

---

27 Rabbis Nosson Scherman and Meir Zlotowitz, general editors, *History of the Jewish People: The Second Temple Era* (Brooklyn, New York: Mesorah Publications, Ltd., in conjunction with Hillel Press, 1982), 159.

"Can we help you, sir?" Monobaz stopped to inquire.

"Only Hashem can help me!" the man groaned. "I lost my father and older brother forty years ago, when Herod's son, Archelaus, massacred three thousand of our people on Erev Pesach,[28] and I just can't bear to see it happen again. In the *zechus* of our peace offerings, may *Hakadosh Baruch Hu* have mercy on us!"

No sooner had the man finished speaking than they heard a rumbling sound akin to thunder.

"Hurry, the stampede has begun!" Amram shouted.

The scene was horrific. *Olei regel*, who just moments before had been in a state of exaltation as they offered their *korbanos*, were now fleeing for their lives. Anyone who stumbled and fell was quickly trampled upon in the great panic that ensued. Amram, who was as familiar with the side streets of Yerushalayim as the back of his hand, pulled the prince and his nephews quickly around a corner into an alley that had not yet been discovered by the hysterical crowd. From there, he led them through a maze of back streets and passageways until they arrived, breathless, at the palace.

Word of the tumult had already reached Helene. She rushed to greet Amram and her family with tears in her eyes.

"*Baruch Hashem*, you have returned!" She sighed. "I am fearful that not all of our brethren will be as fortunate! We must act quickly to help in any way we can!"

"Mother, Amram and I will begin preparing those trampled to death for burial," Monobaz said. "Perhaps we can open an infirmary in the lower level of the palace for the wounded."

"Of course!" Helene replied, clearly distraught. "Moshe, please find the fabric dealer and ask if he will open his store for us. We'll need to purchase clean cotton strips for bandages. Reuven, please start boiling pots of hot water for cleaning wounds."

---

28 Rabbis Nosson Scherman and Meir Zlotowitz, general editors, *History of the Jewish People: The Second Temple Era*, 140.

The palace was quickly transformed into a hospital ward, with both guests as well as family members surrendering their mattresses to the injured. Helene had to remain outside the "hospital" due to the potential for coming in contact with the dead. In her place, Chava worked tirelessly as a nurse. As she tended to a young man, wracked with the pain of broken bones, she could hear him whispering the Shema. Tears streamed down the young girl's face.

Prayer vigils were organized around the clock for the recovery of the wounded. Nevertheless, the fifth day of Chol Hamoed witnessed funeral after funeral for victims of the riot.

So did the inhabitants of Yerushalayim observe the remainder of Pesach that year.

"Uncle, why don't we just fight against the Romans and get rid of them?" Yosef asked, despondent.

"That is a good question, my clever nephew," Monobaz answered sadly. "We must be morally worthy before Hashem will enable us to prevail in war. The sages do not believe that we are in such a position of spiritual strength. I hope the situation changes quickly — or who knows where these events will lead us?"

Chapter Twenty

King Abia relaxed on the silk-covered couch in his throne room as servants fanned him. He was just closing his eyes when a knock on the door interrupted his rest.

"Your Majesty," the chief steward announced, a look of consternation on his face, "this missive was just delivered to the palace by an unfamiliar messenger claiming to hail from Adiabene. He sped off before he could be questioned further."

King Abia pursed his lips. As king of Arabia, the noblemen of Adiabene considered him an ally against King Izates, whose political successes only exacerbated the hatred they felt toward him.

In spite of past failures, they now had a plan that would surely allow them to take revenge on their wayward relative. King Abia, however, recognized Izates's talents and strength and was very wary of him. He fumbled for the scroll and unrolled it nervously.

To His Royal Majesty, King Abia:

It is no doubt well known to King Abia that since the death of Monobaz I, the country of Adiabene is now ruled by Izates, his son. The king may be less familiar with the great affront to our country's traditions that has been perpetrated by our new ruler. Surely, the king, who respects not only your nation's indigenous gods, but also our own, will sympathize with our plight.

It seems that the new king, while still crown prince, traded his nation's customs and faith for that of a small, despised minority. Not content with his private heretical beliefs, this descendant of generations of loyal followers of Zoroaster went as far as to have the self-mutilating circumcision ritual performed on him in order to be considered a full-fledged member of the Jewish faith.

Not only is this treacherous act an insult to us, it presents a threat to our populace from outside. Is it not true that a country must surely be weakened when its ruler follows a ritual totally foreign to the vast majority of its populace? Indeed, such a situation could readily destabilize neighboring states as well!

As loyal patriots of the noble country of Adiabene, we appeal to you, dear king, to help us avoid the consequences to ourselves, as well as to your own people, of Izates's persistent kingship. Our proposal is the following: Your Highness, backed by your valiant soldiers of Arabia, would launch a military expedition against King Izates for which we would forward you the vast sum of one hundred thousand talents of gold. Furthermore, only minimal risk to the king's troops would be posed by such a campaign.

At the approach of your army, a pre-arranged signal will be passed through our camp, resulting in mass mutiny and desertion of Adiabene's army. In this way, we will communicate in no uncertain terms to our "king" that his religion is not compatible with his leadership of our nation. Inflicting such a punishment on Izates will give us, the spat-upon noblemen of the realm, much satisfaction and support. You, King Abia, will achieve great fame for restoring the honor of our Zoroastrian faith to the realm. At the same time, your treasuries will be augmented handsomely.

Signed with great respect and esteem for the exalted King of Arabia, with our heartfelt desire that you carry out this plan posthaste,

The noblemen of Adiabene

A smug smile spread across King Abia's face. Lazy by nature and upbringing, he could be motivated to act swiftly and decisively by the lure of even more luxury and honor.

The king hastily convened an emergency meeting of his top officers, who waited with anticipation and some trepidation to be informed of the latest desires of their impulsive leader. Abia entered the room with pomp, followed by a retinue of servants carrying personal effects, ranging from the king's pipe to his Siamese cat that was always at his side. The chief steward struck the large conference table with a leather mallet to call everyone to order.

"Gentlemen!" the king bellowed. "I have just been informed of a great threat from the kingdom to our north. Assemble the troops! We are going to war against King Izates of Adiabene!"

"If I may inquire of His Majesty," Omar, the chief of staff, began deferentially, "for what wrongdoing is King Izates deserving of attack?"

"He has betrayed his people by delegitimizing their religion and demeaning them in the process!" Abia bellowed self-righteously. "Izates is not worthy of carrying the mantle of his deceased father and must be deposed!"

"Yes, my king, of course you are correct," the chief of staff agreed. "But Izates still enjoys a high level of popularity among his people, and he is a clever strategist. His defeat may come at a significant cost to us."

"Fear not, Omar," King Abia reassured the official. "We have allies on the inside to help assure our quick victory. I anticipate that our goal will be easy to accomplish."

The meeting adjourned, and the king's cabinet bowed to the recumbent king and exited amid low murmurs and head-shaking.

Only several weeks later, King Abia brought a mighty army into the field of battle not far from Adiabene and prepared to launch a fierce campaign against King Izates.

Fortunately, Izates had been given warning of the impending attack, and he was ready with his troops to respond to the first assault. He had spent the previous day fasting and praying for salvation from the dangers of war — for his troops and for himself. Now he was ready to defend his country and his honor.

He could see the enemy approaching over a far hill in the distance. It was time to mount an offense.

"Charge!" Izates ordered.

Instantly, the infantry began to drive their steeds at breakneck speed toward the enemy, churning up dust in massive clouds that resembled a tornado.

The war had begun!

Then, inexplicably, just a few minutes after the start of the stampede, the noblemen, who comprised the front guard of Izates's soldiers, seemed to be stricken by sudden panic. They reined in their horses and, turning their backs on the fast-approaching enemy, fled!

Izates, who had been traveling at the head of his troops, quickly perceived what had occurred and returned to camp, mercifully shielded by the Alm-ghty and accompanied by his faithful officers and servants. He entered his tent purposefully, followed by his chief military advisors. Izates conducted a strategy meeting for one hour and then dismissed his advisors with a wave of his hand.

Once he was sure that he was truly alone, Izates reached for a leather bag beside the table and withdrew a small scroll. It was the book of *Tehillim*, specially written to accompany the king on the battlefield. He opened it to chapter 22, the psalm said by Queen Esther before she was to appeal to King Achashveirosh to save her people. Izates recited it and then sat for a long time, deep in meditation. What he was about to do was totally out of character with his peace-seeking nature. Nevertheless, he was compelled to act for the sake of the people who depended upon him to rule and protect them. He rose heavily from his chair and again summoned his officers.

"Within the next six hours, I want the names of every one of the individuals who deserted me today," Izates demanded. "By dawn, I expect to hear that they have been executed. We will resume the battle tomorrow."

The next day, Izates surprised the enemy with his rapid return to the battlefield, slew the majority of them, and forced the remainder to flee for their lives. King Abia was forced into the Arsamus fortress, which Izates promptly conquered. After plundering the fortress of its abundant contents, Izates returned to Adiabene, albeit without the vanquished King Abia, for once the latter perceived that he was surrounded, he took his own life.

In spite of the clear victory for Izates, the king could not feel totally vindicated. His rule was being challenged from within over and over again. Hashem had come to his aid, making him victorious in conflict after conflict and leaving his opponents wondering about the source of this Jewish king's resiliency.

But when would it ever end?

The following year,[1] Adiabene found itself once again enmeshed in conflict.

The surviving noblemen, not yet ready to abandon their coup, now approached Volgases, the new king of the Parthian empire. A courier was dispatched posthaste to Ctesiphon, the palatial seat of Parthia, where Volgases read with great interest the missive delivered to him. While similar in intent to the one directed to Abia, it was even more explicit in purpose, and clearly venomous in tone.

The noblemen of Adiabene demanded no less than the extermination of King Izates, expressing their deep hatred of him for abrogating the laws of their forefathers and abandoning their nation's customs. Volgases was invited to replace him with a potentate of his choice.[2]

---

1 This occurred in the year 51 CE.
2 Josephus, *Antiquities of the Jews*, 20:4.

"We have an opportunity to eliminate Izates," Volgases said aloud, to no one in particular. "But under what pretext can I wage war on him? Surely, there must be some valid reason." He thought for a few moments, and then his eyes lit up. Volgases stood up and began to pace the room. His mind churned rapidly as he ironed out the details of the plan. Izates would have one week to return the royal honors granted him by Volgases's father, Artabanus — including the right to wear the royal tiara upright and to sleep on a golden bed. If he refused, the entire army of Parthia would be summoned to bring him down.

Volgases clapped his hands loudly.

"Frahatak, bring the royal seal! Santruk, ready a messenger to leave immediately to King Izates in Arbela!"

Great clouds of dust spun above the road leading to the palace, as the horse was pushed to its limit. The pressure to arrive had been so great that the courier could barely catch his breath to announce that he bore a letter of vital importance from King Volgases of Parthia to King Izates.

As Izates read the scroll, his brow tensed and his face darkened.

"In truth," Izates mused, "these perquisites mean nothing to me, but I know that stripping me of them would have great symbolic impact. Out of responsibility to my citizens, I cannot accede to Volgases's demands. Even if I did return the favors, Volgases would not be appeased. I would lose either way." He sighed. "Better to be considered a defender of one's people than to be thought of as a coward. I place my trust in Hashem, my Protector. May He have mercy on me and the people of Adiabene!"

Once he made his decision, Izates quickly swung into action. Desiring his war preparations to remain secret for as long as possible, he summoned only Urud, his prime minister.

"What has happened?" Urud asked fearfully as he entered the study. "His Majesty's eyes look as if they are afire!"

"Urud, Volgases is readying to attack us," Izates responded grimly. "He could arrive in Adiabene within days. We must prepare quickly. I will escort Princess Samacha myself, and I ask you to instruct my other wives and children to pack their belongings to be ready for transport to the fortress.[3] Please prepare attendants for them and sufficient food to last one month. The corn should be put in storage in the citadels and locked up. The hay and grass must be set on fire. Hopefully, if there will be no food for the animals, the enemy's resolve will weaken more quickly. I will pitch my tent at the border of our province to wait for the enemy. Six thousand troops should be sufficient to convince Volgases that we are serious about defending ourselves."

The king of Parthia, accompanied by a great army of horsemen and infantry, arrived at the edge of Adiabene much more quickly than would have been expected. A messenger found Izates not far off with his army of six thousand horsemen and delivered an ominous threat to him.

A missive to Izates of Adiabene, from King Volgases of Parthia, the great empire that extends from the Euphrates to Bactria:

If you fail to heed this warning to surrender, you will be severely punished, as befits a person ungrateful to his lords. The G-d you worship is unable to deliver you from the king's hands.

Izates tried to hide the disgust he felt at Volgases's hubris. He summoned the court scribe to his tent and paused only briefly before dictating his response.

I, Izates of Adiabene, am aware that the power of the king of Parthia is much greater than my own. However, I am likewise aware that the power of the one G-d of the universe surpasses by far the power of all men. Thus, my actions must be dictated by what He would expect of me, and, so, as earthly ruler and protector of my people, I cannot surrender the privileges and authority given me by King Artabanus, your late father.

King Izates of Adiabene

---

[3] Izates left twenty-four sons and twenty-four daughters.

The Parthian courier took the rolled-up parchment from the scribe and quickly left the presence of the king to complete his mission, unaware of the import of the words he carried.

Izates waved his scepter, and the tent was cleared of all servants and advisors. Once alone, he was suddenly overcome by uncontrollable trembling. He threw himself upon the ground in desperate submission. When he finally rose, he scooped some ashes from the fire pit and smeared them prominently on his forehead. He then sent a messenger to the fortress to announce a fast for Princess Samacha, his other wives, and their children.

Izates sat down at his small work desk and reached for a leather sack filled with parchment scroll, as he did whenever he faced a military challenge. Withdrawing the scroll corresponding to *Sefer Bereishis*, he unrolled it to the Torah's account of Yaakov Avinu's preparations for his meeting with his brother Eisav. Izates then prostrated himself upon the tapestry covering the floor and cried out to Hashem to have mercy and to send him salvation. The thought of those dear to him facing risk of destruction brought tears to Izates's eyes, and he called out to Hashem in anguish.

"Oh, L-rd my King, the one and only G-d to Whose goodness I am totally committed, come now to my assistance and defend me from my enemies, not only on my account, but on account of their insolent behavior toward Your great power and authority, since they have not feared to lift up their arrogant tongue against You. For the sake of Your holy Name, I beg the Alm-ghty to put down their rebellion and save Your servant."[4]

Izates finally stood up but remained silent for a long time. Finally, he called to his chief aide, who was standing right outside the tent.

"Gershon, I am going to the fortress. No one must know that I have left the camp. Do you understand?"

---

4   Josephus, *Antiquities of the Jews*, 20:4.

The aide nodded obediently, confused and alarmed at the quick shift in events. Izates donned a disguise and slipped out of the camp, hidden by a moonless night.

When her husband entered her room, Samacha was alarmed by the distress on his face. She rushed to him.

"Dearest Izates, why have you come?" she cried out in panic. "What has happened to cause you such pain? Why do you wear ashes?"

"We are in grave danger," the exhausted king replied. "We must fast and pray that our merits outweigh our sins. I cannot tarry. With Hashem's help, you will be safe here, but I must return to my men."

Samacha tearfully bade her husband farewell. When he had gone, she collapsed to the floor, beseeching the Alm-ghty to protect him.

Izates returned to the camp and continued to pray, and, once again, Hashem saved him. That very night, Volgases received letters that made his expedition against King Izates impossible to implement. An opposition group, despising Volgases, and seeing that he had left the country for an extended period of time, laid waste to Parthia, forcing him to return home without engaging in battle!

Izates wrote to his mother, informing her of his great salvation from the brink of devastating war. Her reply arrived several weeks later. A particular section of the letter gave the king great encouragement.

You know, my son, I now realize how wrong I was in discouraging you from performing the mitzvah of bris milah *so long ago. This reflected a weakness in my own faith of which I am very ashamed. How could I have ever thought that you could be satisfied with the status of a* ger toshav? *How could I have thought that you would be satisfied to adopt only seven of the 613 mitzvos? Contrary to my expectations, the people of Adiabene expressed respect for you and your brother on account of your circumcision. That gratified me, but it merely reflected G-d's kindness, not a validation of the mitzvah. We must constantly ask ourselves, "What does the Alm-ghty want from us?" It is this and only this that must direct our actions.*

In spite of their ranting, the nobles truly care nothing of our religion one way or the other. Theirs is a power struggle, plain and simple. Our conversion merely gives them a pretext to usurp power from its rightful source. You must never yield to them, Izates. It will gain us nothing. I pray that Hashem have mercy on you and on all of His people always.

Your loving mother

"Amen!" the king exclaimed aloud upon finishing the letter.

Little did Izates know that war was being waged against his sons on a different front.

Moshe walked slowly along the cobblestone streets that led from the small *beis midrash* to the palace. He enjoyed these late night walks home and was glad his grandmother had agreed to allow him to dispense with an escort. As far as Moshe was concerned, he had left his royal status behind in Adiabene. He knew his father did not want him to return one day to become king, and Moshe preferred his role as yeshivah student to that of prince. These walks gave him time to ponder the fine points of the Torah he had been learning and to absorb the *kedushah* of the sleeping Yerushalayim. The moon was particularly bright that night, and he felt its presence like a spotlight accompanying him with every step.

Suddenly, his reverie was broken by a figure that moved toward him from the shadow of a building. It seemed almost as if the young man had been waiting for the prince to pass his way.

"Good evening, Moshe, son of Izates," the stranger said cordially. "My name is Shaul ben Gidon. I have heard so much about the prince and your family. If you don't mind, I'm going in the same direction as you are and can walk you home."

Moshe was leery of the youth, but his friendly confidence and refined demeanor set him at ease. Shaul was dressed in the simple robe and head covering of a Perushi, but he seemed to be hiding something.

"Please feel free to accompany me," Moshe replied a bit tentatively.

"Thank you!" Shaul replied heartily. "It would be a privilege to get to know you better."

Moshe nodded but remained silent.

After a few moments, Shaul again began to speak, this time quickly and with urgency in his voice. "Prince Moshe, I actually know quite a bit about you and your family, and I want to protect you from a very real danger that is brewing. I spy on the Romans for the Zealots, and I have found out that you and your family are being carefully watched."

Moshe looked directly into the youth's eyes, trying to hide the alarm he felt.

"Why are we of interest to the Romans?" he asked sharply.

"Although your father has avoided direct conflict with Rome, his negative sentiments toward the Empire are well known. Roman authorities are convinced that he has sent you to the Holy Land with your grandmother and brothers in order to prepare for an insurgency against them. Consequently, they have decided to make a pre-emptive strike against Adiabene and its king, to make an example of your homeland and discourage further rebellion."

How absurd an accusation! Moshe thought. *Surely they have no evidence of any insurrection or spying by any of us!*

Moshe wanted to shout at the youth, but remembered how the Torah stressed the importance of returning insult with silence.

Shaul believed Moshe was listening to him and continued. "The Romans are very nervous these days. They know they are tightening the noose around us, and that our patience is wearing thin. They don't need verified evidence to act, Moshe, but listen to me. I have a suggestion that will almost certainly avert disaster without any harm befalling you."

Moshe wanted to dismiss the youth, putting an end to his doomsaying, but something inside of him pushed him to listen further.

"Yes?" he said warily. "What do you suggest?"

"The best advice I can give you is to pretend to support them. If they think you're on their side, they will give you the royal treatment that is your due, and your father will be spared. In truth, you don't have to deal with the Romans at all. I have many contacts with Jews who are friendly with Roman officials. I can arrange a meeting with them, and they will take care of the rest."

Shaul paused, letting his words sink in. Moshe said nothing.

"Think about it, and meet me in front of the *beis midrash* tomorrow night at eight with your answer. Just be sure not to tell a soul about our conversation. Remember that the walls have ears."

Shaul bowed quickly and disappeared around a corner.

Moshe walked the rest of the way home, deep in thought. He believed that Shaul was trying to trap him, and he was unlikely to be acting on his own. Moshe's grandmother had warned him that such a thing could happen, and that she would help him if it did. He knew he could report the incident to her, but he was hesitant to do so.

I'm an adult, Moshe thought, *and it's my father's honor and safety that are at stake.*

By the time he reached the palace, he had made a decision.

Moshe left the *beis midrash* shortly before eight the next evening and began walking toward the corner where he had met Shaul the night before. The youth was waiting for him, and he gestured for Moshe to follow him down a dark alley. The two wound their way northward through the narrow streets of the Ophel until they reached the entrance to the Upper City. Shaul stopped in front of a large, well-lit stone house and knocked firmly. The door was opened by a man dressed in Roman garb, who appeared to be in his thirties. He ushered Shaul into the room and then turned to Moshe.

"Welcome, honored prince!" he greeted Moshe with exaggerated warmth. "It is so good to make your acquaintance! Please, come in and partake of some refreshments."

As Moshe stepped into the house, he was shocked to see a room filled with men speaking the Aramaic of the Jewish people but who were dressed like Roman aristocrats. He was immediately accosted by a group of three youths, who looked as if they had rehearsed for this moment.

"Prince Moshe," the oldest began, "we are so happy that you chose to join us tonight. Please take a seat on the couch over here. We are great admirers of the royal family, and in particular, your father, who is known as a mighty warrior and strategist in battle."

He smiled obsequiously, and Moshe felt sickened.

"We call our group the 'Friends of Rome,'" the man continued, oblivious to Moshe's reaction. "We pride ourselves in helping our people through our amiable connections with the Roman government. We know how much your family desires to help the Jews here in Eretz Yisrael, and we believe we hold the answer."

"Yes, Your Highness," added a short, stout man. He was dressed in a bright scarlet robe woven of fine wool. "The government greatly prizes your allegiance and is willing to pay for it. This is not to mention the obvious protection it would provide your father, King Izates, whose loyalties have been brought into question as of late."

"Becoming a member of our party also brings with it great honor to you and your brothers," added the third. "We appreciate those of royal blood, certainly more than the poor residents of the Ophel do."

Moshe seethed inside, disgusted to hear fellow Jews speak in such a despicable manner. He quickly composed himself and prepared to say the words he had mentally practiced over and over again.

"Thank you, gentlemen," he began, looking each of the three directly in the eye. "I appreciate your concern for the well-being of my family. However, I must decline membership in your political party. You see, as Jews, our sole loyalty is to Hashem and His Torah, as expounded by the rabbis. This loyalty is inconsistent with any affiliation with a group that looks to Rome for its salvation. As for my father, King Izates has been protected by the Alm-ghty until this day, and we pray daily for His continued protection. I speak for every member of the royal family of Adiabene and respectfully request that you refrain from contacting any of us again."

With those words, Moshe turned around and left the house. It wasn't until the next day that he saw his grandmother and informed her about the meeting.

"Moshe, you have acted appropriately," the queen reassured her grandson. "I think I know who is behind this lowly plot, and with Hashem's help, I believe it can be squelched. But please, continue to be careful."

The queen immediately penned a letter to Salome Miriamne.

Dear Giveret Salome Miriamne,

I hope that this letter finds you and your family well. During your visit to me, you graciously offered to help me in any way you could. I appreciated that offer and am calling upon you at this time with a humble request.

I am aware that you and your family have close connections with the Roman government. My son, King Izates, likewise has a peaceful relationship with Rome. You can surely understand that I was shocked to hear that there are Jews who have tried to blackmail my grandson into allying with the Friends of Rome in order to "protect his father from harm."

I ask you, Giveret, to use your considerable influence and connections to squelch this lowly plot. Again, my son has many friends in Rome. It would surely not be good for the perpetrators if this behavior were to be discovered.

I thank you in advance for your help in this matter.

Queen Helene of Adiabene

Salome Miriamne did not respond. Nevertheless, Helene was left feeling unsettled by this incident. It was clear that there were those within the Jewish people who would try to sacrifice the royal family for their own wicked purposes. If only the hatred would end!

Chapter Twenty-One

As the twelfth of Av in the year 52 CE dawned in the north of Eretz Yisrael, the sunbaked earth greeted another day that would feature blazing sunshine and a cloudless sky.

As soon as it was just bright enough for one man to recognize another, hundreds of *olei regel* began to stream like the Jordan River over hills and through valleys and desert toward Yerushalayim, bringing their *bikkurim* to the Beis Hamikdash. Oxen crowned by wreaths of flowers led numerous parades, followed by men, women, and children riding on donkeys, camels, and horses, as well as traveling by foot. Young boys danced as they blew lilting melodies from handmade flutes and shook tambourines rhythmically.

Once it was fully light, Monobaz viewed the activity with great joy from his vineyard in Gush Chalav. He had arrived several days earlier with all five of his nephews to supervise the harvest and prepare for the journey to Yerushalayim. This was an entirely new experience for him. His native Adiabene was nearly devoid of agriculture. The mountainous terrain was more suited for cattle- and sheep-grazing than the cultivation of grains and fruit trees.

Shortly after his arrival in the Holy Land, the prince had consulted with Amram ben Be'iri as to the best place to purchase a vineyard and orchards. Amram had directed him to the far northwest of the country, the land that had been originally granted to the tribe of Asher.¹ This land was known for its fertility and particularly for its fruitful olive trees, whose silver leaves shimmered in the sunlight. Monobaz had followed his advice and purchased the tract five years ago, and, *b'chasdei Hashem*, he was now reaping bountiful crops. The previous year, he had taken the fruit to eat in Yerushalayim, and this would be the first year that his fruit was permitted to eat anywhere, after the *bikkurim* were brought to the Beis Hamikdash.

For a few moments, the prince allowed himself to be mesmerized by the beautiful display of pageantry, but he quickly shifted his gaze from the horizon to the lush vines before him. Monobaz scrutinized the dark purple clusters of large ripe grapes for several minutes, a look of deep concentration upon his face. Then his face relaxed, and he looked up with a broad smile and a twinkle in his eye.

"Moshe, Reuven! Come here, please!" he called excitedly. Nineteen-year-old Moshe, who had been feeding the donkeys in preparation for their long journey, was the first to arrive at his uncle's side. His eyes followed his uncle's finger to a spot deep within the thick vine.

"Now, watch me!" Monobaz instructed.

His hand disappeared inside a thick set of branches and emerged with a beautiful cluster of grapes that looked different from the others. Wrapped around the fruits, like a ribbon plaited around a girl's braids, was a string fashioned from pliant grass that he had tied around this first cluster to ripen several weeks before. This procedure was continued repeatedly for a number of hours, as *bikkurim* were harvested from the rest of the grapes, as well as the pomegranates and olives.

"Why are there so many first fruits, Uncle?" Yosef asked. "Must we bring so many to Yerushalayim?"

"That is a good question, Yosef," Monobaz answered. "There is no

---

1 Moshe Rabbeinu blessed the tribe of Asher before his passing, saying, *"Blessed with sons is Asher, he shall be pleasing to his brothers, and dip his foot in oil"* (Devarim 33:24).

required amount of fruit to bring as *bikkurim*, but there is likewise no limit."[2]

Just then, seventeen-year-old Reuven emerged from the small house Monobaz had built for his visits to his fields. In his arms was a large straw basket gilded with gold.

"Excellent, Reuven!" Monobaz carefully placed the grapes in the basket.

Eleven-year-old Yaakov, who had been making trips to the nearby communal well to fill jugs with water for their trip, looked up from his task and noticed the basket of grapes glittering in the bright rays of the noontime sun.

"It's so beautiful, Uncle!" he exclaimed. "Is the basket a present to the *kohen* as well as the fruits within it?"

"A good question, Yaakov," Monobaz answered thoughtfully. "For people like us, the answer is no. The Torah says, *Each man according to the portion Hashem has allotted him*. In our case, the golden basket is intended for *hiddur mitzvah*. After being emptied of its fruit, it will be returned to us by the *kohen*. For our brethren of modest means, the modest basket holding their *bikkurim* is considered part of their offering, and it will become an additional gift to the *kohen*.

"Now I will race you to the pomegranate orchard," Monobaz challenged his nephews with a smile. "Let's see which one of you can find the first fruits that ripened!"

"I see them!" Yehudah announced. He stared down the hill at the verdant trees bedecked with bright red fruit hanging like bells from strong branches. "I hope Uncle did not tie the *bikkurim* with red string!"

"You don't think you're up for the task, my dear nephew?" Monobaz quipped.

In response, both Yehudah and Yaakov raced down the hill, determined expressions on their young faces. Monobaz followed Moshe, who carried a wooden ladder.

---

2   *Pe'ah*, mishnah 1:1.

"Uncle?" Moshe said.

"Yes, Moshe," Monobaz answered.

"I learned a halachah yesterday that brings me much joy."

Monobaz smiled. "Please share it with me!"

"It seems that we, as *geirim*, are permitted to recite the declaration of *vidui bikkurim*, even though it speaks of the Land that Hashem promised to give to our forefathers. My *rebbi* explained that since Avraham was the father of many nations, converts can trace their lineage to him, as well, but it is not the same for *ma'aser*.[3] We see that for *bikkurim*, the Torah speaks about the Land that Hashem swore *to give* to us. These words imply that in the future, *geirim* will also be given a portion in the Land. About *ma'aser*, the Torah states, 'the Land that Hashem *gave* us.' Since converts were not given land when the children of Israel entered Eretz Yisrael, they do not say the *vidui ma'aser*."[4]

"You are right to be happy about this, Moshe!" Monobaz replied, proud of his nephew's growing knowledge of Torah. "It makes me very happy, too!"

"I've found two pomegranates for *bikkurim*!" Yaakov announced with glee.

"Good work!" Monobaz praised him. "Add them to the basket!"

"Now, Yosef," he continued, "you'll collect the olives, and Moshe will take care of the figs."

Monobaz watched his nephews busy at work. His heart was filled with joy but also tinged with sadness.

If only my brother could see for himself how his sons perform mitzvos and quote words of Torah! They are becoming scholars and are yirei Shamayim! *What happiness it would bring him to see this firsthand! Surely it would make the great burdens of state he bears feel lighter!*

---

3   Rambam, *Hilchos Bikkurim* 4:3. Others differ with this opinion.

4   *Kapos Tamarim*, as quoted by Yissachar Dov Rubin, *Talilei Oros* (Israel, 1997), *Devarim* 2, 105-106.

As the firstborn, I should have been the one to remain at the helm of the government of Adiabene. But instead, Hashem chose to bestow the crown on my younger brother. This I cannot change. But to be a surrogate father to my nephews, to supervise their education and guide their lives — this I can do most diligently and happily!

"Moshe, Yosef, Reuven!" Monobaz called. "Please come help me assemble the provisions! It's a three-day trip back to Yerushalayim. We'll need lots of water and food for the road!"

"Will we take animals along for the *korbanos* as well, Uncle?" Yosef asked hopefully.

"No, I'm afraid not, Yosef," Monobaz replied gently, knowing the boy would be disappointed. "We can purchase those in Yerushalayim, but we'll join our neighbors who are bringing their oxen, goats, sheep, and doves in the procession to the Beis Hamikdash, so there will be no shortage of four-footed and winged company."

"Do you mean that we will travel with the residents of many other cities?" Yaakov asked excitedly.

"Yes," Monobaz said. "The more Jews who travel together to the Beis Hamikdash, the more Hashem's Name is glorified.

"But enough questions for now!" he said, smiling. "We must ready our belongings and the *bikkurim* for the long trip. We are set to leave with our neighbors at dawn tomorrow morning. Boys, let's get to work!"

By nightfall, Monobaz and his nephews had filled the basket with grapes, pomegranates, figs, olives, and dates, representing five of the fruits of the seven species by which Eretz Yisrael is praised.

"You have done an excellent job, boys!" Monobaz commended his nephews. "Next year, I hope to acquire barley and wheat fields. It is my dream to bring *bikkurim* from each of the seven species that represent Hashem's great bounty in the Holy Land. Then, we will be able to start bringing *bikkurim* in time for the festival of Shavuos, when the grains are ripe, instead of having to wait until the summer for the fruits."

"If you do that, Uncle," Yehudah piped up, "can I use the scythe and tie the sheaves?"

"Let's discuss it next year, Yehudah," Monobaz suggested. "But since you've been such a help this year, I'm giving you the first ride on our new donkey!"

"Oh, thank you, Uncle!" he exclaimed.

After the younger boys had gone to sleep, Monobaz and Moshe stepped outside the tent to enjoy the cool night breeze and crystal-clear sky twinkling with stars.

"Uncle," Moshe said, his voice barely above a whisper.

"Yes, my nephew," Monobaz answered softly, as if reluctant to disturb the still of the night. "What is on your mind?"

"Tu B'Av is not only the day we hope to offer our *bikkurim* in Yerushalayim," Moshe said, sounding a bit hesitant. "It is also a day designated for finding marriage partners. Uncle, I am nineteen years old, and I believe I am ready to marry."

Monobaz smiled warmly and met his nephew's gaze. "I agree, Moshe. You have grown and matured into a true *ben Torah*. Of course, a *talmid chacham* must have a wife worthy of him. I have perhaps been delinquent in not addressing this matter sooner, but I wanted to wait until you approached me yourself. I will have to give the matter serious thought."

"Uncle," Moshe said shyly, "I have already thought about it, and I know whom I desire to marry."

Surprised by this unexpected revelation, Monobaz was silent for a moment.

"So, Moshe," he finally said, raising his eyebrows. "Who is this girl who has won your favor?"

"Chava, Grandmama's adopted daughter. She accompanied Grandmama to the Holy Land after insisting that she would become a Jewess upon her arrival." Moshe's voice grew more determined. "I have heard Grandmama praise her piety, kindness, and modesty on many occasions. These are the *middos* our rabbis have instructed us to look for in a prospective wife."

"You choose well, Moshe," Monobaz agreed. "Chava is a true *bas Yisrael*. Your grandmother has taught her to perform all of the *halachos* pertinent to a Jewish woman, and she has told me that the girl has a pure heart and learns quickly. I hear that she is also a gifted seamstress and a talented cook."

"So, then, you approve, Uncle?" the young prince asked hopefully.

"Yes, Moshe," Monobaz replied. "I most definitely approve of your choice, but we must ask your grandmother's permission for her hand. Since she took responsibility for her as a young orphan, we will have to see if the *shidduch* meets with the queen's approval."

"Thank you, Uncle," Moshe said with a relieved smile. "I was hoping this suggestion would win your favor, but do you think Grandmama will approve?"

"You can be sure that I will give you my highest recommendation!" Monobaz replied, smiling.

It was still dark when Monobaz woke the boys to go to the *beis knesses* before the journey back to Yerushalayim.

By the time they finished the morning prayers, the sun was shining brightly through the cloudless blue sky. The village square was a cacophony of men's voices shouting instructions to family members, the bleating of sheep and goats, the moos of oxen and braying of donkeys, grunts of camels, and the neighing of horses. Men were tightening carriage wheels with tools, while boys ran to and from the well filling large, leather bags with water for the trip.

Nevertheless, within an hour, the caravan was ready to set off southward on a trip through terrain both inhabited and uninhabited that would last three full days. Individuals could be heard reciting the wayfarers' prayer with great concentration, beseeching Hashem to bring them to their holy destination in peace, unimpeded by wicked people, wild animals, or any other misfortune along the way, and to bless them in all their endeavors. The group then proceeded with graceful pageantry. Even the animals seemed to understand the importance of their role in the journey.

Leading the procession was an enormous ox, its horns covered with gold and encircled by a wreath of olive leaves. The animals seemed to strut jauntily to the rhythmic melody wafting through the air as the children frolicked among them.

Monobaz and the boys took their place near the middle of the procession so as to attract the least possible attention. In spite of their modest ways, the prince of Adiabene and his family were well known in the Land of Israel, and their regal bearing made them easily recognizable, even in the large crowd.

A young boy tugged at his father's robe. "Abba! Who is that tall man walking with all of those boys? Could he be a king?"

"No, my son," the man replied, "but I believe he is Prince Monobaz of Adiabene, a righteous *ger*, with his nephews, all of whom are Jews like us. Please try not to stare. I have heard that they disdain special attention."

The travelers were blessed with temperatures cooler than usual and made good progress the first day. As sunset approached, a guide pointed them to a tract of empty land near a spring, where they pitched tents under the open sky. The *olei regel* assembled to pray the evening service, then ate from their provisions and retired for the night.

The following day was spent much as the previous one, in joyous travel through the central part of the Land. Toward evening of the second day, Reuven excitedly tapped his uncle's shoulder and exclaimed, "I see a town in the distance, Uncle! Is this the *ir hama'amad*?"

"Yes, I think it is, Reuven," Monobaz said. "I see *olei regel* from the surrounding villages converging upon the town from all directions. It is from here that we will all make our final ascent to Yerushalayim."

"My *rebbi* taught me about this, Uncle," Yosef piped up. "'*B'rov am hadras Melech* — The glory of the King is increased among the masses.'"

Yehudah, whose pace had slowed markedly over the past hour, asked, "Uncle, will the residents take us in, like we do for others on Pesach?"

"No, tzaddik," his uncle replied reassuringly. "That would be too risky. We could become *tamei* if we stay inside a house. Instead, we will sleep in tents under the stars, as we did last night. Hashem has appointed His Heavenly hosts to watch over us on our way to do this great mitzvah!"

As the sun began to set, the *olei regel* converged on the town of Modi'in, the birthplace of the Hasmonean rebellion against the Syrian-Greeks over two hundred years earlier. Monobaz noticed a distant look in Reuven's eyes, a sign that he was deep in thought. He assumed that the historical significance of this place was not lost on his insightful nephew. Indeed, after a few moments, Reuven turned to his uncle, clearly agitated.

"Uncle, are we not in a situation that is similar to that of the Maccabees? Then, we had two destructive forces — Jewish assimilation and the government's attempt to destroy the Torah. Today, the Tzedokim are imitating the ways of the gentiles, and the Romans dare to perform abominable acts in our holiest place. Where are the Maccabees of our time? Do we not have the courage to defend our faith and rise up against them?"

Monobaz remained silent as he contemplated how to respond to his nephew. Then he turned to Reuven and put his arm around the boy's shoulder.

"Your insights are astute, dear nephew, but we must remember the mitzvah to heed our sages. Perhaps we have insufficient merits in

Shamayim to support a direct rebellion against the Romans and the Tzedokim who ally with them. If the time comes for us to take direct action, our rabbis will tell us to do so. These are troubled times, but remember that Hashem will never abandon us, and that He takes note of every mitzvah we do and every time we refrain from sin. This is our best collateral in times of distress."

Reuven's muscles stiffened, but he did not answer. He knew his uncle was right, but his answer was very difficult for him to accept.

Suddenly, Yosef, who had been lagging behind the others and was unaware of this solemn discussion, ran toward his uncle excitedly.

"Look, Uncle, the people of this town are happy to see us!"

Monobaz smiled as he saw local residents running from their homes to greet the tired travelers. Carrying jugs of water and trays of dried fruits, they warmly welcomed their guests to their city. Animals were watered and fed. Sheep, goats, and oxen were corralled in pens that had been prepared for them, and the children were tucked into straw-mattress beds under thick blankets to keep them warm during the cool night.

"Try to rest, boys," Monobaz encouraged. "It will be a long day tomorrow. If we get an early start and can keep a good pace, we should, *b'ezras Hashem*, reach our destination before nightfall."

Many hours passed before the sounds of densely lodged people and animals settling in for the night finally subsided, and the chirp of cicadas and the soft rustle of the breeze could once again be heard. Before long, it was dawn, and Monobaz was startled awake by a middle-aged man sounding a trumpet. He blew three short blasts from his instrument and chanted, "Arise! Let us go up to Zion to the House of Hashem, our G-d!"[5]

The men and youth quickly arose and assembled for morning prayers. Afterwards, scores of *olei regel* jumped into action, loading their

---

5   *Bikkurim,* mishnah 3:2; *Rambam, Bikkurim* 4:16.

wagons and beasts of burden, and readying them for the trip. Before leaving, however, the travelers, grateful for the hospitality shown them by the town's permanent residents, worked feverishly to dismantle the temporary structures built for their overnight stay. They gathered lost items for return to their owners along the way and cleaned areas where the animals had been kept. Rabbi Ezra, spiritual leader of the group, took formal leave of the town's *rav* and offered heartfelt thanks. Then he gave the signal for the entourage to move forward. Well-wishers lined both sides of the main road, singing and offering their prayers for a safe trip.

A middle-aged man and his family were among the group. He turned to his sons and whispered, "Do you see that tall man and five boys accompanying him? Their features are foreign, but their bearing is regal. I think they must be Prince Monobaz from Adiabene and his nephews. I would announce their presence among us in order to thank the prince for his role in sustaining us during the famine, if I had not heard that he does not like to be recognized."

"Yes, Abba, a man as benevolent as the prince would certainly not look for honor. I will stand at attention for a moment as he passes by, out of respect for his righteousness."

"Your father will do the same, my son," the man responded, proud of the boy's piety.

Hours later, as the procession approached the foothills of Yerushalayim, a wave of excitement passed through the group. Musicians began playing their flutes, horns, and cymbals, while children, riding in carts, perked up and clapped to the beat of the music. This was accompanied by the lowing, bleating, and mooing of animals, a scene that would have been chaotic, if not for the holy purpose that pervaded it.

The summer heat was reaching a crescendo in Yerushalayim, enveloping its environs with intense, dry warmth by day. The cool mountain breezes in the evening made sleep comfortable. Then, morning would break once again, with the temperature escalating rapidly to blazing levels as the sun shone through a turquoise, cloudless sky.

As the prince and his nephews descended the hills surrounding Yerushalayim, they saw whirling white circles amidst the vineyards that decorated the outskirts of the city.

"Why are there so many birds flying around Yerushalayim today?" Yaakov asked his uncle.

Monobaz laughed heartily. "Your eyesight is very keen, my son, but your interpretation is not quite accurate. What you see are not birds but rather the daughters of Israel rejoicing on this very happy day."

"Why are they dancing?" Yaakov asked. "And why are they all wearing the same white gowns?"

"These are also good questions, my boy," Monobaz replied. "Maybe your brother Reuven can answer them for you," he said loudly. Hearing his name, Reuven, whose rapid gait had placed him far ahead of the others, turned around.

"Reuven, can you tell Yaakov what we are seeing below?" the prince asked.

"Yes, Uncle, Rabbi Baruch taught us all about Tu B'Av in yeshivah," he said enthusiastically. "The girls are dancing because they hope to be chosen for marriage by someone still looking for a wife. They wear the same dresses so the wealthy ones won't get more attention than the poor ones. In fact, my *rebbi* told me that they all borrow dresses from each other, so no one is wearing her own clothes! Even the daughter of the king would borrow from the daughter of the *kohen gadol*, and the daughter of the *kohen gadol* from the daughter of the substitute *kohen gadol*, and his daughter from the daughter of the *kohen* who went out to war, and his daughter from the daughter of a regular *kohen* — everyone borrowed from someone else!"[6]

---

6   *Ta'anis* 26b. Another reason why they dance in the vineyards is because Dovid

"Rabbi Baruch has taught you well, Reuven," Monobaz commented. "Who would like to hear more about the story of Tu B'Av?"

"I do!" Yosef and Yaakov shouted.

"I do, too!" Yehudah chimed in.

"Moshe, why don't you begin?" Monobaz suggested.

"Actually," Moshe said thoughtfully, "the original cause for celebration on Tu B'Av occurred during the Jews' sojourn in the desert. Every year since the Divine decree that the generation of the *midbar* would not enter Eretz Yisrael, fifteen thousand Jews died every Tishah B'Av. This continued until the fortieth year, when the last fifteen thousand Jews, who had dug graves for themselves in anticipation of passing away on Tishah B'Av, did not die. They waited until the fifteenth of Av, when there was a full moon, to celebrate the great mercy of Hashem, to be sure that they had not miscalculated the date. It was also at this time that the Alm-ghty resumed speaking with Moshe Rabbeinu, because during the entire time that the Jews were dying in the *midbar*, Hashem communicated with Moshe only in a limited manner.[7] This was another cause for celebration. Just as the generation of the *midbar* was forgiven for its sins, this day became one of atonement for sin, similar to Yom Kippur.

"The joyous celebration originally centered upon Shiloh, where the Mishkan was located at the time. The young girls would go out to the vineyards, where the crushing of grapes to make wine was in full force. They would dance there in circles, just as on Yom Kippur, in hope of being noticed by a potential suitor.

"More than a generation after the tribe of Binyamin had been ostracized by its Jewish brethren for a horrific crime committed by some of its members,[8] the ban on marriage was finally lifted on Tu

---

Hamelech taught (*Tehillim* 128:3), *Your wife will be like a fruitful grape vine.*

7   *Rashi* on *Devarim* 2:16-17.

8   Known as *pilegesh b'Givah*, this occurred during the times of the *Shoftim*.

B'Av, allowing members of that tribe to marry the daughters of the other tribes. On that very same day, it was also ruled that a woman who inherited land could marry a man from any of the twelve tribes, lifting her restriction to marry only within her own tribe.⁹

"So, Reuven is right," Moshe concluded. "Tu B'Av continues to be celebrated as a day when young women throughout the Holy Land dance together in hopes of finding their intended in order to build a *bayis ne'eman b'Yisrael*."

Helene was sitting in the parlor of the palace, a white linen robe on her lap; scores more had been distributed to poor girls in the Ophel earlier that day. She looked at Chava, sitting to her right.

"Your Majesty," Chava said wistfully, "you encourage me to participate in the dancing, and yet, I feel that, as a *giyores*, my presence might be questioned."

"Hashem knows the purity of your conversion as well as that of your heart, my child. You belong with the other young girls just as much as if you had been born a Jewess. And remember, my dear, on this day, we are also celebrating His kindness in accepting the *teshuvah* of the tribe of Binyamin. There are so many reasons to dance!

"And you, my dear child, how you've grown," Helene commented fondly. "You are a young woman now. It is time for me to think about your future."

Chava looked downward, as a pink flush spread across her face. When she raised her eyes, they were filled with tears. Helene embraced her, and Chava started to cry.

"What makes you so sad, child?" Helene asked gently.

When Chava's sobs finally subsided, she spoke up.

"Your Majesty," she said, her voice barely louder than a whisper.

---

9   Eliyahu Kitov, *Sefer Hatoda'ah* (Jerusalem: Kollel Bookshop, 2000), 640.

"Who would ever want to marry me, a *giyores* and a foreigner, when there are so many beautiful Jewish girls waiting to become wives and mothers?"

Helene looked concerned. The path Chava had chosen was not an easy one. How she desired to shield her from all pain! But the only thing she could do was strengthen the girl's trust in the Alm-ghty.

"I have told you before, my dear, that all *shidduchim* are made in Heaven," the queen said. "Forty days prior to the birth of a baby, a Heavenly *bas kol* declares, '*Ploni l'bas Ploni*, this young man is designated for this girl.' My dear, surely you have recited Tehillim frequently enough to know, *Hashem watches over converts; He encourages the orphan and widow.*"[10]

Chava looked at the queen, a spark appearing in her eyes. "Of course, Your Majesty! This was the first chapter you taught me, and since then it has accompanied each of my prayers!"

"Very good, my dear, and may it continue to give you strength!" Helene replied. "*Yeshuas Hashem k'heref ayin* — Hashem's salvation comes in the blink of an eye!"

Helene glanced out the window and saw what looked like an enormous, colorful ball rolling closer and closer.

"They are coming!" she gasped excitedly. "The *olei regel* are almost here! Monobaz and my grandsons must be among them! Come, Chava, look!"

The spectacle was breathtaking! All roads were clogged with people, many of them bearing baskets of fruit on their heads and leading different types of animals. A distant melody wafted through the open window.

"Come, my dear," she said encouragingly. "Let us prepare to offer *bikkurim*!"

A short time later, the queen was seated with Chava on her palanquin

---

10 *Tehillim* 146.

outside the gate as the group approached. Her regal demeanor only slightly masked the excitement she felt on this momentous occasion.

Monobaz arrived, dismounted his horse, and, flanked by his nephews, walked toward the queen. He kissed his mother's hand.

"Mother, I am happy to report that we have arrived with our *bikkurim*, and that they are ready to be offered at the Beis Hamikdash," the prince announced.

"May I please see them, my son?" Helene asked, unable to hide the excitement in her voice.

"Yes, Mother," Monobaz replied. "They are awaiting your inspection."

The palanquin was lowered and Helene alighted. Her ladies-in-waiting quickly moved up to carry the train of her robe. Monobaz signaled for the *bikkurim* to be paraded before the queen, who gasped at the stunning sight of the golden baskets glittering in the sunshine, laden with pomegranates, figs, dates, and olives. Monobaz had sent the grapes ahead to the Beis Hamikdash so as to prevent the queen from coming into close proximity to them.

"How beautiful and well-formed they are! A worthy offering, indeed!" she exclaimed with great joy. "Let us now go together to the Beis Hamikdash!"

The entourage continued their trip from the Lower City to the Har Habayis, ultimately reaching the entrance to the eastern gate leading to the *Ezras Nashim*. The courtyard was teeming with people bearing large baskets of fruits. All movement had slowed to a snail's pace, as the *olei regel* inched toward the Nikanor Gate marking the entrance to the much smaller *Ezras Yisrael*. After a wait of several hours, it was finally their turn. Monobaz and his nephews proceeded through the *Ezras Yisrael* to the *Ezras Kohanim*, to the area between the *Mizbe'ach* and the *Ulam* that was specially designated for the bringing of *bikkurim*.

"Is this another exception to the rule that only *kohanim* are permitted to stand between the *Ulam* and the *Mizbe'ach*, Uncle?" Moshe whispered.

"Yes, Moshe," Monobaz responded. "The Torah dictates that we bring our *bikkurim* to this specific place to demonstrate how dear this mitzvah is to the Alm-ghty, but now, we must be silent. The *kohen* is ready for us."

For a moment, Monobaz gazed at the *kohen* standing opposite him, resplendent in a white linen robe and turban with a multicolored sash of embroidered wool tied around his waist. Then he stepped forward and declared, "I proclaim today to Hashem your G-d that I have come to the Land which Hashem swore to our forefathers to give to them."[11]

Monobaz grasped his basket filled with fruits.

As Monobaz held the basket by its handles, the *kohen* placed his hands under it. The two began waving the basket in each of the four directions, as well as up and down.[12] Monobaz then rested the basket at the southwest corner of the *Mizbe'ach*, his hands trembling.

The prince walked slowly to the entrance of the *Heichal*, tears of gratitude streaming down his face. The *kohen* gave him a moment to compose himself before beginning the *vidui* that Monobaz, as the landowner, would repeat, phrase by phrase, after the *kohen*.[13]

Arami oveid avi… An Aramean tried to destroy my forefather. He descended to Egypt and sojourned there, few in number, and there he became a nation — great, strong, and numerous. The Egyptians mistreated us and afflicted us, and placed hard work on us. Then we cried out to Hashem, the G-d of our forefathers, and Hashem heard our voice and saw our affliction, our travail, and our oppression. Hashem took us out of Egypt with a strong hand and an outstretched arm, with great awesomeness, and with signs and wonders. He brought us to this place,

---

11   *Devarim* 26:3.
12   *Menachos* 81b; *Rambam* 3:12.
13   *Bikkurim*, mishnah 3:7.

and He gave us this Land, a Land flowing with milk and honey. And now, behold! I have brought the first fruits of the ground that You have given me, Hashem![14]

The prince then prostrated himself before the altar and uttered his own personal prayer.

"How can I ever thank You, Hashem, for the kindness You have bestowed upon me? You brought me to Eretz Yisrael and enabled me to harvest from the bounty of Your Land to bring these gifts to Your Holy Temple. Please have mercy on Your people, Hashem, and grant them both physical and spiritual sustenance. May I merit the privilege of coming again next year to offer *bikkurim* before Your Holy Temple, with joy."

---

14   *Devarim* 26:5-10.

Chapter Twenty-Two

Early the next evening, after returning from the *beis midrash*, Moshe requested an audience with his grandmother.

"His Highness, Prince Moshe, seeks to speak with the queen," the butler announced.

"Please send him in," Helene responded, suppressing a knowing smile.

Moshe approached the queen and kissed her hand.

"Good evening, Grandmama," he began hesitantly. "I have come to seek your wise advice."

"While I cannot vouch for my wisdom, dear Moshe, I am always here to listen," Helene answered with a smile.

Moshe looked down and began to speak, his words seeming to stumble over one another. "How does one know when he is ready to be wed?"

Helene was silent for a few moments before responding.

"Moshe, a boy must contemplate the mitzvos and responsibilities of a husband and feel he is ready to fulfill them with a happy heart," the queen explained. "Then, he must find the right girl to be his life partner, a wife who will help him achieve his purpose in life and whom he will help achieve hers."

Moshe looked into his grandmother's loving eyes. "I have accomplished these things, Grandmama, and so I believe I am ready to wed."

"Who, may I ask, is the fortunate girl, my son?" Helene asked, with a seriousness that was partially feigned.

"With your permission, Grandmama, the girl I wish to marry is Chava bas Sarah Imeinu, your adopted daughter," Moshe blurted out.

Helene smiled warmly. She wanted to embrace Moshe just as she had when he was a little boy, but, so as not to embarrass him, she substituted warm words of encouragement.

"Moshe, I wholeheartedly grant my permission for you to ask Chava to marry you. May you merit building a *bayis ne'eman b'Yisrael!*"

"But how do you know she will accept me?" Moshe asked shyly.

"Indeed, I do not know this for certain," Helene replied. "But I have a feeling that your request will be granted." She smiled, her eyes sparkling. "In any case, there is no reason to delay. I will introduce the idea to her tonight, and you can speak to her tomorrow."

"Thank you so very much, Grandmama," Moshe said with a broad grin. "I will await further word."

Chava was soon entering the queen's throne room, wondering why she was being summoned at such a late hour. Helene smiled at her and motioned for her to sit down.

"Chava," Helene said, "do you remember when I told you that all *shidduchim* are determined in *Shamayim*…?"

The two spoke into the wee hours of the morning.

Helene called for Moshe early the next afternoon. Then she summoned Chava.

The girl blushed at the sight of Moshe standing next to the queen.

"Please enter, Chava," Helene encouraged. "My grandson, Moshe, would like to speak with you."

Moshe turned and, summoning his courage, walked forward to greet Chava. He glanced briefly at the demure girl and then met her large, dark eyes with his own.

"I would be greatly honored, Chava bas Sarah Imeinu, if you would agree to become my wife," he said. "I can imagine no finer *shidduch* and hope you will accept me as your husband. My grandmother has granted permission and blesses our union."

"Yes, I accept your proposal," Chava replied in a voice barely above a whisper. "I will strive to be a worthy wife to you."

The *eirusin* was set for the next week. Helene invited a *minyan* to the palace to witness the event. Monobaz escorted Rabbi Yechezkel, an emissary of Rabban Shimon ben Gamliel, into the hall. The sage stood before the *chassan* and *kallah* with a cup of wine.

"Blessed are You, Hashem, our G-d, King of the universe, Who creates the fruit of the vine," he recited.

"Amen!" responded all those assembled.

"Blessed are You, Hashem, our G-d, King of the universe, Who has sanctified us with His commandments, and has commanded us regarding forbidden unions; Who forbade betrothed women to us, and permitted women who are married to us through canopy and consecration. Blessed are You, Hashem, Who sanctifies His people Israel through canopy and consecration."

"Amen!"

Rabbi Yechezkel gestured for the two witnesses to come close and turned to the *chassan*. "Moshe, have you brought the item for *kiddushin* to give Chava?"

"Yes, Rabbi," Moshe answered. "I am giving my *kallah* this gold *Ir Shel Zahav* necklace." Moshe took a leather pouch from his pocket and withdrew a finely crafted piece of gold jewelry.

Rabbi Yechezkel turned to the *kallah* and said, "Chava, do you acknowledge that this necklace is worth at least one *perutah*?"

"Yes," Chava said clearly. "I acknowledge that it is worth more than one *perutah*."

Moshe gave his bride the necklace and recited, "*Harei at mekudeshes li k'das Moshe v'Yisrael* — Behold, you are consecrated unto me according to the laws of Moshe and Israel."

"*Mekudeshes?*" Rabbi Asher questioned.

"*Mekudeshes!*" the witnesses responded emphatically.

Messengers were sent to Adiabene to announce the good news of Moshe and Chava's betrothal to King Izates and Princess Samacha.

It would be another year before the couple would come under the *chuppah* to join in marriage. During that time, Helene assembled a dowry for her adopted daughter befitting a princess.

An atmosphere of anticipation settled over the palace, and the months passed quickly.

Summer was still at its height in Eretz Yisrael, late in the month of Menachem Av. The fruit trees were heavy with their bounty and ready for picking. Places were set in the soup kitchen for one hundred needy guests who would partake of a pre-wedding feast. The queen greeted the women personally, accepting their blessings that Moshe and Chava be worthy to build a house loyal to the ideals of the Jewish people.

Just then, trumpeters outside the palace played a special pattern of notes reserved to announce the arrival of important guests. The queen looked surprised, and then smiled broadly. She quickly excused herself and hurried to the palace entrance, where King Izates and Princess Samacha were exiting their carriage at that moment. Helene rushed toward them. She first embraced her daughter-in-law, and then her son, as tears of happiness flowed on both sides.

"Let us offer thanks to Hashem!" Helene exclaimed joyfully. "My prayers have been answered!"

She turned to Izates and gazed at him, not fully believing that she was finally being reunited with her beloved son again after so many years. He had aged so dramatically since she had seen him last!

Trying to suppress her shock, she quickly composed herself.

"Izates!" Helene exclaimed. She then recited the blessing said upon seeing a loved one after more than thirty days, as did the king.

"How I have yearned to behold your handsome visage, my son! How I have missed you!" Helene cried.

Izates smiled and embraced his mother again. Right then, he was not the monarch of Adiabene. He was simply an adult son reunited with his beloved mother.

"Please hurry and tell my grandsons that their parents have arrived!" the queen requested of her chief butler.

A tearful reunion ensued, spiced by much animated conversation in Pahlavanik, the native language of Adiabene.

"Izates, how are things at home?" Helene questioned her son.

"In truth, Mother, it has been more than a decade now that the Parthian monarchs have been feuding, and I feel as if I am seated upon a tinderbox ready to explode. Each day seems to bring me closer to direct involvement in the conflict, but we know that the future is in the hands of the Alm-ghty."

"I worry about you, Izates. May Hashem continue to protect you from all harm."

The wedding of Moshe and Chava took place the next day amid great joy and celebration. Immediately following *sheva brachos*, King Izates and Princess Samacha emotionally took leave of their dear children. Izates turned to the *chassan* and *kallah*.

"Moshe and Chava," he said, "you are poised to build your very own home in the Holy Land. Never forget what a privilege it is to serve Hashem in this way. Offer thanks to Him throughout the days of your lives for His many kindnesses toward you. Seek His guidance through the holy Torah, and pray for His constant protection. Know that we are always thinking of you and praying for you."

Izates then turned to Reuven, Yosef, Yehudah, and Yaakov.

"My dear sons," he began, his penetrating eyes focusing on the boys. "It has been very difficult for me and your mother to live so far away from you for all of these years, and I am sure it has been difficult at times for you as well. Our purpose in sending you to the Holy Land to learn Torah and to become integrated members of the Jewish people has been well served. With Hashem's great mercy and assistance, each of you has become a true *ben Torah*. Nothing could make your mother and me happier and more thankful to the Alm-ghty. May you continue to enjoy His protection and guidance every day of your lives, and may you always know how much we love you."

No eyes were dry as Izates and Samacha boarded the carriage that would carry them back to Adiabene. Both father and mother were silent as they were led further away from their family, immersed in their thoughts and holding back strong emotions.

Would only the ultimate redemption come soon, when they could be united forever!

Chapter Twenty-Three

A young boy raced through the courtyard surrounding his two-room home and bounded through the door of his family's sukkah.

"I saw it, I saw it!" he shouted, breathless.

"Meir, what was it that you saw?" his mother asked. Her eyes twinkled as she smiled lovingly at her curious son.

"Queen Helene's tall sukkah!" Meir announced, wide-eyed. "Everyone has been talking about it![1] I was able to peek through the gate leading to the royal compound. I have never seen such an enormous sukkah! I overheard someone saying that it has many small rooms within it — and one of these rooms is built differently than the others. Its floor space is small, but it rises up tens of *amos* into the sky! I saw many sages going in and out to pay respects to the queen." Meir looked perplexed. "I thought they'd be upset about seeing a sukkah that is clearly too tall to be valid, but instead, they were smiling."

"Please take a breath and speak more slowly, my son," his father said. "I want to hear every detail."

"Father, I don't understand!" Meir said. "You taught me that a kosher sukkah can be only as high as twenty *amos*. Why would the queen build such a tremendously tall structure if not to fulfill the mitzvah?"

---

1 *Sukkah* 2b.

"Surely, Meir, there must be an explanation," his father replied. "It is common knowledge that Queen Helene acts only upon consultation with the *rabbanim*." He paused thoughtfully. "Maybe she built this sukkah to sit in by herself. Since she is a woman, she is not obligated to sit in the sukkah, and so its restrictions do not apply to her. Perhaps her family is sitting in the other small rooms that make up the sukkah rather than in the tall room with her."[2]

"But why isn't the queen at her palace in Yerushalayim, Abba?" Meir asked. "Why is she here in Lod?"[3]

"That is a good question, my son. As *geirim*, members of the royal family are not obligated to make the pilgrimage to the Beis Hamikdash. Perhaps the queen, in her kindness, has vacated her palace to make room for *olei regel* who need lodging and space to build their sukkahs for the festival."

Meir nodded, planning to return to the royal compound the next day to try to catch a glimpse of those who were sitting inside the great sukkah. He awoke the next day of Chol Hamoed and accompanied his father to the synagogue for morning prayers.

Meir then asked his father's permission to take a walk and turned toward the queen's palace once again. As he neared the beautiful structure, he noticed two men speaking in hushed tones across from the palace gates. They were so engrossed in their conversation that they didn't notice the boy standing nearby.

"Surely this is ample evidence to discredit the queen," the taller man said to the other.

---

2   According to the opinion of Rav Ashi in *Sukkah* 2b.
3   Soon after the completion of her palace in Yerushalayim, Helene purchased a large estate in Lod out of her great affinity for the ocean and her desire to associate with Jews living in the smaller towns that are characteristic of this region. The port city of Lod is located about ten miles from the western Mediterranean coast of Eretz Yisrael, between Jaffa to the west and Modi'in to the southeast. Lod was the site where Rabbi Tarfon had his yeshivah and held his rabbinic court, and so it became a place famous for its *chachamim*.

"Once Helene is shown to disregard the Oral Law, she can be viewed as one of our own. Then it should be relatively easy to convince the Romans that her family is not bent on rebellion."[4]

"Or maybe we can shame her into returning to Adiabene," the shorter man suggested.

Meir's face paled with the realization that he was witnessing a conspiracy against the righteous Queen Helene.

"I must warn her," he whispered to himself.

Looking quickly around him, Meir dashed toward the gate surrounding the building. He looked around him one more time, then quickly climbed over the gate. Relieved that the guards had not spotted him, he sprinted toward the enormous sukkah and peeked inside the tall chamber.

"She is there!" he gasped.

Helene heard a sound and glanced over her shoulder. When she saw the young boy trembling with fear, she smiled warmly.

"Please come here, my child," she beckoned.

Meir approached the throne timidly.

"My visitors have been almost exclusively adults today," she said. "It is so wonderful to have a young guest. My name is Helene. What is yours?"

---

4   There is a discussion between Rabbi Yehudah and the *Chachamim* in the Gemara (*Sukkah* 2b) about Helene's tall sukkah. Rabbi Yehudah holds that a sukkah taller than twenty *amos* can be valid, and cites Helene's sukkah as a proof, since she acted only on the advice of the sages. Some possible reasons as to why the queen would have sat in such a tall sukkah include the need for a queen to have air circulation, reasons of modesty, and as a way for Helene to acknowledge that a woman is not required to sit in a sukkah. A hypothesis is presented that Helene's sukkah consisted of many small rooms, presumably for men and boys, all of which were within the allowed height, while only one room was tall, and this is where she sat. The *Chachamim* maintain, however, that Helene would have wanted to fulfill the mitzvah of sukkah, even though she was not obligated to do so, and she surely would have wanted to sit in the sukkah with the male members of her family, who would require a kosher sukkah. The reason for the tall sukkah is therefore unknown, but all agree that she would have acted only according to the word of the rabbis.

"My name, Your Majesty, is Meir, son of Yehoshua," the boy responded. "I live nearby, but I came for a purpose. When I was walking by the royal compound just now, I heard men plotting against Her Majesty. They spoke of discrediting the queen for not following the halachah."

"How very kind it is of you to be concerned for my welfare, Meir. You are a boy with a big heart and a clear sense of right and wrong. May Hashem reward you for your fine *middos*." Helene smiled and lowered her voice conspiratorially. "I will share with you that I am no longer afraid of these 'threats.' *The Guardian of Israel neither slumbers nor sleeps.*[5] Now, Meir, please do not worry about this old queen. Go into the room right beside mine and make a *brachah* in our sukkah."

Helene smiled as she watched Meir scamper away, but then she sighed. She looked up at the slats of *s'chach* with patches of sky peeking between them. Reminding herself that no one could harm her unless Hashem willed it, she turned her attention to the next guest.

The uplifting Yamim Tovim of Tishrei had passed, followed by a quiet Mar Cheshvan. Helene awoke abruptly one cool morning in Kislev, many thoughts rushing through her mind. The end of the fourteen years since she had made her initial vow had arrived. This much-awaited day would finally grant her the opportunity to fulfill her vow. Tomorrow, all of the hair on her head would be shaved, and she would bring the three *korbanos* of the *nazir* in the Beis Hamikdash. Then she would rejoin society as a new person — and hopefully, a much better person…

Helene looked forward to sharing her feelings with Savta Dina that day. During her journey to the southern side of the Ophel, Helene was so lost in thoughts of her upcoming purification that her arrival at the

---

5   *Tehillim* 121:4.

old woman's home seemed to come unusually quickly. She paused a moment to refocus her thoughts and then knocked on the door, waiting a few moments for the soft but familiar invitation to enter, but it did not come.

Helene furrowed her brow. Perhaps Savta Dina was sleeping, although it wasn't her usual time for rest. She slowly and carefully opened the door, and peeked inside. Savta Dina was indeed sleeping on the straw mattress in the corner of the room.

She gently called to her elderly friend and then rubbed her back to wake her.

"Savta Dina, it is I, Helene, come to visit you," she whispered. When there was no response, Helene repeated her words several times. An eerie silence was her only answer.

Helene pulled a feather from one of the pillows and held it in front of Savta Dina's mouth. When it remained still, she was forced to confront the sad truth. Savta Dina must have surrendered her pure soul to her Maker shortly before Helene's arrival. Tears fell onto the sheet with which she covered her friend.

"*Baruch Dayan ha'emes,*" she recited. "Blessed is the true Judge."

In the midst of her shock and grief, Helene gasped as she realized that she had come into contact with the dead. Her *nezirus* had been violated!

She shook her head and tried to focus. She would deal with this later. Now, all her energy was needed to take care of Savta Dina.

The queen summoned a female neighbor to remain with the deceased, while she hurriedly returned to the palace to make arrangements for Savta Dina's funeral. She knew she must consult with the rabbis as to her own fate, but this would have to wait until after Savta Dina was laid to rest later that day.[6]

---

[6] The holiness of Yerushalayim requires that burial take place the same day.

Helene clenched her hands together as she traveled with Monobaz the following morning. When they reached the *beis midrash* of Beis Hillel, the *shamash* escorted them into Rabban Shimon ben Gamliel's private study.

"Good evening, Your Majesty," Rabban Shimon said kindly. "I understand that you have become defiled in the course of trying to perform a mitzvah."

"Yes," Helene replied steadily. "I accidentally found myself in the presence of a *meis* yesterday — the day I was to complete my term of *nezirus*."

Rabban Shimon looked down, deep in thought, and was silent for several minutes. He then turned to the queen.

"The *meis* was known to be a righteous woman. It was a great *chessed* that Her Majesty took upon herself the mitzvah of helping her." Rabban Shimon paused. "Did the queen know ahead of time that she was deceased?"

"No."

"Did you actually touch the *meis*?"

"Yes."

"Was the bed of the deceased in a totally enclosed room?"

"Yes."

The questions ended, and Rabban Shimon retreated into an inner chamber, where two other *rabbanim* awaited him. Helene and Monobaz were instructed to remain in the antechamber.

After about one hour, Rabban Shimon emerged from the chamber, his wise face wearing a grave expression.

He slowly approached Helene, who rose to honor the great *talmid chacham*.

"Kindly be seated, Queen Helene," Rabban Shimon said, in a voice filled with compassion. "Please forgive the delay, but your question has many ramifications and major implications. Great deliberation was necessary to arrive at a decision.

"Your Majesty became *tamei meis* on the day she would have otherwise completed her vow of *nezirus*," he continued. "A term of *nezirus* can only be completed when it is free of contamination from any of the prohibitions incumbent upon the one making the vow."[7]

He paused, and a tense silence filled the room.

"Because you became *tamei meis* prior to completing your seven-year vow of *nezirus*, it is required that you restart your status as a *nazir* for another seven years," Rabban Shimon ben Gamliel explained.[8] "After that time, you will bring the *korbanos* of the *nazir* and undergo the shaving process to complete your vow."

There was no perceptible change in the serene expression on Helene's face. Masking her emotions from the public eye had clearly been a part of her royal upbringing.

She listened attentively to everything Rabban Shimon ben Gamliel said and remained silent. After a few moments of thought, she was ready to speak.

"Esteemed Nasi," Helene said, intent on making sure that she understood the sage correctly. "I was defiled prior to completing my term of *nezirus*. Therefore, I must begin anew the seven years I originally pledged in Adiabene. If Hashem grants me the merit to complete

---

7 The Torah stipulates that a *nazir* who becomes *tamei meis* must first undergo the seven-day purification process. Then, he must shave all of the hair on his head on the seventh day of this process. On the eighth day, he must bring two turtledoves or two doves to the *kohen* at the entrance of the *Heichal*. The *kohen* will then prepare one as a sin offering and one as a burnt offering. In addition, a year-old lamb is brought as a guilt offering. These offerings grant the *nazir* atonement for becoming defiled by the dead. Then, on the eighth day, he would start counting his days of *nezirus* anew (*Bamidbar* 6:9-12).

8 According to the first opinion in *Nazir*, mishnah 3:4.

my vow successfully, I will undergo the purification process at its proper time."

"Yes, Your Majesty," Rabban Shimon ben Gamliel agreed solemnly. "That is absolutely correct. I understand that my words must be difficult to hear, and they are difficult for me to deliver to Her Majesty. It appears that the *Ribono shel Olam* is pleased by what you have accomplished through your *nezirus*. May there be no stumbling blocks put in the queen's way toward ultimately fulfilling her vow."

"Amen! These words are a balm to my heart," Helene acknowledged gratefully. "When I first heard the ruling of the esteemed Nasi, my initial emotion was one of fear. I yearn to fulfill the promise I made to Hashem so many years ago! Could it be that, due to some sin I committed, I am being prevented from fulfilling my vow? But both situations that forced me to begin my *nezirus* anew were beyond my control. Perhaps the Alm-ghty has determined that it is not yet time for me to cease living the life of a *nezirah*. I accept the decision of the Nasi wholeheartedly and with great humility."

Rabban Shimon was momentarily silent, awed by the eloquence and sincerity of the woman sitting before him.

"Today is *Yom Sheini*. I will send the *metaher* to the palace tomorrow to begin the purification process. He will return on *Yom Chamishi* and again on the following *Yom Sheini* to sprinkle the queen with the purifying waters of the *mei niddah*. On that day the shaving will be performed, and you will bring your *korbanos*."

"Thank you, Rabban Shimon, for making the arrangements," Helene responded. "I look forward to my purification."

The palace was abuzz upon the queen's return. Her ladies-in-waiting were greatly concerned about the emotional state of their mistress, but her face revealed no anguish. After the queen alighted from her carriage and entered the palace courtyard, Moshe and Chava, who had been waiting for her return, whisked her quickly inside, sparing her the need to make conversation with onlookers, as was Helene's custom.

Later that evening, there was a soft knock on the door to the queen's chamber. Helene rose and heard a soft voice murmur, "Your Majesty, it is I, Chava. May I please have a few minutes with the queen?"

Helene opened the door to find the young woman, who had left her apartment in the palace to pay her a visit.

"Please, my dear, come in! Is Moshe well? How long have you been waiting out there?"

After bowing in deference to the monarch, Chava slowly raised her head to face Helene. Tears welled up in her eyes and the words tumbled out.

"My husband, *baruch Hashem*, is well, dear queen, but I feel so sorry for you!" she cried. "Your special day of celebration has been turned into one of disappointment! You have already waited so long to complete your vow, and now it has again been deferred!"

"My child, my dear child," Helene said comfortingly. "Thank you for your concern, but do not be worried or distressed! Everything that happens is designed for our good by Hashem. It is the loss of Savta Dina that is indeed cause for mourning. Her absence leaves a void in my soul, even though I know that she is in a better place, now that she has fulfilled her mission in this world.

"But Chava, do not think that I mourn the extension of my *nezirus*," Helene insisted. "Quite the contrary!" She smiled. "The *hashgachah pratis* is so clear to me. My *nezirus* must be extended because I need more time to work on my *middos*! I am truly grateful that Hashem has brought me this far. May He, in His great mercy, allow me to live long enough to complete my vow."

The next day, a tall, stately man, dressed in white linen robes, arrived at the palace. He was quickly ushered through the gate.

The steward appeared at the palace entrance. "Please come in and wait in the antechamber," he said. "The queen awaits your visit. I will inform her of your presence."

The man was soon summoned into a small room furnished as a study. Helene rose respectfully as he entered.

"Your Majesty, please, there is no need to rise for me. I have come today, on the third day of the week, to begin the queen's purification, to sprinkle her with the *mei niddah*."

"Thank you, sir. I am ready."

As Helene felt the holy water on her hands, she thought about what it meant to be *tehorah*, to be spiritually pure of any impediments to serving Hashem in the best way possible. A weight gradually lifted from her heart.

She would, with Hashem's help, yet complete her *nezirus*.

Chapter Twenty-Four

One of Monobaz's visits to the Holy Land occurred in the year 55 CE, less than two decades before the Beis Hamikdash would be destroyed.

It was three years since the Roman emperor Claudius had appointed the evil Felix as high commissioner. Felix was brought in at the behest of Yonasan, the *kohen gadol*, who was misled into believing that Felix would be less oppressive to the Jews than Cumanus, his predecessor.

What misery the new procurator inflicted during his eight-year rule! Felix, a former slave, was a greedy and heartless oppressor of the Jews who exploited criminal elements within the Jewish community to accomplish his evil goals. He now reported to a new emperor, Nero, the successor to Claudius, who had died the year before. Nero was a corrupt and cruel madman who was too busy pursuing his decadent pleasures to pay attention to the governing of his provinces. This gave Felix free rein to oppress his subjects. Felix took full advantage of severe political divisions among the Jews to pit one against the other.

Yonasan, the *kohen gadol*, complained about Felix's behavior toward the Jews. In response, the procurator hired two Jewish thugs, men loosely affiliated with the Zealots, who murdered Yonasan.

It was against this backdrop that Prince Monobaz and his friend, Amram ben Be'iri, walked together one evening during the peaceful hour just after sunset. The conversation of the two men was drowned out by a group of about a dozen youths who swaggered down the narrow alley, chanting in loud voices:

Woe unto me because of the House of Baisos,
Woe unto me because of their maces.
Woe unto me because of the House of Hanin,
Woe unto me because of their incantations.
Woe unto me because of the House of Kathros,
Woe unto me because of their pens.
Woe unto me because of the House of Ishmail, son of Piachi,
Woe unto me because of their fists.
For they are High Priests, and their sons are Temple treasurers.
Their sons-in-law are trustees, and their servants beat the people with staves.[1]

The words of the young men bespoke frustration with the corrupt *kohanim* and those under their authority whom they used to extort and oppress the vulnerable. It was clear from their tattered dress that the youths were from poor families. The turmoil in their eyes reflected the pain of internal conflict that was afflicting the Jewish people. Amram and Monobaz were shaken by their passion and tried to comprehend its meaning.

"I see a troubling change in Yerushalayim since my last visit a year ago," Monobaz said sadly. "There is terrible strife among the people. The poor and elderly wear expressions of raw fear! In truth, Amram, the persecution of the weak by the Tzedokim and their rich cronies is even more frightening to me than the persecution we endure from Felix, the Roman procurator, himself, and we certainly know how evil he is! Felix uses criminal elements among the Jews to do his dirty work for him, turning the other way in the face of their lawlessness. The stress of the Roman oppression is written on the faces of the people I see everywhere. Please, dear friend, explain to me what is happening! There must be something we can do to help."

---

1 *Pesachim* 57a.

"You are correct, Your Highness," Amram agreed. "I am afraid that we are sometimes our own worst enemies. We respond to the Roman beasts by outdoing them with our own self-destruction. The sad reality is that we are aiding the enemy through our own actions. Yitzchak Avinu blessed Eisav that he would live by his sword and serve his brother — but when his brother transgresses the Torah, he may cast off his yoke."

Amram sighed and was silent for a moment.

"To explain it as simply as I can, there are three main factions operating here," he said. "The Zealots are ready to go to war against Roman domination. Then there are the Moderates, who support the goals of the Zealots but would like to avoid armed confrontation with Rome. Finally, there are those whom we call the 'Friends of Rome,' who are loyal to Rome. Many Tzedokim belong to this party. Most Jews consider themselves Moderates, but, as time goes on, the ranks of the Zealots are growing. This is what you may perceive as a change from your last visit. Unfortunately, the numbers of Zealots are being swelled by gangs of violent individuals, whom we call the Biryonim. They terrorize innocent Jews while attempting to accomplish their goals. I fear we are headed for civil war."

"I don't see how they can fail to understand the impact of what they are doing!" Monobaz commented. "The lawlessness, the infighting, the bitter hatred of one faction toward the other is devastating. I tremble to think what this all means in Heaven."

"Of course," Amram replied. "How can we fail to see the path of destruction we are paving for ourselves? How can a society operate without the authority of, and respect for, the court? It has been well over a decade since the Sanhedrin left the Beis Hamikdash and relocated to the Chanuyos area, outside its walls. Since then, there can be no trial of capital cases. Why did the judges do this? They were merely recognizing reality. It is better not to try them at all than to convict them and not be able to carry out the sentence. Woe to us!"

Monobaz heaved a sigh as he listened to his friend speak.

"For twenty-five years, the great sage and tzaddik of our generation, Rabbi Tzadok, has been fasting and praying that the Temple should not be destroyed," Amram said sadly. "How can we fail to respond to his pain? From within the Temple itself, Hashem has sent us sign after sign to convince us to do *teshuvah* and to know that everything we hold dear is at stake. It has been nearly two decades since the lot for the Yom Kippur offering has come up in the *kohen's* right hand! And to our great dismay, the ribbon tied on the goat offered to Hashem has remained red, instead of turning white. The western light of the Menorah has failed to remain lit all night and all day, and, as we both witnessed, the doors of the *Heichal* now open by themselves. May the Alm-ghty have mercy on all of us!"[2]

The two men continued to walk in the dark, which now seemed somehow oppressive.

"Since the first King Agrippa's murder by Greeks living in the Holy Land eleven years ago, our situation has worsened markedly," Amram said. "Agrippa was not qualified to be a king over the Jews due to his mother's Edomite ancestry, but he did try to protect the Jewish people to the best of his ability. During his reign, there was peace, and he advanced the position of the sages within the administration, bringing honor to Israel.[3] Since his death, the power of the Roman procurators has been increased — and with it, their persecution of our people. They have set the tone for other Roman officials and gentiles residing in the Holy Land. The result has been an attitude of disdain toward Jews in

---

2   These miracles were all signs of Divine favor. During the last forty years of Jewish autonomy in Eretz Yisrael, the devastating absence of these miracles, as well as the miraculous opening of the doors of the *Heichal* for the enemy, were Heavenly signs that the sins of the Jewish people would soon bring about the destruction of the Beis Hamikdash and subsequent exile.

3   Rabbis Nosson Scherman and Meir Zlotowitz, general editors, *History of the Jewish People: The Second Temple Era*, 156.

general, backed by terrible acts of lawlessness that go unpunished by the Roman bureaucracy.

"So, returning to your question, Your Highness," Amram continued, trying to keep his voice calm, "in my humble opinion, there are two things you can do to assist us. First and foremost, pray for the salvation of our people, for our fate is in the hands of Hashem alone. Also, stand strong against the Tzedokim. Make it clear to them and to all whose eyes will be trained upon you that you recognize the authority of the rabbis alone in determining halachah and the proper way to act."

"With all due respect, Amram, as a foreigner and a convert, I doubt that my opinions would be of much interest," Monobaz commented.

"My dear friend, you are clearly unaware of how truly influential a dignitary you are," Amram said, chuckling. "Your coming to Yerushalayim was preceded by all sorts of rumors and speculation about which side had your sympathy. Stories of your great piety likewise circulated freely, but some believed that due to your great wealth and royal background, you were encouraged to immigrate to bolster the political fortunes of the Tzedokim. Surely, their reputation and power could be much enhanced by the support of royal *geirim*.

"Tomorrow, G-d willing, I will take Your Royal Highness to visit one of the greatest sages of our generation, Rabbi Tzadok, to whom I am privileged to be related on my father's side. You will surely be granted a blessing for your undertakings. Please meet me in the *beis knesses* for afternoon prayers. We will set out shortly afterwards. Rabbi Tzadok is very frail and cannot accept guests late at night. Besides, my friend," Amram added, "I see now that walking the streets for any distance after dark is no longer safe. I certainly would not want to put you at any added risk."

Heavy clouds sent sharp needles of rain against the cobblestones.

"May these showers be *gishmei brachah*," Amram said in an undertone, as he walked with Monobaz the next day. Then he recited some verses from *Tehillim*.

Clouds streamed water, heavens sounded forth,
Even Your arrows went abroad.
The rumble of Your thunder rolled like a wheel,
Lightning bolts hit the world, the earth trembled and roared.[4]

"You know, dear prince," Amram mused, "when I watch the rain, I see two images. One is that of tears drenching the earth, tears of sorrow from Heaven for the degraded state to which the Jewish people have descended. The other is one of sharp arrows pounding the earth, arrows of retribution for the corruption of the Holy Land perpetrated by those who manipulate the meaning of the Torah to serve their greedy purposes."

Monobaz walked silently with his friend. The only sound was that of the rain pounding the hard stones. Suddenly, the prince was startled by a loud thunderclap. He recited the blessing said when hearing the first clap of thunder during a rainstorm.

"Hear, oh city of Yerushalayim!" he then declared. "All power belongs to Hashem and not to hoodlums, nor to the wealthy and well-connected. The power is His alone!"

Amram and Prince Monobaz continued down the cobblestone alleyways of the Ophel to the tiny stone house where Rabbi Tzadok dwelt. Monobaz felt especially uneasy at the prospect of meeting the sage, who was known as a "prophet of doom."

Amram knocked on the stone door. It was opened by the tzaddik's wife. She motioned them to follow her into a small room furnished with only a bed, two wooden chairs, and a small table upon which sat a plate of dried figs. That was the sole food Rabbi Tzadok would allow himself to eat.

---

4   *Tehillim* 77:18-19.

The sage lay on the bed, a small, shriveled figure so still that both men shot each other worried glances before approaching closer. Then they saw the thin lips of the saintly *rav* moving ever so slightly in prayer. His eyes were closed. Those eyes could no longer see when open, but it was not long before the elderly sage sensed the presence of visitors. Rabbi Tzadok partially pulled himself up on the bed and faced his guests.

"Rabi, Mori, my *rav*, my teacher! It is I, Amram ben Be'iri. I have brought my dear friend, Prince Monobaz of Adiabene, to visit. He seeks the Rav's blessing."

"Yes, my nephew," Rabbi Tzadok said weakly. "I have heard of your friend. He has given up power, fame, and great wealth in his home country to join our people in our Land. Why, Prince Monobaz, have you chosen to do this at such a time of decline and shame for the Jewish people? Surely you see the sorry state into which we have plunged!"

"Esteemed Rabbi Tzadok," Monobaz answered, trembling. "Throughout the history of the Jewish people, there have been great triumphs and devastating defeats. Nevertheless, Hashem has promised us that He will never completely abandon His people, and His unchanging Torah will continue to support the existence of the world. I seek the truth, Rabbi Tzadok, and in Torah, I have found the absolute truth. This is why I have become a Jew."

"Your answer is a worthy one, my son," the holy man whispered. "Pray for your people and its land," he continued, mustering all his strength. "May the aspirations of your pure soul be heard in Heaven, and may they bring us salvation!"

"Amen!" Amram said softly.

Monobaz looked down, overcome by the tzaddik's words.

Assuming their audience had ended, the prince began to walk backwards, out of respect, toward the door. He had taken no more than a few steps when he was shocked to see Rabbi Tzadok again struggle to sit up. He began to speak, his voice sounding stronger.

"Many *geirim* accomplished extraordinary things," he declared. "Mashiach will come through Rus. Why is this? It is true that the foundation of greatness is Torah scholarship. The efforts of Yissachar in the *beis midrash* have been, and always will be, the main focus of Torah. Nevertheless, there is another aspect of Torah, and that is giving up something for Torah. We must not forget that the Jews followed Hashem into the wilderness to a desolate land. This kind of sacrifice does not come easily to those born into Jewish families today. The *mesorah* is a path already forged for us, and we follow it.

"When Moshe Rabbeinu gathered Bnei Yisrael together on the last day of his life, he included the men, women, and children, as well as the convert. The Torah elaborates on the *ger* further, saying, *From the hewer of your wood to the drawer of your water.* What does this mean?"

Amram and Monobaz waited silently for an answer.

"The Torah is describing Canaanites who came to Moshe Rabbeinu desiring to convert. This presented a problem. The Jews did not circumcise their infants in the desert because it was potentially dangerous for them, but there can be no full conversion without *bris milah*! We learn that the halachah is different for a Jew and a non-Jew. Nearly every mitzvah can be abrogated in the face of life-threatening danger to a Jew, in the hope that many more mitzvos can be performed by that individual in the future. One who is becoming a *ger*, on the other hand, is allowed to risk his life in order to acquire the ability to perform all of the mitzvos of the Torah! The Canaanites who underwent *bris milah* were appointed by Moshe Rabbeinu to be woodchoppers. In the future, these converts would chop the wood for the altar. This was such an important task that the day the wood was brought to the Beis Hamikdash was declared a Yom Tov! The Canaanites who chose not to have *bris milah* became water drawers, a lesser function, since this job is not directly involved in the *avodah* of the Beis Hamikdash.[5]

---

5   *Panim Yafos L'Ba'al HaHafla'ah* in *Yalkut Olas Shabbos* 21, *Parshas Nitzavim.*

"When a *ger* is successful as a Jew, he is showing tremendous love of the Torah. He is making a *kiddush Hashem*."[6]

Rabbi Tzadok slid back into a reclining position, sapped of his meager energy.

Amram and Monobaz bowed and took leave of the great sage. Rabbi Tzadok's wife escorted them to the door, and the two walked home as silently as they had come.

The high-pitched wails of the infant reverberated throughout the synagogue. Monobaz stepped forward to give the child his name, while Rabban Shimon ben Gamliel, the *sandek*, held the baby on his lap.

"Our G-d and the G-d of our forefathers preserve this child for his father and mother, and may his name be called in Israel… Avraham ben Moshe!

"…And I said to you: 'In your blood, live!' And I said to you: 'In your blood, live!'

"Give thanks to Hashem, for He is good. His kindness endures forever!"

Monobaz's eyes filled with tears. The *bris milah* of his great-nephew was so different from his own! A new generation was being born. Baby Avraham would grow up as a Jew in the Holy Land … or would he?

The prince's joyous face suddenly became solemn. So much strife from within and from without buffeted the *kedushah* of Eretz Yisrael. Even the Beis Hamikdash was not safe from infringements of its sacred laws. How long would Hashem wait for them to do *teshuvah*?

Quickly composing himself, Monobaz led the assembled heartily in song. "*Siman tov u'mazel tov u'mazel tov u'siman tov!*"

Still, as Monobaz gazed at the baby's innocent face, he shuddered inwardly. *May the Alm-ghty extend His mercy and bless this child!*

---

6   Adapted from comments on *geirim* from the *Pri Tzaddik*.

Chapter Twenty-Five

The final seven years of Queen Helene's *nezirus* were filled with joy and fulfillment as her family blossomed and grew. Four of the queen's grandsons were married and blessed with children, and nineteen-year-old Yaakov had just become a *chassan*. Helene celebrated her seventy-fifth birthday[1] physically frail but still filled with her trademark enthusiasm for life.

As the completion of Helene's vow of *nezirus* drew near, she requested that Rabbi Yechezkel teach her the laws of the required sacrifices. After a period of intensive study, she felt prepared for the momentous day.

Finally, the day arrived. The queen opened a small scroll filled with numbers and marked off the last entry. Her gaze became distant, as if she had temporarily lost her connection with the present. She sighed, turned her attention back to the scroll, and uttered a silent prayer.

Ribono shel Olam, *just as You saved my son from war and have brought me to this day to offer the* korbanos *of the* nazir, *may You continue to watch over my sons, grandsons, and all of Klal Yisrael during these tumultuous times and always.*

Helene's attendants dressed the queen in a simple but elegant Shabbos garment — a silk brocade tunic of pure white, with a row of white roses embroidered into the hem. Around her snow-white hair

---

[1] This occurred in the year 60 CE.

they wound a turban of matching white silk, to which was attached a long drape of fabric that flowed down her back, reaching the hem of her robe. She wore no jewelry.

Helene emerged from her chamber and greeted her son. Monobaz stared at his mother. She appeared like an angel, her face suffused with an almost other-worldly glow.

"Good morning, Mother," he said. "The carriage is waiting to take us to the Beis Hamikdash."

Monobaz, who had traveled once again to the Holy Land to mark this long-awaited milestone at his mother's side, and Helene's five grandsons, accompanied the queen to the Beis Hamikdash. They traveled in two carriages, Monobaz and his nephews in one and the queen in the other. A large group of curious onlookers had assembled outside the palace gate, hoping to catch a glimpse of the queen on her way to complete her vow of *nezirus*. The gatekeepers had received instructions not to disperse them. The crowd was subdued and respectfully quiet as Helene's carriage passed through the gate. They were there to show respect for this woman who had extended great kindness to them and who had dedicated herself so wholeheartedly to fulfilling her vow as a *nezirah*. Their encouraging presence was met by the queen's famous, warm smile.

Upon reaching the marketplace outside of the Beis Hamikdash, Monobaz purchased a male lamb for the *olah* offering, a female lamb for the sin offering, and a ram as a peace offering.[2] He also purchased the unleavened loaves that would accompany each offering and placed them in a basket.[3] His nephews helped him carry the loaves and lead the animals to the Shushan Gate at the eastern entrance to the Har Habayis, where the carriage bearing the queen was waiting for them.

---

2 These were all unblemished animals and would comprise the *korbanos* of the *nazir* (*Bamidbar* 6:13-21).

3 There were ten loaves of fine flour mixed with oil and ten wafers smeared with oil.

Helene descended from the carriage and walked serenely, supported by her son, until they reached the southern gate leading to the *Ezras Nashim*, which was designated for women. Monobaz and his nephews entered through another gate and then joined Helene in the courtyard to traverse the length of the *Ezras Nashim* up to the area just in front of the twelve steps leading to the Nikanor Gate. There, Helene transferred the animals to a waiting *kohen* and was led back toward the *Lishkas Hanezirim*, in the southeast corner of the *Ezras Nashim*. The animals were promptly slaughtered and prepared as *korbanos*.

Soon after Helene was seated in the chamber, another *kohen* entered the *Lishkas Hanezirim* carrying the large foreleg of the ram from Helene's peace offering. He placed it into an enormous kettle over a fire and added water to begin the cooking process.[4] Before exiting the chamber, the *kohen* turned to speak to the queen.

"It is written in the Torah that on the day his status as *nazir* is completed, he shall bring himself to the entrance of the Tent of Meeting. When other offerings are brought for purification, like those of the *sotah* and the *metzora*, the person who comes to be purified is brought by the *kohen*, who is vested with the authority to purify him.

"It is different for the *nazir*, Your Majesty. The purification of the *nazir* that comes about through the shaving of the hair on the head transforms the *nazir* into a new person. Hair represents clarity of wisdom, just as products of the vine represent understanding, and contact with the dead represents knowledge.[5] Through abstaining from products of the vine and remaining ritually pure, you have detached yourself from man's animalistic nature and reached such an elevated level of wisdom, understanding, and knowledge, that there is none higher than you to cause your purification. Therefore, you are able to bring yourself to the Beis Hamikdash."[6]

---

4   Once cooked, the foreleg would be waved together with two of the loaves by both Helene and the *kohen*, after which it became the *kohen's* property.
5   *Chizkuni*, as quoted in *Otzar Toras Hakorbanos* 146.
6   *Seforno*, as quoted in *Otzar Toras Hakorbanos* 145.

"It is with thanks to the Alm-ghty and humility that I exercise this privilege," the queen replied softly.

The *kohen* exited the chamber. A female barber was waiting for the queen behind a linen curtain. The queen's turban was unwound, letting loose a mane of white tresses that reached to her waist. All of the women present gasped. Her Majesty looked angelic as she stood briefly before sitting down.

The barber made a swift cut with her scissors, being careful to catch all of the hair in a linen sack prepared especially for that purpose. Then she shaved the remaining hair from Helene's head and added it to the sack. The queen did not flinch. Her attendant carefully wound the turban once more around the queen's head.

A soft smile brightened Helene's face, expressing her relief and joy. After twenty-one years, she had finally merited to complete the term of her *nezirus*.

"This is the day made by Hashem; we will rejoice and be glad on it!"[7] she whispered, then added a prayer of thanks to Hashem for watching over her until this time. She gazed, wide-eyed, as the sack containing her hair was emptied onto the blazing fire beneath the kettle containing the cooking ram. The smell of its incineration quickly filled the chamber.

"May the destruction of my hair truly purify my soul," she prayed silently.

The queen was aroused from her reverie with a gentle tap on her shoulder. It was time to approach the *Azarah* with her *korbanos*. Before leaving, she was given a platter upon which to lay the foreleg of the ram and one loaf of each type of unleavened bread. The *kohen* on duty was waiting and gestured respectfully for her to approach. Helene held out the platter toward the *kohen*. He nodded to acknowledge her presence and began to wave the offering in every direction.

---

7   *Tehillim* 118:24.

"You have completed the obligations of a *nezirah* and are now free to consume the produce of the vine," the *kohen* said, his voice reflecting both the solemnity and excitement of the event. "Restrictions on cutting your hair or on having contact with the dead are hereby canceled."

The words reverberated in Helene's ears. She bowed her head and prayed quietly.

Ribono shel Olam! You plucked me from a gentile nation and allowed me to join Your Chosen People. You saved my son Izates from almost certain death at battle and enabled me to fulfill my vow to You out of my deep feeling of hakaras hatov. *You extended my period of* nezirus *threefold, as this must have been the time I needed for my purification. You preserved my health all of this time, allowing me to come to the Beis Hamikdash on this great day to offer the* korbanos *of the* nazir. *Were my mouth as full of song as the sea, and my tongue as full of joyous song as its multitude of waves, and my lips as full of praise as the breadth of the heavens, and my eyes as brilliant as the sun and the moon, I still could not thank You enough, Hashem, for even one of the thousands of thousands and myriads of myriads of favors that You performed for me.*

I am an old woman, Ribono shel Olam, *and I feel my strength beginning to ebb. Please permit me to use whatever additional time You grant me to perform mitzvos according to Your will as a member of Your holy People. Please preserve the righteousness of my offspring for generations to come. Please let them study Your Torah in peace and give honor to Your holy Name through all their actions.*

Helene was so deep in her thoughts that she did not notice an enormous crowd of women gathering in the *Ezras Nashim* to be near her. As she walked by, looking downward, hushed comments could be heard.

"Even now, she is so beautiful!"

"How straight and gracefully she walks!"

"And to think that she is a woman of over seventy years!"

"I hear she does nothing without first consulting the rabbis!"

Before entering her carriage, the queen addressed the assembled women.

"My dear daughters, it is not I who deserves any honor today, but rather the rabbis who lead us in the ways of the Torah of Hashem. Always look to them for guidance, and you will be assured of walking in His ways and thereby fulfilling your purpose in life."

Chapter Twenty-Six

Soon after Helene's fulfillment of her vow, word reached the palace that King Izates had passed from this world two weeks prior. The messenger bearing the sad news handed the queen a parchment bearing the royal seal. Trembling, the queen was assisted to her private chambers and then left alone to read her son's final letter.

Dearest Mother,

My days have been blessed and full. Hashem has shown His bountiful mercy toward me by allowing me to merit joining His Chosen People. I am grateful that I have lived such a good portion of my life observing the holy Torah and Hashem's mitzvos, and I am thankful that I share my faith with my wife, her children, my mother, and brother. How great are the wonders of the Creator!

Mother, your guidance and love have sustained me through my many challenges all of these years. While your absence from Adiabene has been sorely felt, your presence in the Holy Land and your dedication in raising my five sons in the ways of the Torah have nourished my soul and given me strength to continue on, even while surrounded by those who hate our people.

But now I feel the time for me to leave this world is approaching, and I want you to know that I have chosen my older brother Monobaz over my sons to succeed me. I have discussed the matter with him, and he has agreed to accept the crown. I am relieved to be able to entrust our homeland into his able hands. I could never repay the goodness he showed me after our father's death, when he preserved the government until my arrival home and gave it up to me with a full heart. It gives me great peace of mind to know that a compassionate, G-d-fearing man such as he will be at the helm of the government.

Please forgive me for any and all wrongdoing I may have committed toward you during my lifetime. May you be blessed with many days and years of continued blessing, in good health.

Your loving and admiring son,
Izates

Tears streamed down the queen's cheeks. When she finished reading the letter, her lips moved in prayer before she collapsed in grief. Giving herself little time to recover, she summoned her grandsons and relayed to them as gently as she could what had happened. There was a stunned silence as each of their faces took on an expression of disbelief. Then, one by one, each of Izates's sons hugged their grandmother and sobbed.

They cried for the loss of their father and for the circumstances that had made it necessary for them to be separated by such a great distance for so long. They cried for a father who had set aside his desire to raise his sons to adulthood so they could have the opportunity to develop to their full potential as Torah Jews. They cried for a life of *mesirus nefesh* well lived and now ended.

Rabbi Yechezkel came to the palace immediately upon hearing the sad news. He instructed the queen and her grandsons to recite the blessing of *Baruch Dayan Ha'emes*. Then he helped Izates's sons tear their garments as a sign of mourning. A female attendant helped Helene tear *kriah*.

Since Izates's death had occurred within the past thirty days, a complete week of *shivah* was observed. People from all walks of life streamed into the palace from morning to evening. Sages came not only from Yerushalayim, but from Bnei Brak, Teveria, and even from outside of Eretz Yisrael, as did other foreign dignitaries. Residents of the Ophel came to comfort Helene and her grandsons, as distraught as if they had lost a member of their own family.

Upon completing *shivah*, Helene requested an audience with Rabbi Yechezkel.

"Esteemed Rav," she began, "my broken heart pulls me to return to Adiabene to be a source of support to my son Monobaz, who is now the king. At the same time, my soul cleaves to the holiness of Yerushalayim. I am acquainted with the halachah that one who has gone up to live in the Holy Land should not live again in *galus*. Would it be permissible for me to visit Adiabene with the fervent wish to return again to my holy Yerushalayim?"

"Yes, Your Majesty," Rabbi Yechezkel replied. "It would be permissible for you to visit Adiabene to give support to your son and to ease his transition to power."

"Rabbi Yechezkel's answer to my question is bittersweet to me," Helene confessed. "I am seventy-five years old. Hashem has blessed me with longevity and good health, for which I am very grateful."

"May it be His will that you merit returning to the Holy Land at a propitious time," Rabbi Yechezkel blessed the queen.

"Amen!" Helene responded, a smile returning to her face. "Thank you. You have comforted me."

Helene returned to the palace and spent a long time alone in the parlor. Then she summoned her grandsons. The door opened, and Moshe, Reuven, Yosef, Yehudah, and Yaakov entered with somber expressions on their faces.

Helene's gaze rested on Moshe, now a handsome young man completing his third decade and raising a growing family.

Ribono shel Olam, she prayed, *please continue to watch over Moshe, his brothers, and their families, and protect them from all harm, both spiritual and physical.*

Helene composed herself and began to address her grandsons.

"You boys are as dear to me as life itself. You are the future of our family and of the Jewish people. Your father would be so proud to see what you have become. Let me read you the letter I have just received from your dear mother. Since it was addressed to me, I opened it, but it is intended for you."

My dearest sons,

Receiving your letter lifted my spirits and filled my heavy heart with such joy! How proud I am to be the mother of talmidei chachamim *like you. How I have missed you during our years of separation, but the ache in my heart has been eased by knowing how much you have grown. My sons, you have used to the utmost your opportunity to live and learn in the Holy Land. You have done what your late father, may his memory be for a blessing, so yearned to do but was unable to accomplish due to his responsibilities here. You and your children are his legacy.*

Your father, of blessed memory, requested in his will that all of his sons remain in Eretz Yisrael rather than return to Adiabene upon his death. Your uncle, Monobaz, has readily agreed to assume the kingship, so that you can continue to live in the Holy Land. It is my fervent wish that I be able to join you there soon.

May we all be comforted in our mourning.

Your loving mother

Helene looked at her grandsons, tears in her eyes.

"There is little that I can add to the heartfelt words of your dear mother," she said. "Her *mesirus nefesh* in sending you to Eretz Yisrael to learn and live as Jews is unfathomable. I was entrusted by your parents to bring you up as they would have done. While I could never substitute for them, I have loved you as my own children, and I am proud beyond words of your many accomplishments. You are all *yirei Shamayim* and *talmidei chachamim*, and there is no greater praise for a man in this world."

Helene paused and looked each grandson in the eye.

"We are living through very difficult times, and you will inevitably be swept up in the flow of events. Emotions will be strong. I pray to Hashem to bring you safely through the maelstrom and to give you the strength to refrain from taking any action without the sanction of our great sages, for even the wisest mind can be persuaded by the exigencies of war to act imprudently. Hashem in His great kindness has given us rabbis so great that they have the ability to rule on the most difficult and painful questions."

Helene kissed her grandsons and gave each one a personal letter.

"Please wait until I have left before opening these," she requested, managing a small smile. "I hope they will please you. They were written with much thought and love."

Queen Helene left her beloved Yerushalayim shortly thereafter to return to her birthplace, Adiabene, propelled by a sense of duty and motherly instinct. When her younger son departed this world, she felt drawn to the place he had vacated.

Helene's return was quite dissimilar to her departure. Fourteen years had passed. She had left a country still in turmoil over the conversion of its royal family, an act viewed by some as traitorous to the Adiabenean people. In the interim, hundreds of her countrymen, impressed with tales of the royal family's good deeds in the Holy Land and intrigued by their attraction to this alien faith, sought out rabbis and wise men to teach them the principles of the Torah. Many became full-fledged converts to Judaism. The queen's mission in life had been fulfilled, and within just a short time after returning to her homeland, she, too, surrendered her pure soul to her Maker.[1]

---

1 Josephus, *Antiquities of the Jews*, 20:4.

Monobaz sent his mother's remains and those of his brother, Izates, which had been temporarily interred in Adiabene, to Yerushalayim. They would be buried in the tomb Helene had built during her lifetime, about half a mile from the city. A funeral procession consisting of thousands of mourners wound through the streets of the Ophel, heading toward the tombs near Mt. Scopus.[2] As the entourage passed the palace, the entire staff stood tearfully at attention, together with an honor guard sent from Adiabene to pay its respects to its queen. Bystanders, wearing expressions of pain and sadness, lined the streets, many openly weeping at the loss of the foreign queen in their midst.

Rivka ben Be'iri looked on tearfully as her husband served as a pallbearer for Queen Helene. Standing far back in the crowd was Giveret Salome Miriamne, paying her last respects to a woman whom she had come to highly respect.

A girl of about eight tugged on her mother's robe. "Ima, why are you crying?"

Her mother composed herself before turning to her daughter. "I am sad because Queen Helene gave us food when we were hungry and I never thanked her..."

As the *tallis*-draped bier of King Izates, carried on the shoulders of the pallbearers, made its way through the crowd, a hush swept over the onlookers. Few of them had ever met the deceased king of Adiabene. Although he had visited the Holy Land on a few occasions over the past decade and a half, he purposely kept a low profile, preferring to make his pilgrimage as a simple, G-d-fearing Jew. He had been a *ger tzedek*, risking his life and career as king for the sake of observing the mitzvos of the Torah.

No empty space could be found on the immense thirty-foot wide staircase leading down to the tombs. Helene had directed Monobaz to

---

2   Jacqueline Schaalje, "Jerusalem's Tombs," [www.jewishmag.com/47mag/jerusalemtombs/jerusalemtombs.htm], October 31, 2007.

build the three pyramid-topped tombs years before for herself and her two sons.[3] Before long, the entire courtyard was filled with mourners and the sound of sobbing. Soon a respectful silence descended, reflecting the reverence felt by all present for the great woman and her son who were to be interred there.

Izates's oldest son, Moshe, eulogized his father, citing the king's dedication to the Torah and his *mesirus nefesh* in sending his dear sons so far away from him to live the lives of religious Jews in the Holy Land.

Then Moshe read the eulogy he prepared for his grandmother, based on verses from *Tehillim*.[4]

> *You love righteousness and hate wickedness,*
> *Accordingly has G-d, your G-d, anointed you with oil of joy above your peers.*

Feeding the hungry during the famine and the poor in your own palace, you fought injustice and *sinas chinam* through acts of boundless kindness. Performing these acts gave you great happiness.

> *Myrrh, aloes, and cassia are all your garments, which are from ivory palaces that bring you joy.*

Yes, dear grandmother, your beautiful garments were a wrapping for your pure, refined soul, and the sweet fragrance of your good character inspired all you met to reach for higher levels of spiritual attainment. You were a Jewish queen in every sense, always seeking to achieve closeness to the Alm-ghty through strict adherence to the dictates of the Torah.

> *Hear, O maiden, see and incline your ear,*

---

[3] The tombs were hewn into the bedrock of what was once a quarry. The wide entrance of the tomb was graced by two Ionic columns standing between two additional pillars that projected from the side walls. Above, the building was topped by three pyramids (R. Steven Notley and Jeffrey P. Garcia, "Queen Helena's Jerusalem Palace – In a Parking Lot?" *Biblical Archeology Review*, May/June 2014, 32-34).

[4] Selected verses from *Tehillim* 45.

Forget your people and your father's house;
Then the King will desire your beauty, for He is your Master — bow to Him.

You left your nation of birth, turning your back on the worshippers of idols, leading young maidens to follow in your footsteps in recognizing the one, true G-d. The sincere converts you inspired have brought glory to His holy Name.

You left everything familiar behind in order to fulfill your great desire to perform mitzvos in the Holy Land, to fulfill your vow as a *nezirah*, and to care for and encourage us, your grandsons. Hashem in His mercy granted you success in each of these endeavors.

You accepted unquestioningly everything the sages told you, rejecting not only the idols worshipped by your forefathers but also all attitudes held by Jews that were not consistent with their teachings.

The complete glory of the princess is within;
Surpassing golden settings is her raiment.
In embroidered apparel she is brought to the king,
The maidens in her train, her companions, will be led to you.
They are brought with gladness and joy.

As a Jewish mother and grandmother, you held court in the privacy of your home, preserving modesty in its highest sense, while still serving as a leader and role model to the daughters of Yaakov.

They enter the palace of the King.
Your sons will succeed your fathers.
You will appoint them as leaders throughout the land.
I will commemorate Your Name through all generations,
Therefore the nations will acknowledge You forever and ever.[5]

Moshe's words were met with quiet sobbing, as the crowd attempted to comprehend the enormity of their loss.

---

5 Translation from *The Artscroll Tanach Series: Tehillim*, 567-575.

Izates's sons lodged together in a room in the palace the night following the burial of their father and grandmother. They didn't want to disturb their wives and children so early the next morning. It was well before dawn when the five men arose and quickly readied themselves, entering a waiting carriage in the still-dark early morning. The horses trotted in an easterly direction toward Har Hazeisim. Once there, they descended from the carriage and joined a large group of people, some with their animals, who stood silently, peering to the west, each lost in his own thoughts.

Suddenly, Yehudah called out excitedly, "There it is!"

All of those present glanced briefly at the beam of light emanating from the *nivreshes* hanging in front of the entrance to the *Heichal*. The top half of the Beis Hamikdash was bathed in light, while the portion below was still cloaked in eerie darkness.

Queen Helene's family, together with the scores of Jews who were assembled on Har Hazeisim, joined together with the *kohanim* and *levi'im* on the Har Habayis and the rest of the inhabitants of Yerushalayim in reciting "*Shema Yisrael! Hashem Elokeinu, Hashem Echad!*"

The holy words reverberated over the hills and across the valleys of Yerushalayim, converging on the Beis Hamikdash. The small, golden ornament shone, uniting the population of the Holy City in declaring the Unity of the one G-d. Perhaps not all of those assembled knew to whom they owed thanks for the ability to sanctify His Name at the earliest possible moment, but King Izates's sons knew.

This was the legacy of their grandmother, a foreign proselyte queen, who understood the eternal mission of the Jewish people — to declare and bear witness to the Unity of the Alm-ghty, from generation to generation, forever.

Epilogue

69 CE, Yerushalayim

The general Vespasian had left the battlefront to assume his position as emperor in Rome, consistent with the prediction of Rabbi Yochanan ben Zakkai. In his place he left his son, Titus Flavius, to take over the military command of the Roman troops in Judea. While internal political strife tore Yerushalayim apart, Titus marched toward Yerushalayim, accompanied by sixty thousand seasoned soldiers. The sages had urged the Jews to surrender, but the desperation of the people and the internal strife that had been tearing the country apart for forty years left no room for reason.

Titus and six hundred of his select horsemen rode unchallenged from the north to Yerushalayim. As they neared the northern wall of the city, a group of Jewish rebels ran out from the Women's Gate and split the cavalry in two. The larger group retreated, isolating Titus with just a few horsemen, trapping the Roman general. Titus charged into the group of Jews, who fired arrows and spears at the general. Not a single arrow or spear touched him. Titus managed to trample some of his enemies and join the group of horsemen who had retreated. The Roman general's invincibility was clearly a Divine decree.

Just opposite the site of this battle, another imposing building witnessed the impending tragedy. It was the tomb of Queen Helene and King Izates, and it would be the final resting place of her son, Monobaz, who was still king of Adiabene at the time.¹ The queen, who had passed from this world only about nine years prior to the war, would surely have mourned the impending doom that this battle foretold — the destruction of the holy Beis Hamikdash and the decimation and exile of her adopted nation.² Ultimately, the fierce fighting concluded with the destruction of the Temple and exile of the Jewish people.

The great palace was another casualty of the battle to destroy Yerushalayim. The enemy dismantled the walls of the immense structure, causing the massive stone frame and ceilings from upper stories to collapse onto the basement. Nevertheless, the assaulters left much evidence of the grandeur, strength, and leadership that the royal palace represented. There were massive foundations, walls more than fifteen feet tall built of stones weighing thousands of pounds, halls that were at least two stories tall, a basement riddled with vaults and *mikva'os*, and the remains of multi-colored frescoes. Modifications had apparently been made to the structure for wartime. Narrow openings in the basement level probably served as a means for its inhabitants to escape before the Romans destroyed the building.³

Sadly, two members of the royal household who fought against the Romans, one also named Monobaz and the other Kenedeus, were killed on the very day the Roman general, Cestius Gallus, was pushed back by

---

1 These were not the only buildings associated with the royal family of Adiabene to be caught up in the conflict, as reported by Josephus in *The Jewish War*. He writes that Shimon, the Zealot leader, "held the Upper City and the Great Wall as far as the Kidron, down to the palace of Monobaz, king of Adiabene. He also held the Fountain and part of the Citadel, or Lower City, as far as the palace of Helene, the mother of Monobaz."

2 The tragedy would have been personal as well as national. It is documented that members of the royal family of Adiabene were well represented in this opening campaign between Titus and the Zealots in Yerushalayim, and they fought against Rome until the end. During the earlier Roman conquest of Judea and Shomron in 67-68 CE, Adiabene sent not only provisions to the besieged Jews, but also troops. Throughout the conflict, they supported the Jewish side.

3 Etgar Lefkovits, "Second Temple Palace Uncovered," *The Jerusalem Post*, December 24, 2007.

Jewish warriors in a shamefaced retreat while attacking Yerushalayim.[4] This was to be only a temporary victory for the Jews, for the end was soon to come. When Titus ultimately entered Yerushalayim to conquer it, he found additional children and relatives of Izates. He spared their lives, transporting them to Rome as hostages, together with many of their Jewish brethren.[5]

Adiabene's existence as a sovereign nation lasted only about sixty years after Izates's death. The last king of an independent Adiabene was Meharaspes, who ruled around the year 115 CE. The following year, the country was invaded by the Roman emperor Trajan and became a part of Assyria, under the Roman Empire. Just one year later, in 117 CE, the emperor Hadrian discontinued Roman control over Adiabene.[6] Nevertheless, Jewish life in Adiabene continued after the deaths of Queen Helene and her family, and the many non-royal subjects of Adiabene who converted during that time continued to practice their new religion. Thus, the positive impression made by the righteous Queen Helene and her family bore lasting fruit — but this was only one aspect of her legacy.

During a time when Jewish society was poisoned by wanton hatred, Queen Helene and her family injected the antidote of boundless love. During a tragic era marred by challenges to the authority of the sages, Queen Helene and her family exhibited total deference to the rulings of the sages and their guidance. Although the royal family's kindness and scrupulous observance of the mitzvos were exemplary, they were not sufficient to annul the Divine decree of destruction and exile. Surely their deeds influenced subsequent generations of survivors of the *galus*. May the souls of the royal family of Adiabene plead successfully on behalf of their beloved Jewish people!

---

4 Josephus, *The Jewish War* (New York: Penguin Books), 166.
5 Josephus, *The Jewish War*, 354.
6 Jonah Gabriel Lissner, "*Adiabene, Jewish Kingdom of Mesopotamia*," 6.

Glossary

Avodah – sacrificial service

Azarah – the Temple courtyard that contained the large altar and the *Heichal* building

Baruch Hashem – thank G-d

Bas kol – a Heavenly voice

Bas Yisrael – a Torah-observant Jewish woman

Bayis ne'eman b'Yisrael – a Jewish household in which the laws of the Torah are observed and safeguarded

Beis din – a Jewish court conducted according to the laws of the Torah

Beis knesses – synagogue

Beis Hamikdash – the Holy Temple

Beis midrash – Torah study hall

Ben Torah – a Jewish man whose life is focused on the study of Torah

Bikkurim – first fruits brought as an offering to the Temple and given to the *kohen*

Brachah – a blessing

Chachamim – sages

Chametz – leavened foods

Chas v'chalilah – G-d forbid

Chassan – bridegroom

Chavrusa – Torah learning partner

Chessed – an act of kindness

Chol Hamoed – the intermediate days of the festivals of Sukkos and Passover

Chuppah – marriage canopy

Dayan – judge for a Jewish court

Duchan – three-staired platform located in the *Azarah* of the Temple upon which the *levi'im* sang and played their instruments

Eirusin – betrothal ceremony of a bride and groom

Emunah – faith in G-d

Eis ratzon – a time when our prayers gain special acceptance in Heaven

Erev – evening

Eruv – a technical enclosure that surrounds both private and otherwise public domains, creating a large private domain in which carrying is permitted on Shabbos

Ezras Kohanim – the portion of the *Azarah* between the *duchan* and the large altar

Ezras Nashim – women's courtyard; the easternmost courtyard of the Temple, containing the balconies reserved for women, four rooms for specialized functions, and the fifteen steps leading to the Nikanor Gate at its western end

Ezras Yisrael – area west of the Nikanor Gate between the *Ezras Nashim* and the *duchan*

Galus – exile

Ger toshav – a gentile living in Eretz Yisrael who accepts the authority of the Torah and the rabbis upon himself specifically as applied to gentiles, i.e., to observe the seven Noachide laws incumbent upon gentiles and certain other religious and cultural traditions under Jewish law

Ger tzedek – a righteous convert to Judaism who accepts all the laws of the Torah

Gid hanasheh – the sciatic nerve of an animal, which may not be eaten by Jews

Gishmei brachah – beneficial rains

Giyores – a female convert

Hachnasas orchim – the mitzvah of providing hospitality to guests

Hakadosh Baruch Hu – the Holy One, blessed be He; G-d

Hashem – G-d

Hashgachah pratis – Divine intervention

Heichal – the Temple building housing the *Ulam, Kodesh,* and *Kodesh Hakadashim*

Ir hama'amad – a city where people from the surrounding villages would assemble prior to making their way together to Jerusalem in order to perform the mitzvah of *aliyah l'regel* (pilgrimage) in the most beautiful way

Kallah – bride

Kapparah – atonement for sin

Kares – a punishment for certain serious sins that can result in dying before age sixty, dying without children, or the soul being cut off from the World to Come after death

Kedushah – holiness

Ketores – incense offering

Kiddush Hashem – an act that sanctifies the Name of G-d in the world

Kiddushin – betrothal ceremony; another name for *eirusin*

Kodesh – portion of the Beis Hamikdash that housed the Menorah, *Shulchan* with showbreads, and golden incense altar

Kohen hedyot – a regular member of the priestly class

Kohen (pl. *kohanim*) – member(s) of the priestly class

Kohen gadol – high priest

Korban Hager – offering brought by one who is converting to Judaism

Korban Pesach – the Passover offering, consisting of a young sheep or goat

Korban (pl. *korbanos*) – sacrificial offering(s)

Korban Tamid – twice-daily offering of a sheep, accompanied by a meal offering, wine libation, and incense offering

Korban Todah – thanksgiving offering

Kriah – the act of tearing a garment as a sign of mourning

Ma'aser – tithe

Mekudeshes – a woman who is betrothed, sanctified in marriage

Meis – a dead person

Melamed – a Torah teacher of young children

Middos – character traits

Mikveh (pl. *mikva'os*) – ritual bath(s)

Mizbe'ach – altar upon which animals were offered in the Temple; smaller *Mizbe'ach* where incense was offered was called the "golden altar," or altar of incense

Nasi – religious and political leader of the Jewish people at the time of the second Temple

Nazir – one who has taken the vow of the nazirite

Neitz hachamah – sunrise

Ner hama'aravi – western lamp of the Menorah

Nesachim – poured offerings

Netilas yadayim – ritual washing of the hands

Nezirus – the period of time during which the vow of the nazirite is observed

Olah – elevation offering

Oleh regel (pl. *olei regel*) – pilgrim(s) to Jerusalem

Parah adumah – red heifer

Perutah – coin of minimal value

Rachamei Shamayim – mercy shown from Heaven

Ribono shel Olam – Master of the world

Sandek – person who is honored with holding the baby during the circumcision ceremony

Semichah – leaning of the hands of the person bringing a sacrifice on the head of the animal as part of the process to atone for sin

Seudas hoda'ah – meal of thanksgiving

Shatnez – a garment or other fabric consisting of a mixture of wool and linen

Shamash – assistant to a rabbinic figure

Shalmei simchah – thanksgiving offerings of joy offered during the three pilgrimage festivals

Shamayim – Heaven

Shechitah – ritual slaughter of animals

Shemoneh Esrei – fundamental prayer originally consisting of eighteen blessings

Sheva brachos – festive meals held during the first week after marriage in which seven blessings are recited following the grace after meals

Shidduch (pl. *shidduchim*) – proposed marital match(es)

Shivah – seven-day period of mourning for a departed relative

Siyata d'Shmaya – Heavenly assistance

Sotah – woman suspected of adultery

Talmidei chachamim – Torah scholars

Tamei – ritually impure

Tamei meis – ritually impure due to contact with the dead

Tefillah (pl. *tefillos*) – prayer(s)

Tehillim – Psalms

Terumah – obligatory gift from crops given to the *kohen*

Teshuvah – repentance

Tikun – means by which a spiritual flaw can be corrected

Tumah – spiritual impurity

Ulam – entrance hall to the *Heichal*, which led to the *Kodesh* section of the sanctuary

Yamim Nora'im – Days of Awe

Yiras Shamayim – fear of Heaven

Yom Tov (pl. *Yamim Tovim*) – holy day(s), referring to the three pilgrimage holidays, Passover, Shavuos, and Sukkos, and the High Holidays

Yovel – jubilee year

Zechus – spiritual merit